THE ENGLISH ROAD TO ROME

THE ENGLISH ROAD TO
ROME

BRIAN BAREFOOT

Published in 1993 by
Images,
13 Old Street,
Upton-upon-Severn,
Worcs WR8 0HN.

in conjunction with Brian Barefoot

© BRIAN BAREFOOT 1993

This book is copyright. No part of it may be reproduced in any form without permission in writing from the publishers except by a reviewer who wishes to quote brief passages in connection with a review written for inclusion in a newspaper, magazine, radio or television broadcast.

British Library Cataloguing in Publication Data

A catalogue record for this book is available from the British Library

ISBN 1 897817 08 8

Designed and Produced by Images Publishing (Malvern) Ltd.
Printed and Bound in Great Britain.

CONTENTS

	Page
Introduction	9
The Pilgrims' Road: From the Seventh to the Sixteenth Century	15
Rediscovery of Italy: From the Mid-Fifteenth Century to 1615	53
Giro d'Italia and Grand Tour: The Seventeenth and Eighteenth Centuries	81
To Rome for the Winter: From the Napoleonic Wars to 1870	135
The Modern Way to Rome: From 1870 to 1944	197
Conclusion	223
Notes	237
Bibliography	241
Acknowledgements	251
Index	253

LIST OF ILLUSTRATIONS

	Page
1. The Appian Way (by Piranesi)	16
2. St. Paul, Covent Garden	77
3. Ickworth Rotunda, Suffolk	134
4. Frascati (by James Hakewill)	148
5. Villa of Maecenas and Cascatelle, Tivoli (by James Hakewill)	149
6. The Coach for Rome (by James Hakewill)	151
7. Ruins of the Palace of the Caesars (by James Hakewill)	154
8. Part of the Colosseum (by James Hakewill)	173
9. A 1901 Passport	204

LIST OF MAPS

1. The Roman Roads to Rome from Britain	25
2. Passes of the Alps	33
3. Some typical roads to Rome	114
4. Rome showing sites of Anglo-Roman interest	236

INTRODUCTION

The genesis, construction and deliberate limitations of this book call for some prefatory remarks.

When my wife and I lived (newly-married) in Rome, from 1953 to 1954, we explored the city, on foot, with the assistance of an ordinary tourist guide-book. This contained a short chapter, written in exuberantly odd English and not devoid of some wild inaccuracies, on some of the English and American celebrities who had visited Rome during the two thousand years when Rome and the English-speaking world had been aware of each other's existence. It seemed to me that this subject was worthy of fuller treatment, and my original intention was to write a series of biographical essays related to this general theme.

Much of my spare time for several years after that was occupied with preliminary research and tentative writing along these lines; but about 1960 the course of my life was such that I no longer had any spare time. The Rome project had to be set aside indefinitely. As happened to Edward Gibbon, if I may introduce the august simile, " . . . several years elapsed, and several avocations supervened" before I was able to resume work on the book. I now proposed to approach the subject-matter in a different way, relating, in the form of a straight historical narrative, the story of the English traveller to Rome through the centuries.

"A man who has not been in Italy," wrote Samuel Johnson, who himself never went further than Paris, "is always conscious of an inferiority." If this is true it was inevitable that a book such as this would be bound to afford space to a very considerable *dramatis personae*. Everyone who has visited Italy has at least wished that he could include Rome in his itinerary; and there is surely no city anywhere abroad which has become the repository for so many memorials of our own history, literature, art and science. In this sense Rome is more important to us than Florence, Venice, Vienna or Lisbon, more important even than Paris; and to mention everyone who has been to Rome would require not a book but an encyclopaedia.

Yet it also needed to be borne in mind that not everyone is terribly excited by the idea of Rome, perhaps because of its close association with the Christian religion. To non-Catholics, the long succession of similar popes does easily arouse boredom, and the concept of the pilgrimage now seems somewhat anachronistic. When we think of Italy, isn't the first image called up one of the Tuscan cities (Siena, Florence, Lucca), the Tuscan countryside, or the canals of Venice? I had also to persuade the potential reader that Rome too has its artistic attraction, and that a journey to Rome could be something other, and something more, than a pilgrimage.

One of the first necessary limitations, then, lay in deciding what – and whom – to leave out. It seemed to me that I should allot the most space to those English and American travellers whose journeys to Rome were of the greatest importance to their own development or their subsequent career. This means that, for example, the journeys not only of Inigo Jones (who is well known) but also of Anthony Munday (who is not) are described in some detail, while important figures such as Sir Walter Scott (whose visit to Rome had no significance at all for literature) are barely mentioned. From this angle, Augustus Hare seems more important than John Keats, Hilaire Belloc more significant than D.H. Lawrence, and so on. I have tried to keep to this principle throughout the book; but at the same time, so that the record should be as complete as possible, I have allotted at least a passing mention to as many English-speaking people as possible who have visited Rome, including of course not only Englishmen and Americans, but also Scotsmen, Welshmen and Irishmen. Even this left a dubious borderline area peopled by such characters as the Hanoverian secret agent Philip von Stosch, who was born in Brandenburg, spoke little English, and wrote his despatches from Rome in French, under his English pseudonym John Walton.

It was necessary to decide also when the story should start, and when it should come to a close. With some regret, I left out the first four centuries between 55 BC, when Julius Caesar made his first and singularly unsuccessful landing on the Kent coast, thus linking Roman and British history for the first time, and 410 AD when, the Visigoths having captured Rome, the Emperor Honorius sent a message to the British cities to the effect that in future they would have to rely on their own military defence.

Those four hundred years were of vital importance to British history, and it could be said that at no later time were the fortunes of Rome and Britain so closely linked; but the fact remains that we know almost nothing, save by inference and deduction, of the actual living people who travelled between Britain and Rome at that period, nor of their opinions concerning Rome, nor of their daily life either in Rome or in Britain.

This was an insuperable difficulty. Even about Caratacus, who carried on a guerrilla war for nine years against the troops of Aulus Plautius (the Emperor Claudius' invading general) in AD 43, and later against those of Ostorius Scapula, we have little reliable information. We know only that he was taken captive to Rome in AD 51, presumably by the then usual route across Gaul to Massilia (Marseilles) and then by ship to Ostia, the port of Rome. He was displayed at a great military review and he made a speech in which he urged his captors to use him and his people with *clementia* rather than *atrocitas,* the two alternative policies between which the Romans chose, when dealing with ferocious beaten tribes. We know that his life was spared. But what did he think of Rome? What did his daughter think, who is said to have married a Roman? We do not know and probably never shall.

Other characters who might be introduced in order to illustrate this period are equally elusive. There is nothing more to be said about Claudia Rufina, who came to Rome from Britain in the third century, married a Pudens and fitted well into Roman society, although she came from the furthest periphery of the Empire. We should not know even this much had not the lady been the subject of one of Martial's epigrams.

Pelagius, the early heretic who is one of the great archetypal figures in English thought, is the first character who appears in depth. He is said to have been a large man, broad-shouldered and bull-necked in youth, corpulent as he grew older. Possibly of Irish origin, he reached Rome from Britain about AD 384, and stayed there, studying and practising theology, for some twenty-five years. His theological ideas were strongly opposed to those of the established Church in relation to predestination and free will, but they won a good deal of influential support. Pelagius was three times tried and acquitted of heresy, and was finally condemned in 418 by both the Roman Emperor and the Roman Bishop. Although discredited, he lived on to a ripe old age, and ended his days somewhere near the eastern borders of the Roman Empire – thousands of miles from the remote western islands where he was born. We know nothing about his early days, nor about his journey to Rome, nor about his life there. But some of his ideas on practical Christianity (for example, that it is possible for any man, if he wishes it and strives for it, to live a life free from sin) strike such a modern, Protestant note that we wish we knew more.

The year 418 affords only a glimpse of Anglo-Rome: Pelagius was declared a heretic, while far away in the north the last Roman troops have embarked for Gaul, abandoning the Romanized Britons to the sea and to the barbarians. We pass on, through another 180 years of legend or baffling silence, to the year 597, when St. Augustine and his monks arrived at Canterbury, set up a monastery and initiated a period that I have called the Pilgrims' Road.

Introduction

It was also necessary to decide when to end the historical narrative. Dramatically though somewhat arbitrarily, the date chosen is the 4th of June 1944, the day on which units of the US Army entered Rome from the south. It was only eight months short of two thousand years since Julius Caesar, commanding the VII and X Legions, had established a beach-head at Deal and spent a few fine autumn days campaigning in the Kentish hills.

Rome, however, still appears to be an inexhaustible mine for historical researchers, and many important and interesting books on this subject have appeared in English since 1944. I have referred to them, where appropriate, in a Conclusion in which I summarize briefly what has remained to the present day of the traditional British visit to Rome.

THE PILGRIMS' ROAD

FROM THE SEVENTH TO THE SIXTEENTH CENTURY

In the year 596, when Gregory and Augustine were discussing, on the Caelian Hill in Rome, their plans to send Benedictine monks to England in order to convert the Anglo-Saxons to Christianity, the fortunes of Rome were at a very low ebb. It was three hundred years since the Roman Empire had been divided into East and West, and much of the tradition and material attributes of Roman civilization had been transported from Rome to Constantinople, almost two hundred years since the Visigoths had captured Rome, a hundred and fifty since the city had been carefully plundered by the Vandals, just over a hundred since the Western Roman Empire had been brought formally to an end. The dominant powers in the Western world were the Byzantine Empire, Islam and the Vikings, the two greatest and most prosperous cities in the Mediterranean basin were Constantinople and Cordoba, capital of Muslim Spain. Rome lay helpless in between – a degenerate, half-deserted place with waterless aqueducts and ruined palaces, huddled on the right bank of the Tiber which, with a few springs and wells, constituted its only water supply. Its greatness lay, to all appearances, entirely in the past. It had only just escaped the fate of Nineveh and Babylon, and of the countless urban settlements founded by the Romans all over Europe, of which today only the names and the archaeological sites survive.

APPIAN WAY – Not all the Roman roads were built as solidly as the Appian Way, illustrated here. But many were, and provided one firm reason for the constant travel to Rome across Europe down the centuries. This picture is from Le Antichità Romane, G.B. Piranesi, Vol.III, Plate VII, first published in 1756. The legend translates into English as follows:

View of the ancient Appian Way as it passes beneath the walls, already described in the previous plates, of the Ustrino; at the present time covered by the ruins of the same. A. Bed of earth, well consolidated and rammed with piles before spreading the main body of the filler to the height of one palmo, so that it resembles paving composed of lime pozzolana, and chips of flintstone, and above this the paving stones B. are placed bodily in rows; they are cut on the reverse side with a diamond point. C. Other stones are placed like wedges; they press against and firmly enclose the said paving stones, which pave the road aforesaid, and among this, at intervals of thirty palmi, there occurs a stone D. which is higher and more prominent than the others; this was perhaps used by persons who mounted or dismounted from horses, and served as a resting place for wayfarers. This and other lower stones are placed in rows above a wall of filler of similar chips of flint, but larger than those mentioned above.

Drawn and engraved by Piranesi, Architect.

The resurgence of Rome was due to the city's more recent connexion with Christianity: to the fact of Christianity having been adopted as the official Roman religion late in the days of the Empire; to the martyrdom of Saints Peter and Paul, and the cults that grew up around the sites of their martyrdom; as a result, therefore, of the establishment of the Papacy, and of the emergence of Rome as the administrative capital of the Church. Without that slender thread connecting ancient Rome to renaissance Rome, the city might never have assumed the outstanding importance that it achieved, in the eighteenth and nineteenth centuries, as an art centre; and there would not have been enough English visitors to Rome to justify a book on the subject.

But at the beginning of the seventh century, Rome was scarcely a pilgrim centre. The first pilgrimages of the Christian era did not end in Rome – they started there. Most of the holy relics by which the pilgrims were later to set such great store were not in Italy at all – they were in Palestine. So the earliest pilgrims of whom any record remains were found trudging the roads of Asia Minor or the shores of Galilee, their goal not Rome but Jerusalem. There must have been an occasional Romanized Briton or Anglo-Saxon among them, to judge by the slightly incredulous comment of a Roman woman pilgrim in the fourth century, to the effect that even "the Briton, remote from our world"[1] could be encountered in the Holy Land. Latin writers had been in the habit (which in due course was handed down to the Italians) of regarding the Britons as uncouth colonials. Britain, which had been on the periphery of the Empire, was equally regarded as being on the furthest fringe of Christendom. The bands of monks sent by Pope Gregory to Kent were not without their fainthearts, who doubted the wisdom and the practicability of carrying the Christian message so far into the wilds.

Thus, for the first hundred years of the Pilgrims' Road there was scarcely a road *to* Rome as far as the Anglo-Saxons were concerned; there was only a road *from* it. The first five Archbishops of Canterbury were all Italian pupils of Pope Gregory; the sixth was an Anglo-Saxon who concealed his identity under a Latin name (Deusdedit), but never went to Rome; and the seventh (Theodore) was a Greek from Asia Minor. Their road started from Rome, reached Canterbury, then spread out to the other ecclesiastical birthplaces of our islands – to York, Lichfield, Glastonbury, Lindisfarne, Iona.

But by the eighth century there was a small but growing tide in the opposite direction – southward through the kingdoms of England to Canterbury and thence across the Strait of Dover, and on towards Rome. By this time Rome was not only the centre that had to be visited to have an ecclesiastical office confirmed, or to plead a case with the papal authorities; it had sufficient holy places of its own to justify a visit for that reason too. Nearly everyone who had been to Jerusalem from the West came back through Rome; most returning pilgrims had presented a relic or two to one of the Roman churches. Jerusalem was a long and dangerous way off; it was very gratifying to the slightly less ambitious pilgrim that great kudos might also accrue from a personal

18

visit to Rome which, though far enough to travel, was not nearly as far as the true birthplace of Christianity.

A number of Anglo-Saxon kings, princes and bishops visited Rome, including Alfred the Great, who was first sent there in 853, at the age of five. He accompanied his father, Aethelwulf, to Rome again two years later. Earlier than this, King Caedwalla of Wessex went to Rome in 689, while still a young man and a pagan, and was baptized there by Pope Sergius I; but he was taken ill and died shortly afterwards. He is the only English king (if the exiled Stuarts are excluded) who has the distinction of having been buried in St. Peter's. He was soon followed by King Coenrad of Mercia and Prince Offa of Essex, both of whom arrived in Rome in 709 and died there some time later. King Ine of Wessex, who resigned his kingdom in order to go to Rome and remain there, arrived in 726. The first English-born Archbishop of Canterbury who is known to have visited Rome (though before he was elected to the office) was Nothelm, who was there while Gregory II was Pope – thus, sometime between 715 and 731. The second Archbishop of York, Egbert, also visited Rome about this time. In 716 Wethburga, the first Englishwoman known to have made the pilgrimage to Rome, found there "the quiet life she had so long sought".[2]

Of greater significance, perhaps, were the Roman journeys of such men as Benedict Biscop, a Northumbrian nobleman who founded the monasteries of Monkwearmouth and Jarrow, and visited Rome no less than six times, bringing back from one of these journeys a volume on cosmography that Bede thought "a wonderful work", and the poet and scholar Alcuin, also a Northumbrian, who became Bishop of Tours and advised Archbishop Ethelheard of Canterbury. His solemn warning (in 798) about Italian food strikes a decidedly modern note:

> *Italy is an unhealthful country, and grows harmful food. Therefore give most cautious thought to what, when, and what kind of food you eat; and especially avoid devotion to drink, since the heat of wine usually kindles in the uncautious the flame of fever.*

19

Another pilgrim was a Wessex nobleman, Willibald, nephew of Boniface, who set sail for France from the Hamble river near Southampton in 720, together with his father, and his elder brother Winnibald. The following year they reached Lucca, where their father was suddenly taken ill and died, being later adopted as a saint by the people of Lucca under the name of *Richardus rex*, though there is no other evidence that this was his name or that he was in any way connected with royalty. The two brothers went on to Rome, where they suffered from malaria, and in 723 they continued their journey towards Jerusalem. Returning to Italy seven years later, Willibald became a monk at Monte Cassino and then first bishop of Eichstätt (near Munich). The *Vita Willibaldi* that he dictated in his old age is the earliest extant book of travel by an English pen. Most of it lacks interest today, but there is an engaging glimpse of this adventurous Anglo-Saxon striving to climb the volcano at Stromboli but failing to reach the summit.

Not all the English pilgrims, however, were impelled by strictly pious intentions to take the road to Rome. Even at this early date we find travellers with ignoble motives. Some were merchants who tried to slip their wares unobtrusively across the frontiers, some were plain vagabonds, and some of the women pilgrims fell by the wayside in more senses than one. St. Boniface, in 747, expressed the view that Englishwomen should not be allowed to make the journey to Rome, since "there are very few cities in Longobardia, in Francia or Gaul, where an English adulteress or prostitute is not to be found, "*quod scandalum est et turpitudo ecclesiae vestrae.*"[3]

It seems that there were already two modes of travel – one for the rich, the other for the poor. The wealthy pilgrims could expect to be entertained in one bishop's palace after another, as Willibald and his party were. But many of the pilgrims were not rich, while some preferred to travel in the traditionally humble way – on foot, wearing the wide-brimmed hat, carrying the knobbed staff, with scrip, bag and wooden bowl (sometimes also shoes) suspended from a leather belt. Such pilgrims relied on charity for overnight lodging, or even begged their way to Rome. This double pattern of travel hardly changed in a thousand years. In 1802 J.C. Eustace was explaining that the reason the inns in Italy were so bad was that only the poor were lodged in "such receptacles"; the rich were accustomed to break their journeys at the villas of the nobility.

It became the custom in the eighth century for the newly elected Archbishop of Canterbury to go to Rome in person in order to receive from the Pope his pallium of office. The first Archbishop who did this was Cuthbert, in 740; and of the twenty-three Anglo-Saxons and one Dane who held the office of Archbishop of Canterbury between the time of Theodore and the Norman conquest, nineteen went to Rome for this reason or some other. The most interesting of these visits historically was that of Ethelheard, who was Archbishop from 791 to 805. He had been obliged to depart rather swiftly from Kent, for reasons of personal safety, when the Kentish nobles decided to elect a king of their own; and he took refuge in Mercia, where there was, at that time, a third English archbishopric, at Lichfield. The purpose of Ethelheard's mission to Pope Leo III, in 801-2, was to ask for the restoration of the rights of the see of Canterbury. The mission was entirely successful, and Ethelheard returned to Canterbury, where he remained for the rest of his life. The wording of the papal document confirming his authority stated that:

> . . . *the see archepiscopal from this time forward (shall) never be in the monastery of Lichfield, nor in any other place but in the city of Canterbury, where Christ's Church is; and where the Catholic faith first shone forth in this island, and where holy baptism was first administered by St. Augustine.*

As a result of the journey of a later Archbishop of Canterbury – Sigeric, who held the office from 990 to 994, and went to Rome for the pallium in 990, we have for the first time an account of the actual route followed "from Rome to the English sea". This was written by a man in the Archbishop's entourage, and described an itinerary which was probably a standard one. It took three months to complete, and involved seventy-nine stops of a night or more; but it seems to have been exceptionally slow for the period, due to the Archbishop's advanced age – though he must nevertheless, have been a determined old man, for it is recorded that while in Rome he visited twenty churches in two days.

One of the interesting aspects of this journey is that it was based on the old Roman roads – indeed, the Archbishop and his party trod the actual *summum dorsum* or paved surface of the Roman road between Rheims and Besançon. These roads, of course, had originally been systems of military communication, running dead straight through the countryside from camp to camp rather than from town to town, with the post-stages (where there were changing-stations or *mutationes*, with fresh horses available, and rest-houses or *mansiones*, where travellers could put up for the night) set at regular twelve-mile intervals along the whole length of the road.

Nothing so efficient as the Roman roads would be seen again in Europe for many centuries after the Roman Empire collapsed; not until the sixteenth century would a traveller be able to mount his first horse at Southwark and ride post all the way to Rome. Professor Richmond has pointed out, however,[4] that the Imperial Post "was not, like the modern Postal service, a government institution run for the benefit of the public, but a service operated at public expense for the use of the government." Thus, the upkeep of these roads and of the Post service imposed a very severe financial burden on the communities through which the main roads passed. As soon as the central authority ceased to be able to exercise control over the communities, the roads fell into disrepair. It is a tribute to the excellence of their construction that they were still (in parts) available for Archbishop Sigeric and his party, nearly six hundred years after the last Roman troops had left Britain.

Reversing the route given for the Archbishop's journey, the first stage would have taken him from Canterbury to Dover, whence he crossed to Wissant. From here the Roman road ran straight across north-eastern France, through Amiens (formerly Samarobrivas) to Rheims (Durocotoro). From that city the road ran south-eastwards through Langres to Besançon (which in Roman times had been Vesontione), and then through the Vallorbe gap into Switzerland, and so to Lausanne (Losum Losonne), which used to be the last posting station in Gaul. This road to Rome involved crossing the Alps over the Great St. Bernard pass (the present Swiss town of Martigny is on the site of the Roman Octodurno), and down into the Po valley through Aosta (Augusta Pretoria). The next cities on the route were Pavia and Piacenza. Then there was another mountain range to cross – the western Apennines – before reaching Lucca, which in Imperial Roman times had been an important traffic centre, since from this city the traveller could easily reach any of the three main roads that led to Rome – the Via Aurelia, which ran through Pisa (Pisis); the Via Clodia, through Siena (Sena Julia); and the Via Cassia, through Florence (Florentia). Archbishop Sigeric's party followed the route of the Via Clodia, stopping at San Gimignano, Montefiascone and Viterbo; and they would have crossed the Tiber, as most other English travellers to Rome were to cross it, during the next thousand years, at Ponte Milvio (once Pons Milvius), and would have entered the city of Rome at the Porta Flaminia.

The Anglo-Saxon pilgrims lodged in the "Saxon" quarter of Rome, on the right bank of the Tiber at the foot of the Vatican hill. Even at that early date the English were somewhat insular. They firmly called their district the *burh* or borough, and the name has survived to this day as the Borgo. Its origin has become slightly obscured by legend, but certainly everyone would like to believe that the Schola Anglorum (the word *schola* meaning, however, only "district" in this context) was founded about 720 by Ine – the same admirable King Ine of Wessex who ruled from 688 to 728, passed a law forbidding the selling of his fellow countrymen into slavery abroad, and gave up his kingdom in order to make the pilgrimage to Rome and end his days there as a monk. It has also been maintained that King Offa of Mercia founded the hospice. It was well established by 799, when the Vatican records show that it consisted of a number of wooden houses in the area where the modern church of S. Spirito in Sassia now stands. In 818, a fire broke out in the Saxon quarter and destroyed a number of buildings. It was feared that it might spread to St. Peter's; and the Pope (Paschal I) was roused from sleep to supervise fire-fighting operations. All the four foreign communities living near St. Peter's (Saxons, Franks, Frisians and Lombards) were obliged to render military service in times of war. This obligation was put severely to the test when the Saracens invaded Rome in 846 and caused great destruction.

After these calamities, the Saxons set to work to rebuild their borough once again, erecting among other buildings their parish church of St. Mary. This church, St. Mary of the Saxons (*Sancta Maria quae vocatur Schola Saxonum*) was built in 850, during the papacy of Leo IV. This same Pope placed the Saxon hostel under the authority of the Abbot of St. Martin's Monastery, near St. Peter's. The earliest information about the organization of the hostel (from the time of Leo IX, 1049-54) shows that its head was an archpriest, appointed by the Pope, and that under him were assistant priests, and *scholenses* (laymen in charge of the hospices), who were appointed by the Abbot of St. Martin's. The Saxons had their own cemetery, in which they buried English pilgrims who died while visiting the city. It was about this time that King Canute visited Rome. He was there in 1027 to attend the coronation of the Holy Roman Emperor, Conrad II, and was the only English ruler ever to assist at such an occasion. He wrote a letter to his subjects describing his visit. The *Schola Saxonum* remained the hub of English life in Rome for about four hundred years – until, in 1201, it was expropriated by Pope Innocent III, in order to set up the new foundation of Santo Spirito in Sassia, so called after the French order of Santo Spirito which was to administer it. At the time of its expropriation, this English church owned not only its immediate buildings and the Hospice for Englishmen, but four Roman churches and their possessions, besides four vineyards and nine other plots of land. But this impressive housing concealed an institution that disposed of less and less internal vigour.

The Pilgrims' Road

The Roman Roads to Rome from Britain

One of Thomas Becket's correspondents wrote from Rome about 1160:

> *This church has now dwindled to such poverty that there can now be found but a few clerics and almost no laymen for the service of the church or the care of pilgrims.*

The Anglo-Saxons by that time no longer existed as a separate people, and before long the English would need a new centre in Rome, across the river in the medieval city. There was left of St. Mary of the Saxons only the sentimental connexion with its successor, and the endowment that King John was persuaded to present to Santo Spirito so as to preserve the English continuity.

The Norman Conquest at the same time strengthened the ties between England and Rome and kept them further apart. On the one hand, the new Norman aristocracy was more intimately connected with the Continent than the Anglo-Saxons had been. The Normans ruled almost half of what is now France, as well as Sicily, and even before 1066 they had infiltrated southern England. Edward the Confessor had spent 27 years of his life in Normandy, and he surrounded himself with Norman favourites when he became King of England, so that by 1050 all the chief offices of State were filled by Normans; and by 1070, only two sees in England retained native bishops. On the other hand, the Norman kings deliberately kept themselves apart from Rome. Unlike the Anglo-Saxon kings and princes, they never went to Rome either as kings or pilgrims, and sometimes they found themselves in violent antagonism towards the Pope of the day. King John, for example, flatly refused to accept as Archbishop of Canterbury Stephen Langton, who had lectured in Rome on civil law with conspicuous success (1198-1206), had been created Cardinal in 1206 and consecrated Archbishop by the Pope at Viterbo in 1207. Not until the Pope had first placed England under an interdict, and had then excommunicated the King, did the latter give way and accept Stephen Langton, who a year or two later was present at the signing of the Magna Carta.

During the Norman period in England, the Papacy gained considerable ground as regards integrity, competence and consequent prestige. It had not been so at the start of this period. About the year 1000 the Papacy had hardly more than a local importance; the holders of the office were either nominees of the Holy Roman Emperor or of a local faction – and usually there was an anti-pope set up in opposition to whoever had been officially elected. In 1046 there were no less than three popes pontificating in Rome at the same time, the least disreputable of whom had paid for his office in hard cash. But after the election of Leo IX in 1049 there was a real movement for papal reform, which made Rome much more than a pilgrim centre. It became the headquarters not of a local bishopric, but of a world-wide Church. The college of Cardinals was set up, and gradually it came to be accepted that the cardinals would elect the Pope. Many of the most brilliant men then living in Europe came to work in the Curia. Many of them were English – or perhaps, since the idea of nationality had not yet taken root in Europe, it would be more accurate to say that they originated from England, studied on the Continent, and served the Roman Church wherever they happened to be.

Such men, who all lived and worked in Rome during the middle of the twelfth century, were Robert Pullen, who taught at Exeter and at Paris before being called to Rome about 1144 by Lucius II; John of Salisbury, the most widely read scholar of his age, who went to Chartres to study grammar and rhetoric, to Paris to study logic and theology, and then to Rome, afterwards entering the service of Thomas Becket; and Nicholas Breakspear, a close friend of John of Salisbury, who became Pope in 1154 – the only Englishman ever to be elected to this office.

The Breakspear family was closely connected with Hertfordshire. At Harefield on the Hertfordshire-Middlesex border there is a country house which has been called Breakspears since at least the end of the twelfth century. A family of the same name occupied the house until 1420, when it passed by marriage to another family, Ashby, who owned the property until 1769. Robert Breakspear, Nicholas' father, became a monk at St. Albans, and his son was born probably at Abbot's Langley, a village which was under the direct influence of the Benedictine monastery.

Very little is known about Nicholas Breakspear's early life. He enters history in 1135 as Abbot of St. Rufus in Provence, where the strict rule that he instituted caused some grumbling among the less puritanically minded of the monks there, and led to the Abbot being called to Rome to defend himself, which he successfully did. In 1146 Eugenius III appointed him Cardinal Bishop of Albano, and sent him on a mission to Scandinavia, where he set up for the first time a Norwegian Archbishopric at Trondheim (then called Nidaros). Nicholas returned from the North to find that in the meantime Eugenius III had died; and after a brief period of seventeen months when the aged Anastasius IV was Pope, he was himself elected to the Papacy under the title of Adrian IV.

It suited the medieval monastic biographers to portray Nicholas as a man of obscure origins, who through his own piety and almost by accident found himself raised to the highest office in the Church. Today it seems obvious that this could hardly have been the case. A man who counted among his close friends a scholar of the calibre of John of Salisbury, and who studied in the monastic schools of the twelfth century (the leading intellectual centres of Europe at that time) before going on to work in the Curia in Rome at a time when the papal reforms were beginning to bear real fruit; a man who occupied the papal chair at the same time that Henry II of England was ruler of Anglo-Normandy, Anjou, Aquitaine and Gascony, and at the same time that Frederick Barbarossa was Holy Roman Emperor, and William II was the Norman King of Sicily, was no simple rustic who had successively achieved the status of monk, prior, abbot, cardinal bishop and finally Pope by the will of God rather than by his own efforts. He was, on the contrary, a highly educated and erudite man by the standards of the twelfth century, thoroughly versed, according to his secretary Boso, in the English and Latin tongues, and accomplished also in French and Norse. Boso also claimed that he was a kind, gentle and patient man, a cheerful giver (*hilaris dator*), a sweet singer and an eloquent preacher. The Paternoster that he is said to have sent to Henry II was translated at the time into words which, even if they do not emanate directly from Nicholas Breakspear, at least illustrate the simplicity that his erudition had not obliterated, and are recognizably in our own language, not Anglo-Saxon:

> *I belieue in God Fadir almichty Shipper of Heuen and Earth, and in Ihesus Christ his onelethi son vre Louerd, that is iuange thurch the Holy Ghost, bore of Mary Maiden. Tholede pin vnder Pounce Pilat, picht on rode tree, dead and yburiid. Licht into helle, the thridde day from death arose. Steich into heauen, sit on his fadir richte honde God Almichty. Then is cominde to deme the quikke and the dede. I beleue in the Holy Gost, all Holy Church, mone of alle hallwen, forgiuenis of sine, fleiss uprising, life withuten ende. Amen.*

The five years of Adrian IV's Papacy were not, however, a period during which there was much opportunity for the Pope to display either erudition or simplicity; they were years of power politics, in which the chief protagonists were the Pope, the Holy Roman Emperor and William II of Sicily. As such, these years belong rather to European and ecclesiastical history and politics than to the story of the English in Rome – except that the Pope *was* of English origin.

Adrian IV was in alliance with William II, and therefore incurred the displeasure of Frederick Barbarossa – whom he nevertheless finally crowned in St. Peter's on June 18th, 1155, after the Emperor had agreed to perform a token act of homage to the Pope. A less formidable opponent of Adrian IV was a radical preacher, Arnold of Brescia, who had stirred up a good deal of opposition to the Papacy in Rome. The Pope was obliged to put the entire city under an interdict before the unfortunate Arnold, who had not learned the fundamental political lesson that he should have played off his two formidable enemies – the Emperor and the Pope – against one another, was captured by the Emperor's forces, handed over to the Pope's, and executed.

The only one of Adrian IV's political acts that much affected the British Isles was his authorization for the invasion of Ireland that was sent to Henry II. Whether the document is genuine or not does not greatly matter. Henry intended to invade Ireland in any case, but he did seek the Pope's consent, which was what the Papacy desired. The invasion was postponed for sixteen years, but Ireland was then brought into the Roman Catholic Church by force of arms, and remained there long after England had repudiated Rome.

Adrian IV might have played a much bigger part in European history had he lived longer. He was not disposed to give way to the Holy Roman Emperor, and a showdown between the two men was imminent. But Adrian then suddenly died, and there is nothing to show in Rome today of his short, eventful reign apart from the church of SS. Giovanni e Paolo, on the Caelian Hill, the church he restored during his term of office, and his tomb in the Vatican crypt – a plain tomb, with nothing to distinguish it from the scores of other papal tombs that surround it.

In the twelfth and thirteenth centuries it was still usual for the Archbishops of Canterbury and York to go to Rome in person to receive the pallium from the Pope. Between 1066 and 1294, fourteen out of twenty-six archbishops went to Rome for this purpose – including the unfortunate Ralph d'Escures, elected Archbishop of Canterbury in 1114. He made the long, difficult and dangerous journey although he suffered from gout, only to find at the end of it that the Pope had been chased out of Rome by a faction of his enemies. Thomas Becket was one of the minority who were excused from making the journey, but he had already been to Rome twice previously – first when he accompanied Archbishop Theobald in 1148, and again two years later when he was sent to Rome on a mission.

Robert Kilwardby, Archbishop of Canterbury from 1273 to 1278, resigned his office in order to go to live in Rome, but he died only a few months after leaving England. His successor John Peckham made the journey in 1279, but found the expenses of the Roman visit greater than he had anticipated; he was obliged to borrow money from the Pope for his return journey to England and his enthronement at Canterbury. The last Archbishop of Canterbury who went to Rome for the pallium was Robert Winchelsea (in office 1294-1313). He had to wait a year in Rome until a new Pope had been elected, and was finally consecrated by Celestine V at Aquila.

After the martyrdom of Thomas Becket at Canterbury in 1170, appeals to Rome in ecclesiastical suits developed greatly. Sometimes, too, cases were heard by papal delegates sent to England from Rome. In both cases, this meant more traffic to and fro.

The path over the Great St. Bernard remained one of the standard routes; eleventh and twelfth century English coins have been found on the pass, indicating that some English travellers came this way. To one of them – Brother John, a monk from Canterbury, who crossed the pass in 1188 – these mountains were "a place of torment", where:

> *... the marble pavement of the rocky ground is ice, and you cannot safely set a foot down; where, strange to say, though it is so slippery that you cannot even stand, the death into which you are given every facility to fall is certain death. I put my hand in my scrip to scratch out a word or two to your sincerity; behold, I found my ink-bottle filled with a dry mass of ice. My fingers refused to write; my beard was stiff with frost, and my breath congealed in a long icicle. I could not write.*[5]

Though there was a hospice on the Simplon pass by 1235, another on the Septimer pass as early as 831, and the St. Gotthard pass was practicable for travellers from 1220, no surviving evidence points to the use of any of these routes by English travellers in the twelfth and thirteenth centuries. But now another of the old Roman roads comes into the story – the road through France and over the Mont Cenis pass. First mentioned in 756, it remained the most frequented route for passengers on foot until at least the seventeenth century. Matthew Paris compiled an illustrated itinerary of this road in 1253. It ran from either Boulogne or Calais across France, passing through Paris or by-passing it to the north, through Rheims and Auxerre; then through Beaune, Mâcon and Lyon, and by way of the Mont Cenis hospice to Susa, on the Italian side of the pass.

This section of the journey took from eighteen to twenty-two days. It was based on the route of the old Roman road, which had started at Geseriac (Boulogne) and ran southwards to Samarobrivas (Amiens) which, then as now, was an important road junction. From Samarobrivas the Roman traveller would have crossed Gaul to Augustodunum (Autun) and then to Lugdono (Lyon); or he could have reached Lugdono by going first to Luteci (Paris) and then to Cenabo (Orléans) and Ebirno (Nevers), which later became the post-road from Paris to Lyon. From Lugdono he would have followed the river southwards to Vigenna (Vienne) and then up into the mountains, crossing the Mont Cenis pass and entering Italy at Segasione – the modern Susa.

The thirteenth century traveller would have needed from sixteen to eighteen days to reach Rome from Susa, going via Pavia, Piacenza, Lucca, Siena and Montefiascone; the Imperial Roman traveller would have posted to Augusta Taurino (Turin), then to Placentia (Piacenza); and then by the roads mentioned earlier.

About the end of the thirteenth century the journey to Rome from England would have lasted six weeks on horseback, longer on foot. Seven weeks had been the average time a century earlier. In 1188 Brother John and his party from Canterbury took at least forty-nine days to reach Rome, and this was also the time taken by messengers sent from St. Albans Abbey to Adrian IV in 1157. But one papal letter was carried from Rome to Canterbury, in 1188, in the then extraordinary time of twenty-five days.

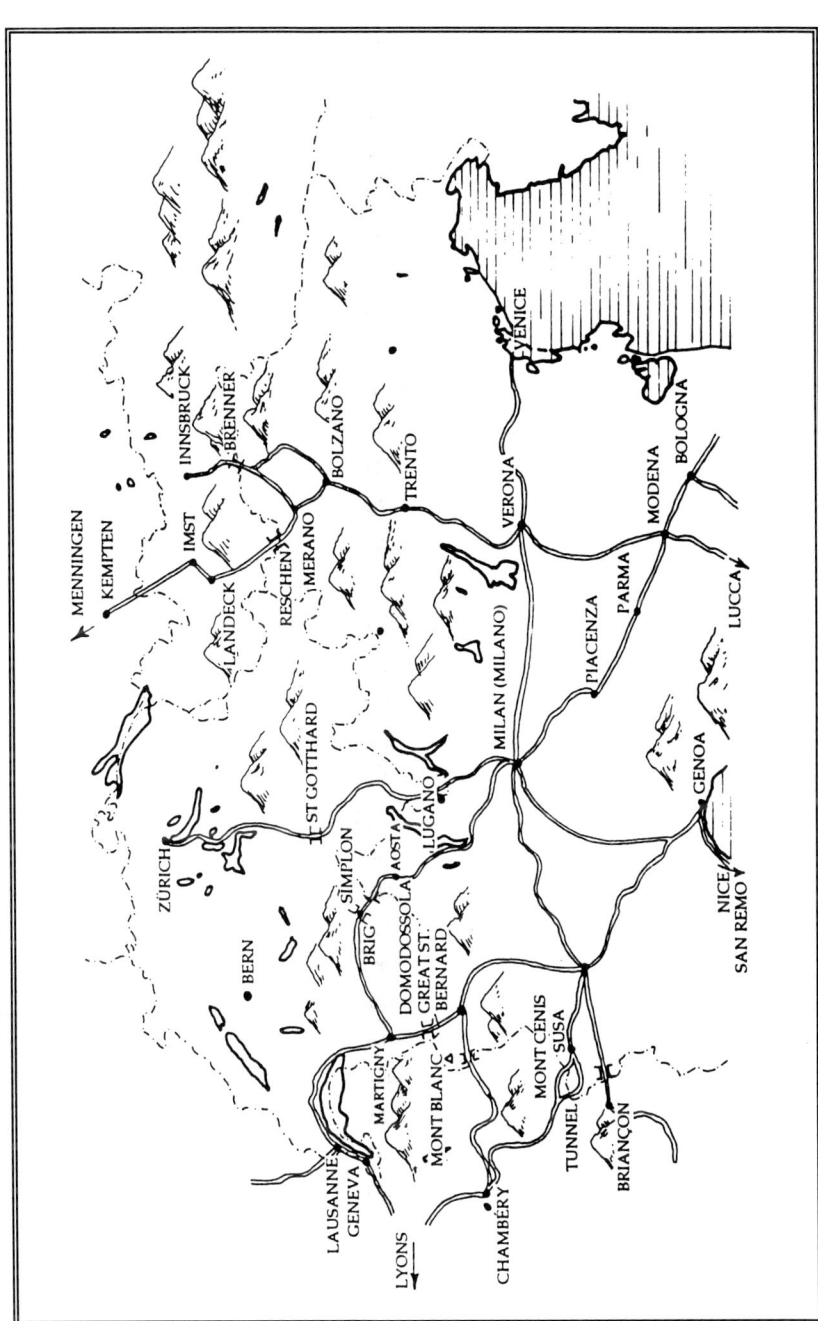

Passes of the Alps

The English Road To Rome

The year 1300 was an important date in the history of travel to Rome. In that year the first Holy Year was held, and an unprecedented concourse of pilgrims travelled over the Alpine and Apennine passes in order to reach Rome, which by now had become the leading pilgrimage centre in Europe – more important in this respect than Santiago de Compostela in Galicia or Rocamadour in central France – and as important as Jerusalem.

In the Holy Years the popes had certainly discovered a highly successful way of attracting the ordinary pilgrim to Rome. Formerly, the bishops throughout Christendom had exercised the privilege of granting indulgences – that is, they could commute the months and years of penance, fasting or self-mortification that were imposed as a punishment for sins, releasing the debt of temporal punishment that the sinner still had to discharge. To obtain an indulgence in earlier centuries, there had been no need to go further than to one's own bishop. But now the popes decided to keep this valuable privilege to themselves, which meant that a personal visit to Rome was necessary in order to obtain the more prized of the indulgences. For example, if the pilgrim had the good fortune to be present at the showing of St. Veronica's handkerchief, on which the image of Christ was believed to be imprinted, he would qualify for nine thousand years of pardon if he came from a country on the mainland of Europe, or twelve thousand years if from beyond the sea. One third of his total sum of sin could be wiped out, if he merely entered the church of SS. Vitus and Modestus. During the Holy Years, the Pope would grant plenary indulgence – i.e., total remission of all sins committed to date – to anyone who made the pilgrimage to Rome.

Not only this, but the pilgrim who went personally to Rome would have the satisfaction of having set eyes on all kinds of marvellous and improbable things – the table that bore the Last Supper, remains of the magnified loaves and fishes, the infant Jesus' swaddling clothes, a piece of his umbilical cord, hay from the stall at Bethlehem, bits of wood, nails and thorns associated with the Cross, a sample of the Virgin Mary's milk and miscellaneous objects of all kinds connected in some way with the innumerable saints.

The response to the first Holy Year, promulgated by Pope Boniface VII, was overwhelming. The Church was rewarded by the personal appearance in Rome of no less than (it is said) 30,000 pilgrims every day – which would have been equal to the total resident population of Rome at that date. Two million pilgrims are supposed to have come to Rome in 1300. There is no way of checking these clearly exaggerated figures, nor of the equally extravagant claims that were made for later Holy Years. In 1350 (when the popes were not in Rome at all, but in Avignon) there are supposed to have been two million visitors to Rome between Christmas and Pentecost; in 1450, forty thousand every day. Yet the sandalled footsteps of these innumerable travellers have left very little trace in the sands of history. In 1300, for example, only four travel licences were issued in England to persons specifically described as pilgrims.

During the fourteenth century, the simple piety of the earlier centuries seems to have become somewhat tainted, in a variety of ways. In the first place, the Papacy was less respected than it had been. It was beginning to condone not merely the issuing of indulgences, but their frank sale; and their sale not only in Rome, but throughout Europe, by the pardoners.

> . . . *a gentil pardoner* . . .
> *That streight was comen from the court of Rome* . . .
> *His walet lay byforn him in his lappe,*
> *Bret-ful of pardoun come from Rome al hoot* . . .

Chaucer's Pardoner is in one sense a fictional character but, as J.J. Jusserand pointed out:

> *The description may seem today improbable and exaggerated; but it is not. A verifying from authentic sources*

> *and a search for documents only shows once more Chaucer's marvellous exactness; not a trait in his picture that may not be justified by letters from papal or episcopal chanceries.*[6]

The principle behind the activities of the pardoners was that they offered Christians a few grains of the heavenly wealth that had been stored up by the popes, as successors of St. Peter, in return for a similar small contribution from their own worldly wealth – a simple and pious idea in its origins, which was obviously prone to abuse on a massive scale. Chaucer's Pardoner simply made his living out of it, and his attitude, which was typical of the later fourteenth century, was completely cynical:

> *What! trow ye, whiles that I may preche*
> *And wynne gold and silver for I teche,*
> *That I wil lyve in povert wilfully? . . .*
> *For I wol preche and begge in sondry londes,*
> *I wil not do no labour with myn hondes . . .*
> *I wol noon of thapostles counterfete,*
> *I wol have money, wolle, chese, and whete.*

Such was the disorder in Rome in the fourteenth century that when a French Pope was elected, he removed the court altogether to Avignon, where it remained from 1306 to 1370. This meant many fewer official visits to Rome. Only three out of eleven English archbishops were consecrated by the Pope in the fourteenth century, and the last English cardinal to visit Rome in his official capacity was Adam Easton, who lived there from 1381 to 1397, and was buried in the church of St. Cecilia, in Trastevere.

There were other reasons why the road to Rome was particularly difficult in the fourteenth century – and perhaps attractive to pilgrims for that very reason. Although the Hundred Years War was a royal rather than a national war (Chaucer never mentioned it; nor did Langland, except to express disapproval), the disruption to civilian life that it caused must have made for dangerous travelling. A still more potent deterrent was the Black Death, the bubonic plague, which was severely epidemic in Europe in 1348, 1361, 1371 and 1382. The outbreak in 1348-9 is said to have caused the death of half the population of England.

The idea of the pilgrimage was now thoroughly implanted in English life. It did, at least, bring out much that was good in medieval Christianity: the need for public penance and atonement for sins; faith in God's inexhaustible store of grace, which was manifested in the form of indulgences and relics; endurance of the incidental discomforts of the journey – the muddy roads, the insanitary inns, the prowling highwaymen, the devastating wars, the stealthy plagues. All this was an unavoidable mortification of the flesh – which to the medieval Christian was a very important and necessary part of his faith.

Pilgrimages constituted the only form of travel that was officially sanctioned, and herein lay the seed of their future decay. People who had their own irreligious or anti-religious reasons for travelling, such as the canny merchant and the wanton woman, could so easily assume the role of pilgrims.

> *[Others] went like gypsies to a fair and tried to gather money by begging; some went for the pleasures of the journey and the merriments of the road and of the inn; so that satirists, paying more attention to the abuse than to the less visible good that came along with it, began to raise a cry which grew louder and louder until, at the time of the Reformation, it was something like a storm.*[7]

At the same time, it followed that any opposition to the prevailing form of society could develop within the pattern of the pilgrimage. If a popular leader had been executed and subsequently canonized, what could be more innocent and seemingly devout, and at the same time more annoying to the king, than to make a pilgrimage to his tomb? If a man wished to leave the country, to earn better wages under a new master, what more natural disguise could he assume than the pilgrim's scrip and staff? So the pilgrimage gradually became one of the vehicles whereby, through commercialization of its purpose, infiltration of undesirable elements, and waning of belief in its efficacy, the system itself was brought to the ground. In the ninth century, the "false pilgrims" were few; in the fourteenth, they were regarded by the Church as a threat; and at the end they often unconsciously helped to overthrow the universal rule of the Church.

But even in the fourteenth century, not all Englishmen approved of pilgrimages. Langland considered that people would do better to practise their religion at home:

> *Right so, if thow be religious – renne thou never ferther*
> *To Rome ne to Rochemadore.*

Not that all visitors to Rome were pilgrims. Sir John Hawkwood was a mercenary general who sold his services to nearly every state in Italy that possessed an army at that time. He fought for Pisa against Florence, for Milan against the Pope and against Verona, for Padua against Verona, for Florence against Milan, and for the Pope against anyone who wanted to attack the temporal rule of the Papacy. He commanded the Pope's mercenaries in 1374, but not having received his pay, went over to the anti-papal forces three years later. In 1378 he met Geoffrey Chaucer in Milan; in 1382 he was English Ambassador in Rome; and in 1394 he died, and was buried in the Duomo at Florence.

The Romano-Britons had started from Southwark for Rome. So did the fourteenth century pilgrim. He would ride from Southwark to Rochester (and could hire a horse for 12 pence for this stage), from Rochester to Canterbury (12 pence also), from Canterbury to Dover (6 pence); and while at Canterbury he would not fail to visit the shrine of St. Thomas, the most famous in England and one of the most famous anywhere; it attracted visitors from other countries, including Louis VII, the first king of France ever to visit England.

In the fourteenth century Englishmen going abroad were forbidden to take more than a very small amount of coin of the realm with them. Even merchants were not permitted to pay for goods in foreign countries with English money. Thus the system of bills of exchange and letters of credit developed. These were invented by Italian merchants living in England and elsewhere who, until the Bank of England was founded, had the monopoly of money-changing and banking generally. Hence the name Lombard Street in London.

Diplomats and merchants travelling "beyond the sea" in these early centuries might be granted a Safe Conduct, or licence to travel, signed personally by the monarch. However, the humble pilgrim would usually have no formal travel document at all. It was not until about 1540 that passports were issued by the Privy Council, which exercised this right until 1685. Attempts were sometimes made by the authorities to control foreign travel. In 1389 the government of Richard II, in the course of a dispute over papal subsidies, tried to stop the pilgrim traffic. It forbade visits of any kind to Rome, stopped the issue of letters of credit, and ordered all English clerics in Rome (with the exception of a few who represented the king there or were engaged in other essential business) to return home. But the hindrance to Dover's pilgrim trade was only temporary. By the sixteenth century the town appeared to a Greek traveller, Nicander Nuceus, to consist entirely of hotels.

Having paid his sixpence to be conveyed across the Channel (or two shillings if he took a horse with him), the fourteenth century pilgrim would lodge at Calais in a "Maison-Dieu" – a charitable foundation "for the sustenance of the pilgrims and other poor folk repairing to the said town to rest and refresh them".[8] Then he would proceed to Boulogne (where there was a miraculous Virgin), to Amiens (head of St. John the Baptist), thence usually to Paris, and by the way of Mont Cenis over the Alps.

The shortest practicable route by the Mont Cenis crossing has been estimated by combining several actual itineraries that were recorded in detail – those of Sir Richard Guylforde and Richard Torkyngton, who set out for the Holy Land in 1506 and 1517 respectively, crossing the Channel from Rye to Dieppe; that recommended in the oldest printed book of English travel, the *Information for Pylgrymes vnto the Holy Londe* (1498); and that of an anonymous merchant who left a detailed itinerary from Avignon to Rome (via Mont Cenis) about 1350. The total length of this route was 1159 miles from Calais to Rome – an average of 32½ miles a day. The road continued from Boulogne through Montreuil-sur-mer, Abbeville, Amiens and Clermont to Paris (180 miles); Paris to Lyon, via Cosne and Varennes (304 miles); Lyon to Susa, via Chambéry and St.-Jean de Maurienne (169 miles); and Susa to Rome, via Piacenza, La Cisa pass, Siena, Acquapendente and Viterbo (506 miles).

Sometime in the fourteenth century the old pilgrim route over the western Apennines to Lucca ceased to be used. The reason probably was that the greatly increased Holy Year traffic led to an urgent need for a better and quicker road to Rome inside Italy. The direct road from Bologna to Florence was repaired and improved with this in view. This was good for Bologna and Florence, bad for Lucca. Indeed Lucca was thereafter very little visited by pilgrims, and only recaptured a certain amount of tourist trade when the coast road from Genoa to Pisa became popular in the seventeenth century.

A further development within Italy was the increase of direct tourist traffic to the Holy Land from Venice. This was a godsend to Venice, whose commercial trade had been badly hit by the Portuguese discovery of the sea-way to India; but it meant that the Jerusalem pilgrims no longer used the Apulian ports. The roads leading to them fell into disuse; the main roads between Venice and Rome, which enabled the pilgrims to visit either Assisi or Loreto, became more important. From the fifteenth century onwards, pilgrims often came to Rome by the western route (through Florence and Siena) or by the central route (Forli – Bagno di Romana – Perugia – Assisi – Foligno), and then returned to Venice by the eastern route (Foligno – Ancona – Loreto – coast road to Ravenna – road or sea to Venice). Thus for the first time a circular tour became standard. The tour which in later centuries became known as the Grand Tour of Italy.

During the fourteenth and fifteenth centuries, when the road through France was often dangerous because of war, plague, or other hazards, another route became popular among English pilgrims. This was "the Dutch way", which took the traveller through Flanders and up the Rhine valley, and then over the Great St. Bernard pass or, in the fifteenth century, through Bavaria and the Tyrol. One of these roads was followed by Adam of Usk, in 1402. He sailed to Bergen-op-Zoom in the Netherlands, went overland to Maastricht and Cologne, up the Rhine valley, and over the Great St. Bernard pass "in an ox-waggon and half dead with cold, and with mine eyes bandaged lest I should see the dangers of the pass"; then down to Como, Milan and Piacenza, across the Apennines to the valley of the Arno, and through Siena to Rome, which he discovered to be a distressed and squalid city of some seventeen thousand people. The Lateran Palace, which before 1306 had been the papal residence, was uninhabitable, and the popes had gone to live at the Vatican.

Better documented in fifteenth century records is the standard "Duche way", as followed by the chaplain William Brewyn (who went to Rome before 1469, and about 1470 compiled a guide-book to the principal churches of Rome) and by John of Wheathampstead, Abbot of St. Albans (who visited Rome between 1423 and 1424, accompanied by two chaplains and at least seven servants, his main object being to attend the Council of Pavia, at which it was expected that English monastic privileges would be attacked by certain English bishops).

Wheathampstead's journey was not recorded in detail, but Brewyn left a number of interesting particulars. First he crossed to Calais, then along the Flemish coast to Dunkirk, Nieuport ("a good town and walled") and Ostend, then inland to Bruges (where there were facilities for changing money) and Ghent, thence to Diest and Hasselt, across the Maas at Maastricht and so into the Rhineland at Aachen ("a good town or city and there is a great pilgrimage to St. Mary's because her shift is there in the hall"), and then to Cologne. The route then followed the Rhine to Ulm ("a beautiful city", thought Brewyn, and he noted that pilgrims who here displayed their tonsured heads might escape the tax levied on travellers). Beyond Memmingen the mountains began, and the road climbed tortuously through little Alpine villages and towns – Vils, Nassereith, Imst, Landeck-am-Inn; then over the Reschen pass and down the Val Venosta to Merano ("take note of the market"); then to Trento, Verona and so into the plain of Lombardy.

Abbot Wheathampstead may have crossed the Alps by one of the more central passes, because the Tyrolean route does not seem the obvious way to approach Pavia. As it happened, it was the traditional hazards of the English journey to Rome – disease, bandits and the heat of summer – that made it possible for him to visit Rome at all. The Council had started its deliberations at Pavia, and the Abbot had made a spirited reply to Richard Flemmyng, Bishop of Lincoln, who had brought out the expected attack on monastic privileges. But the heat of summer was so intense, and the dreaded plague so prevalent (the Abbot had himself already been delayed in Cologne a fortnight through a fever), that it was decided to adjourn to the cooler air of Siena. Here, one of the English bishops who opposed monastic privileges fell ill, which gave the Abbot a great opportunity. Rome was only a few days' journey away; and it was Holy Year. He obtained a safe conduct from the Duke of Milan, set out for Rome, reached it safely . . . and then went down with dysentery. He was so ill that it was thought he would die; the Pope sent him plenary indulgence by the resident English envoy in Rome, Thomas Polton, Bishop of Chichester. But he recovered, was able to see the churches of the city, and was received in audience by the Pope, who granted the monastery fresh privileges. This fully justified the extra journey from the Abbey's point of view (the complete journey, each way, would have cost from £100 to £150 in modern values for each member of the party), and the Abbot, though he had not actually done very much either at Pavia, Siena or Rome, had succeeded in the main purpose of his visit. Moreover, he had seen

Rome; and he had even made contact with the new Italian humanism – in Pavia he inspected the Visconti Library, with its collection of Petrarch manuscripts, and on the road between Pavia and Florence he fell in with a man who turned out to be a Venetian humanist – possibly Guarino, who later, at Ferrara, taught both Robert Flemmyng (nephew of the bishop who had opposed Wheathampstead) and John Free. However, despite his keen interest in the new movement, and the endless pains he took to make himself well read in the classical authors, the Abbot never caught the spirit of it. He remained, for all his erudition and his opportunities, attached to the tradition of orthodox scholasticism. England in any case was not yet ready for the new ideas. Just as, in architecture, the early Renaissance motifs that came into England in the sixteenth century were so alien to the native fashion that they were only adopted as a quickly-dying craze, so, in philosophy, theology and literature there were not yet enough English scholars who had assimilated the classics at their source.

Meanwhile, William Brewyn was occupied with the more mundane problems of foreign exchange, which were as confusing to the English traveller as they have been ever since. He found he needed "plakks and stufyrs" at Ostend, "blafforths" of Rhenish money beyond the Rhine at Speyer, "bylles" at Verona, "crucifers" to pay the ferryman who took travellers across the Po and Panaro rivers, and papal "groats" or "carlyns", and Cologne pence as well. Fortunately English money could be changed in Rome. He himself exchanged nine shillings for two ducats, and was able to do the same for others by means of a letter of credit that he had obtained in London on the bank of Jacopo de Medici. He was also able to buy eleven Rhenish guilders in the bank at Bruges, in exchange for forty English shillings.

When the English pilgrims finally reached Rome, many of them would find accommodation in the hospice that had been founded in the Via Monserrato in 1362, "for the use and comfort of poor Englishmen, sick, needy or wretched." This institution, the English Hospital of the Holy Trinity and St. Thomas of Canterbury, has a history rather similar to that of its predecessor in the Borgo which ended as the

Santo Spirito hospital. It started in a modest way, in a single-storey house and garden provided by its first warden, John Shepherd, a dealer in rosaries. Because there was a real need for an institution of this sort, it began to flourish immediately for several reasons: there were many English pilgrims in Rome for the Holy Years; there had been no hospice catering specifically for the English since 1201; and the centre of Roman life had shifted across the river to the district around the Via Giulia and the Campo dei Fiori. By 1383 the hospice had five houses and three plots of land; in 1396 a branch was opened in Trastevere (the hospice of St. Edmund), which by 1449 had nine houses of its own, with gardens and vineyards. Finally the two hospices, St. Thomas's and St. Edmund's, were combined to form a single administrative unit. Thereafter the English Hospice suffered the usual fate of institutions with a top-heavy administration and too little vigour at the core. It acquired an official status, its warden and chamberlains being nominated by the English ambassador instead of being elected by the members themselves. At the end, in the sixteenth century, it was ripe for expropriation and re-endowment as the Venerable English College, just as King Ine's hospice had been taken over and re-endowed as the Santo Spirito foundation, three hundred and eighty years previously.

Once in Rome, the pilgrims rested, got out their guide-books, and considered how best to make the prescribed tour of the seven stations of Rome, and to see the many remarkable relics that were preserved in the churches scattered all over the city. They were not interested in anything else. The ancient Roman ruins were just heaps of rubble to them, or else they were pagan remains at which they refused to look; and their guide-books reflect that lack of interest. These express neither wonder nor admiration concerning the ruins of ancient Rome; they concentrate on the churches, their relics, their shrines, the indulgences associated with them; they ignore the triumphal arches, the great baths, the imperial palaces and the ancient temples. Even Master Gregory, an English visitor in the twelfth century, who was one of the few who admired the sight of the old ruins, and gave a sympathetic description of the Pantheon, passed over it "briefly because it was once the image of all the gods, that is, the demons."

For more than four centuries, from about the tenth to the fourteenth, the standard guides to Rome were loosely classified as the *Mirabilia Urbis Romae*. They appeared in innumerable versions, at first in manuscript, later crudely printed. They enumerated the holy places in great detail, together with various extravagant legends which were often repeated word for word by later writers. *The Stacions of Rome*, written in the fourteenth century, was a rhymed impression of Rome by an unknown English traveller; and about 1450 there appeared *The Solace of Pilgrims* by John Capgrave, Prior of Kings Lynn and Provincial of the Augustinian Friars, who was in Rome for the Holy Year. Although this work contains the usual details of all the churches, with their relics and indulgences, it does also mention aspects of the city which were to become so much more familiar to the seventeenth and eighteenth century travellers – "the multitude of paleys", "the multitude of arches in rome rered for dyuers uictories", the "fayr place clepit *Ars coeli*", and so on. Capgrave was the first Englishman to describe the catacombs; they are now "desolate for horrible darknesse and disuse of puple", he wrote.

By this time the humanist revival had all but reached Rome, but the pilgrim writers still clung to the ancient superstitions. William Brewyn's work, which appeared soon after Capgrave's, displays no awareness of the New Learning. He repeats all the old legends that the earlier writers had themselves got at second hand, and meticulously assigns to every church its precise value in terms of indulgences. He was completely medieval in his outlook – yet he lived in Rome only twenty years before the English humanist scholar Linacre arrived there.

From about the middle of the fifteenth century, in fact, until the official break between England and Rome of which the symbol is the Reformation, two differing attitudes on the part of the English people towards Rome can be discerned. They might be called the "humanist" and the "traditional" attitudes; and as the humanist attitude gathered strength and adherents (as will be described in the next chapter), so the traditionalists very slowly lost support, while retaining absolute control

The English Road To Rome

over the apparatus of State and Church. At the end of the fifteenth century, it might have seemed to an impartial observer that the Roman Catholic Church would remain the only arbiter and controller of everything in English life for ever. Hospitals, schools, the law – everything came under ecclesiastical management. Humanism was confined to academic circles, and every art, in order to secure any support at all, had to have a religious background or purpose. The Church had never been so rich; the papal collectors lived like millionaires, while tithes, dues and profits from the sale of indulgences poured into Rome. In 1509, when Henry VII died, his funeral was accompanied by a Catholic pomp that today would seem extravagant even in Spain. At the same time the devoutness of the English was then proverbial throughout Europe. It was they, the English considered, who had remained loyal to Catholicism; it was the profligate Roman Bishop and his court who had betrayed the ideals of the Church and were draining the countries of Europe of their wealth. When the disillusioned traditionalists finally united with the humanists against Rome, the result – as much a political as a religious event – was the Reformation.

From that time onwards it is again possible to discuss the English attitudes to Rome in a single chapter. But for about a hundred years, the two attitudes ran parallel, and must be dealt with separately. The remainder of this chapter, therefore, will be concerned with the declining though still powerful "traditionalist" attitude to Rome. It will end with the passing of Henry VIII's Act of Supremacy in 1534, and with the brief reign of Queen Mary from 1553 to 1558.

The kings of England had long ceased to visit Rome in person; but they still found it necessary to send ambassadors. From the 13th century onwards, the king's business in Rome had generally been carried on by a king's Proctor, who was usually resident in Rome but would not necessarily be an Englishman. One such proctor was William Swan, an Oxford graduate who lived in Rome off and on between 1404 and 1429. About the same time (1413) John Cateryck was given power to "undertake, carry on and dispatch all other business whatsoever at the apostolic see". He was the first resident ambassador in Rome from the

King of England (1413-15, 1417-19) and, like his non-resident predecessor Sir John Hawkwood, he died and was buried in Florence. He was succeeded, up to the year 1510, by about twenty other resident envoys and about the same number of diplomats sent to Rome for a specific purpose. The Pope preferred the resident envoy to be called a proctor, reserving the term "ambassador" for the initial period of the envoy's visit. Resident and special envoys might combine in order to provide diplomatic representation at special functions. John Shirwood, Bishop of Durham, represented the king in Rome for nearly twenty years, and died in 1493/4. His body was carried from his residence in the English Hospice, and then buried, attended by the households of four cardinals. The most influential English envoy was Christopher Bainbridge, Archbishop of York and later Cardinal. He was in Rome from 1509 to 1514, attended the Lateran Council in 1513, and died suddenly, it is alleged as a result of poison, in 1514. His tomb can still be seen in the present English College.

It was soon after 1500 that the revival of the Imperial Roman practice of riding post was introduced –that is, changing horses at regularly-spaced posting stations along a recognized route. It remained, for the next three hundred years, the fastest means of getting to Rome from England by land.

A large party, for which there would be no facilities for changing horses, would still need six or seven weeks to complete the journey; but Stephen Gardiner, riding post, went from Dover to Rome in fourteen days in 1529. The record may have been held by another messenger who covered the same distance in the same year in a mere thirteen days; but this would have been a remarkable feat in any age, since it meant *averaging* 89 miles a day, over some extremely rough and hilly country; only a professional rider in hard training could have achieved it.

Using the post system, and sending out envoy after envoy on the Mont Cenis road to Rome, Tudor diplomacy made its last two great efforts to bring the Roman Church to its side. The first of these concerned the hoped-for election of Cardinal Thomas Wolsey as the second English Pope. Wolsey himself never went to Rome to canvass his election; he relied on the king's envoys and on Italian agents in Rome. At the time of his first attempt, in 1521, there was no resident English ambassador in Rome (though Henry VIII's palace, today the Palazzo Giraud-Torlonia, was always available for the ambassador's use); but there were numerous Italian agents, as well as a special English envoy, John Clerk, and the king's secretary, Richard Pace, who did not arrive until after the election. Wolsey never had a real chance, however, and in due course Adrian VI was elected. He died the following year, and Wolsey's name was put up again. His candidature was supported by Clerk and Pace, who had stayed on in Rome, and by Thomas Hannibal, the English envoy in Spain, who came to reinforce them. But again Wolsey failed in his greatest ambition.

The second and final effort was in the matter of Henry VIII's divorce. Beginning in 1527, when Rome had just been pillaged by the Imperial troops, and the dispute can hardly have seemed as vital to Clement VII as it was to the King of England, Henry sent a constant stream of envoys into Italy in the hope of annulling his marriage with Katharine of Aragon, so that he could marry Ann Boleyn. First the king's new secretary, Dr. William Knight, was sent to Rome; then, in 1528, Stephen Gardiner and Edward Foxe. Four more envoys, Sir Francis Bryan, Peter Vannes, Stephen Gardiner (again!) and Gregorio Casali, were despatched the following year, instructed to search the papal archives until they found a document which Katharine's nephew, the Holy Roman Emperor, had lodged with the Pope. It was necessary not only to find the document but also to prove that it had been forged; the Pope would then be obliged to declare the King's first marriage annulled. If the document could not be found, then the Pope's decision must be delayed by all possible means. For if the Pope pronounced judgment in the absence of that vital document, the outcome would be the worst possible as far as the king's pride was concerned: he would be summoned to Rome to justify his action before the supreme head of the Church. And Henry VIII would be no more likely to abase himself before Clement VII than the Emperor Frederick before Adrian IV four hundred years earlier.

The first envoys had no success in finding the document. A more substantial delegation was sent out in January 1530, with similar instructions. It consisted of the Earl of Wiltshire, Ann Boleyn's father (his selection as leader of the delegation seems in the circumstances to have been supremely tactless); Dr. Cranmer, future Archbishop of Canterbury; Dr. Lee, recently envoy to Spain and future Archbishop of York; Dr. Stokesley, future Bishop of London; and Dr. Edward Carne, a Glamorganshire lawyer who had been one of the commissioners for the dissolution of the monasteries, a post which had conveniently enabled him to buy Ewenny Abbey in his native county. This eminent company had no more success than its predecessors in the search for the missing marriage document. At Bologna they split up, the Earl of Wiltshire and Dr. Lee returning to England, while Cranmer and Stokesley went about other business in Italy, and Carne went on alone to Rome.

Dr. Carne's importance in the ensuing negotiations was that he could very suitably be used to prolong the hearings as long as possible. He had no credentials from the King; that presumably was deliberate. Yet he purported to be present in the capacity of "excusator", representing the English people in their protest against the threatened summoning of their king to Rome.

This posed a delightful series of problems for the English and Italian lawyers on both sides. Should Dr. Carne, or should he not, be admitted to the hearings? Should he be allowed to take part in the discussions? Should there not be a more precise ruling from London concerning his right to be there at all? All the legal experts threw themselves with professional zeal into the elaboration and obscuration of all the arguments for and against these and similar propositions – and the work of the court proceeded at an infinitely slow pace.

The discussions went on and on. All the protagonists were fully conversant with the technicalities of curial practice, and they utilized their knowledge to the utmost. From time to time the court was suspended for vacations. Messengers were sent to England with despatches, and it would be six to eight weeks before a reply was received and the hearing could continue. For more than three years the case was deliberated upon. Dr. Carne settled down in Rome and liked it there.

At last the judgment could not be held up any longer. In May 1533, Pope Clement VII finally ordered King Henry VIII to appear before him. In July, he declared void the King's remarriage to Ann Boleyn, which had taken place the previous winter. There was nothing more for Dr. Carne to do but to return to England, which he did in October 1533.

Henry still had hopes that the judgment might be postponed, or even reversed. Early in 1534 he again sent Dr. Carne to Rome, accompanied by another lawyer, Dr. William Revett. This time, procrastination was not the object; they were instructed to ride post to Rome, in an effort to hold up the judgment as best they could. But they were too late. At Bologna they were informed that the Pope had given his final decision. In the eyes of the Church, Henry VIII had not divorced Katherine of Aragon, nor was he married to Ann Boleyn. Once again there was nothing Dr. Carne could do but lodge a protest, and return empty-handed home. The King's reply, the following November, was to pass the Act of Supremacy, which effectively detached the English Church from Rome.

After the remaining nineteen years of Henry VIII's reign (during which Dr. Carne, soon to become Sir Edward Carne, continued his life as a career diplomat), and the short reign of Edward VI, the "traditionalists" had their last years in power during the reign of Queen Mary. Sir Edward Carne was sent, together with the Bishop of Ely and Lord Montague, to make submission to the Pope on behalf of the Queen; and he remained in Rome as resident ambassador.

At the same time the see of Canterbury was given to Reginald Pole, who of all the Archbishops of Canterbury perhaps had the closest ties with Rome. He was a relative of Henry VIII who had studied under Linacre at Oxford, and later at Padua, and visited Rome about 1527. He was in Rome again in 1536 and was created Cardinal, and later returned to Rome as legate of the Patrimony of St. Peter. In 1549 he was a candidate for the Papacy – which he very nearly secured, since at one time he had a majority of two-thirds of the votes. As soon as Mary became Queen of England, Pole was appointed papal legate to England, though he did not arrive until November 1554. After again standing for election as Pope, he became Archbishop of Canterbury as well as Chancellor of both Oxford and Cambridge Universities. Some of his theological views were unpopular in the Curia, and he was charged with heresy and summoned to Rome; but Queen Mary refused to let him go. He died – probably very conveniently for himself – on the same day as Mary.

Elizabeth I was now Queen of England, and the break with Rome was complete; but Sir Edward Carne still stayed on in Rome. According to the diplomatic protocol of the day, it was his duty to ask permission to return to his own country and seek fresh instructions from his new sovereign. His wife and children were in Glamorgan; it was expected that he would want to return to them. But Rome had become his second home: he was nearly seventy, and he may have known that he had not long to live. Further, he was a convinced Roman Catholic, his new sovereign was not.

He asked the Pope to detain him in Rome, but the story that reached England ran that he had been refused permission to leave. This not unnaturally caused a great outcry. To hold a sick, harmless, elderly and much respected diplomat, whose only desire was to see his wife and children again before he died – could the evil faithlessness of Rome go further?

Sir Edward Carne kept his secret; his family and property went unharmed. When, in 1560, Elizabeth asked Philip of Spain to intercede on behalf of the former ambassador, the Spanish king's representative in Rome obtained the true story from Carne, but only on condition that it should not be transmitted to England until it could do no harm. This condition was kept; Sir Edward Carne had brought off his last and most masterly diplomatic success. At what personal cost, we shall never know.

In the meantime he had another employment in Rome, though it can hardly have been more than a sinecure. For the past half-century the Wardenship of the English Hospice had usually been held by the resident English ambassador or his nominee. The last effective chiefs were Cardinal Pole, who controlled the hostel from 1538 to 1540; and Thomas Goldwell, Bishop of St. Albans, who was Warden in 1540-1 and in 1553. Bishop Goldwell left for England in 1555 to take charge of his diocese, and Sir Edward Carne, arriving in Rome the same year, took over the post of Warden, which he retained until relieved of it by Pope Pius IV in 1560.

The hospice, now two hundred years old, was not what it used to be. There were fewer students, and those few were inclined to be less studious and more boisterous. There were allegations of drunkenness, even of rioting in the streets, and the hostel had very little money. As had been the case with its twelfth century predecessor in the Borgo, people at home were more ready to applaud the college's aims than to send contributions to the funds. In fact the hostel, which finally had been plundered during the sack of Rome in 1527, was moribund. In 1555 there were still a few students living in its rooms; but there could have been little for the Warden to do. In 1578, the English Hospice was expropriated and began a new life as the Venerable English College.

But in 1560, when he ceased to be Warden, Sir Edward Carne was himself moribund. He died in Rome on 19 January 1561, and appropriately he was buried in the church which more than almost any other in Rome has intimate associations with England – the church of S. Gregorio at the foot of the Caelian Hill, whence St. Augustine set out in 597 to re-convert the English to the Church of Rome. The funeral monument to the old diplomat, placed in the atrium in front of the old church by his friends Geoffrey Vaughan and Thomas Freeman, may still be read.

REDISCOVERY OF ITALY

FROM THE MID-FIFTEENTH CENTURY TO 1615

There was, of course, never a precise moment in history when mankind suddenly realized that books need not be confined to monasteries, but could also be a guide to the art of living; that the human body could itself be the subject of great painting and sculpture; that architecture, politics, war and even sport could be practised for their own sakes and not only for purposes sanctioned by the Church. Those who lived in Europe in the fourteenth and fifteenth centuries saw nothing specially remarkable about their own era, and today an anti-Romantic swing of opinion leads us to doubt, not only the genesis of the Renaissance (a word that was not even used until the nineteenth century) by the wandering Greek scholars, but even the existence of the Renaissance itself.

The new humanist learning certainly displaced monasticism, but it did so gradually. Some of the new ideas associated with humanism appeared as early as the twelfth century, others not until the Reformation. Individual liberty came first, then the re-birth of letters, then that of art, finally the reform of religion and the gradual elimination of superstition. In fact, the slow flowering of humanism during the last centuries of the Middle Ages coincided with the slow withering of the scholastic tradition. The process began early, and was complete somewhere about the middle of the sixteenth century. But the classical art and architecture of Italy was not rediscovered by the English until nearly a hundred years after that.

The movement for the emancipation of the human spirit did not originate in Rome. It spread down the peninsula, as it spread across the Alps, from a focus in the north of Italy, and especially from Venice.

During the fifteenth century, the north of Italy was the target for those who sought the new learning at its source. There were few enough Englishmen among these seekers after knowledge. The Italians still persisted, perhaps not unreasonably, in regarding the English as living on the uttermost edge of the civilized world – but at Bologna the university contained an English "nation"; there was even an English rector at the university of Vicenza; while the medical school at Padua, then considered the best in Europe, had a considerable colony of English students. Most of all, Venice fascinated the English of that century and the succeeding one because of her riches and her position on the route to and from the East, because of her unique constitution and her sea-power, because of the luxury and magnificence of her way of living. Venice was the first Italian state to which England sent a resident ambassador. Venice remained the embodiment of the exhilarating Italian magnificence to which the name Renaissance was much later applied.

Thus, the few English scholars who set out on the long road to Rome in the fifteenth and early sixteenth centuries, did so after they had been introduced to humanism in the northern Italian cities. To a limited extent, they were themselves instrumental in bringing humanism to Rome.

A typical example was John Free, born in Bristol about 1430, who studied in Oxford between 1445 and 1454, arrived at Ferrara in 1456, studied the classics there for two years, then moved to Padua, where he studied medicine as well as civil law, and set out for Rome in 1462, with the aim of persuading the Pope to grant him an ecclesiastical appointment. He completed a translation of a work by the Greek writer Synesius of Cyrene and dedicated it to Pope Paul II, who acknowledged the compliment by appointing Free to the vacant bishopric of Bath and Wells. But Free never took up the office – he died almost as soon as he had been appointed.

A contemporary of John Free's was Robert Flemmyng, who also studied at Padua, and was in Rome between 1458 and 1461, when he was king's proctor at the *curia*, and again from 1473 to 1477, when he knew the papal librarian Platina. During Flemmyng's second visit to Rome he composed his *Tivoli Meditations* (*Tiburtinae Lucubrationes*) during the hot summer months when the papal court was in *villeggiatura* at Tivoli. This poem is noteworthy as the first imaginative work printed by an Englishman in Rome, or for that matter in Italy, and as the only contemporary description of mid-fifteenth century Rome by an English writer. However, its literary merit is very slender. It is purely a panegyric of Sixtus IV and his rebuilding of Rome.

A generation later another group of humanists travelled to Rome in a similar fashion to that of Free and Flemmyng, but had a far more lasting and profound effect on English intellectual life. To the activities of Thomas Linacre and his colleagues we owe the introduction of the study of Greek to our schools and universities, as well as the implantation of an English tradition of Greek scholarship, which by the end of the century was so far advanced that English students no longer needed to go to Italy for their Greek studies. They could just as easily acquire Greek at Oxford, from Linacre, his colleagues and their successors.

Linacre was born about 1460. He went to Italy in 1487, after graduating from Oxford. He was in Florence for about two years and then went on to Rome. He was admitted to the confraternity of the English Hospice in 1489, and, unusually for a wandering scholar, was elected warden of the hospice in 1491, presumably for the usual period of one year. After this he studied medicine at Padua and graduated from that university in 1496. He returned to England in 1499, and became a scholar-physician. He taught Greek at Oxford, moved to London, became king's physician, and in 1518 founded the institution which became the Royal College of Physicians. His work included the composition of two Latin grammars and the translation of Galen and Aristotle from Greek into Latin.

William Grocyn, William Lily, John Colet and William Latimer all helped to bring the Greek language and Greek scholarship to England. All studied with Linacre in Italy – Grocyn probably in Florence, Lily and Colet in Rome, Latimer probably in Padua. Grocyn was the first to give lectures on Greek at Oxford (1491), Colet founded St. Paul's School, the first school in England to include Greek in its curriculum (1509), and Lily, who was admitted to the English Hospice at the same time as Linacre, became first headmaster of St. Paul's. Latimer was also regarded in his day as a leading Greek scholar.

These visits of Free, Flemmyng and the Linacre circle account for almost everything that England gained from Rome during the three-quarters of a century between 1453, when Constantinople was taken by the Turks, and 1527, when a mixed Spanish, German and Italian army owing allegiance to Charles V – the Flemish-born, Hapsburg King of Spain who became Holy Roman Emperor – captured and sacked Rome. During this period, Michelangelo, Raphael, Botticelli, Perugino and Pinturicchio were all working in Rome. Palaces such as that of St. Mark[1] and of Farnese were being designed and erected. The foundation stone of the new St. Peter's was laid in 1506. But at the same time Italy was swept by marauding soldiers and the plagues that they spread. Syphilis, in particular, made a shattering entry into Europe in 1500, having been brought to Naples from the West Indies by the Spaniards. Politically there was complete disunity in Italy, only the Venetian Republic being able to hold itself aloof both from the Spaniards and the Emperor on the one hand, and the Pope on the other. But the Pope commanded less and less authority and obedience, and the sack of his city by forty thousand mutinous soldiers (as many soldiers as there were people living in the city at that date) left him with a capital two-thirds ruined, in which scarcely a corner had escaped the tide of looting, rape and murder that the invading force had released.

By the mid-sixteenth century most of Italy was in a state of political decline or even degeneracy, and it was this that particularly struck the next significant English traveller to Rome, twenty years after the sack of the city. In his *History of Italy*, published in London in 1549, he tried to show how this disunity had been brought about, and to warn Edward VI and his advisers that a similar fate could befall the Tudor monarchy if due heed was not paid to the lesson provided by Italy.

This traveller was William Thomas, who typified a new trend, since he went to Italy not on a religious pilgrimage, not solely in order to study, but to see contemporary Italy itself. He has been said to represent, in his own life and reasons for travel, "almost exactly the transition from the renaissance scholar to the Tudor student of good manners".[2]

William Thomas travelled in Italy between 1545 and 1549. He is known to have visited Venice, Bologna, Padua, Ferrara, Genoa, Urbino, Florence, as well as Rome, where he arrived in 1547. He "tarried but a small time" in Rome according to his account, but this does not mean that he considered the city to be of small importance. On the contrary he describes Rome with objectivity and sympathy, as can be seen from the following passage:

> *"Of the ground contained within the wall, scarcely the third part is now inhabited, and that not where the beauty of Rome has been, but for the most part on the plain to the water side, and in the Vatican: because since the bishops began to reign, every man has coveted to build as near the Court as might be. Nevertheless those streets and buildings that are there at this time are so fair, that I think no city does excel it, by reason they have the beautifullest things of the "antiquities" before rehearsed to garnish their houses withal."*

His account of Rome forms part of the *History of Italy*. He began with the Tiber and the four bridges that spanned it, and then went on to describe the ancient and medieval remains – the walls, the gates, the

Seven Hills, the aqueducts, the baths, and so on through triumphal arches, circuses, temples, pillars, obelisks, "colosses and images", hippodromes, granaries and arsenals. In later centuries it became usual to introduce most of these objects into any description of Rome; Thomas was the first English writer to do so. In this and several other respects, he had no predecessor. True, his comments are at times a little naive. His statement that "there be three kinds of pillars – round, square and striped" does not greatly elucidate classical architecture for us. But he looked at what he saw, unblinded by prejudice, and he liked it. Rome for him was "the only jewel, mirror, mistress and beauty of this world, that never had her like nor (as I think) never shall";. It grieved him to see her "desolate and disfigured", even though, as a good Protestant, he considered the wretched condition of Rome to be a judgment on the Romans themselves for their "infinite blood shedding".

William Thomas might have had a very much greater effect on English thought and ways of living if his subsequent career had not been a particularly unfortunate one. In fact it ended only four years after *The History of Italy* was published. On his return from Italy he had been appointed Clerk of the Privy Council, and was in charge of the young King Edward VI's training. But Edward VI died in 1553 at the age of sixteen, and immediately the group of men closely connected with him, Protestants too early in their country's history, became themselves the victims of absolute monarchy. William Thomas was one of those arrested on the orders of Queen Mary, and charged with high treason. He was condemned to death, hanged, drawn and quartered. *The History of Italy* was suppressed, copies of it being publicly burnt by the common hangman.

He had so nearly escaped that fate. The previous year he'd written to Sir William Cecil, asking if he could be sent on a diplomatic mission to Venice. "Considering the stir of the world is now like to be very great those ways," he wrote astutely and somewhat wistfully, "I could find it in my heart to spend a year or two there if I were sent . . . " Had he been sent, he might have weathered out the storm of Mary's reign in Italy, and returned to play a more important role in Elizabeth

I's. But history, alas, is full of such *if's*.

William Thomas had written two other books while he was in Italy. One of them, *The Pilgrim*, a eulogy of Henry VIII, was published in Italian in 1552, but in English not until 1774, by which time it was scarcely even of historical interest. The other one, *The Principal Rules of the Italian Grammar*, first published in 1550, is of interest as the first textbook of the Italian language to be printed in England. It comprised a grammar and an Italian-English vocabulary, and was written, states its preface, "after that William Thomas had been about three years in Italy" – in other words, about 1548. Not being of a tendentious character, it was allowed to remain in circulation, and indeed was not superseded as a standard work for fifty years.

Its publication draws a sharply-defined line across an epoch. For the first time the English traveller, if he was going to acquire anything worthwhile from his visit to Italy, needed more than his native language together with Latin. Travel had become, and was to remain for two centuries, an educational process. The object was to put one's accumulated knowledge to the service of the State, as well as to "gain personal force, social effectiveness – in short, that mysterious 'virtu' by which the Renaissance set such great store."[3] It really seemed as though, for the first time, travellers actually enjoyed travelling, and did not travel, as the pilgrims had often done, chiefly in order to mortify the flesh.

Of course this new class of traveller did not always live up to the high ideals that had been propounded by the armchair theorists of travel. Many a young gentleman was so overjoyed by the prospect of a year in Italy, a land reputedly unrivalled for the practice of dissipation, that he gladly put up with the necessity of having a "governor" or tutor in tow, and of writing his periodic "relations" or reports on the Italian states and cities that he passed through. Before long the travelled Englishman, with the absurd Italianate habits that he had picked up, became a figure of fun at home. Fathers began to doubt the wisdom of sending their sons on an educative tour abroad. They might return from their travels with nothing more dangerous than such novelties as forks

The English Road To Rome

or table-linen, but they might also come back infected with the deadly canker of popery.

But soon after William Thomas' visit to Rome, that city had become practically inaccessible except to convinced Catholics. Between 1570, when the Pope declared Elizabeth to be no longer a rightful Queen and her subjects absolved of any duty of allegiance to her, and 1604, when peace with Spain was finally concluded, Rome was as difficult and dangerous for a loyal Englishman to visit as Paris in 1793 or Petrograd in 1917. Turler, who had himself been to Italy, wrote in 1575 that "our countrymen usually bring three things with them out of Italy: a naughty conscience, an empty purse and a weak stomach." Roger Ascham, who had not been and did not intend to, pronounced in 1576 that young men who chose to go to Italy risked being engulfed by popery and filthy living. Philemon Holland, in 1600, advised Englishmen not to visit Rome, since the journey was bound to be long, tedious, pointless and expensive, the modern Romans a degenerate crew and the adventure "for hazard of religion, conscience and good manners, exceeding dangerous." If such head-shaking from the ancients is always liable rather to encourage young men of spirit to go and see for themselves a country where they can enjoy the sensation of exposing themselves to such tempting vices, some at least were deterred by public opinion, now almost unanimous in regarding Rome as a hot-bed of subversive activity.

And there was one man who appears to have calculated deliberately that if he could safely get to Rome and back, investigate the source of this subversive activity – that is, the English College – and use the results of his investigation as literary capital, his reputation and subsequent career would be assured.

This man, Anthony Munday, is labelled "poet and dramatist" by the Dictionary of National Biography, and as "an Elizabethan man of letters" by the author of the only full-length biography of him. However, to his contemporaries he was none of these things, but simply a story-teller, an entertainer, a money-spinner, a writer ready to turn his literary gift to any purpose that might bring his name before the public. He was, in a word, a journalist: a man who knew what the public wanted, and was able to supply it copiously, in the current idiom. During the course of his long career he wrote, or collaborated in the writing of, nearly a score of plays. He composed ballads and lyrics, translated romances from the French, Spanish and Italian, wrote popular guides to religion, physics and music, and compiled also (that irresistible temptation to popular writers) a universal history "from the creation of the world to this instant". In later life he was responsible for the scripts of the annual City pageants, and he rounded off his career by editing Stow's *Survey of London* for publication after its author's death. He died at the age of eighty, a prosperous member of the Drapers' Company who could afford to pay for an elaborate monument to be erected over his grave.

Thirty years later the monument, together with the church in which it stood, collapsed beneath the flames of the Great Fire of London. This was symbolic of the fate of all his works, for only the titles of most of them have survived, and only a handful have achieved, or perhaps deserved, modern reprinting. It is ironical but not inappropriate that today, in the heyday of popular journalism, he should be completely forgotten by the type of reader for whom he wrote, and remembered only by the literary specialist.

In 1578, when he decided to go to Rome to find out what he could about the "English Romans", he was unknown to anyone, a mere stationer's apprentice, aged twenty-five, with only two minor works to his credit. He broke his indentures, left his master, and with his companion Thomas Nowell landed on the continent of Europe at Boulogne. He gave as the reason for his journey the innocent one that he desired to see foreign countries and learn modern languages.

Almost immediately the two travellers ran into one of the everyday hazards of sixteenth century travel. They were held up by marauding soldiers and robbed of all their possessions. Arriving at Amiens destitute, and having heard that there was an old English priest there, they applied to him for help. It is clear that Munday and Nowell completed their journey to Rome on Roman Catholic money and with Roman Catholic letters of introduction. There was, it is true, no other way in which Englishmen bereft of funds could at that time possibly reach Rome. This later involved Munday in awkward explanations, of which he did not make a very likely tale.

They continued their journey, passing through Rheims and Paris, where they spurned the English Ambassador's offer to repatriate them, and were "very courteously entertained" by Roman Catholics along the road to Lyon, Milan, Bologna, Florence and Siena, whence they arrived in Rome at the beginning of February, 1578-79, "upon Candelmas evening when as it drew somewhat towards night." Lodging for the night in the city, they reported next morning at the English College, "a house both large and fair, standing in the way to the pope's palace, not far from the Castle Sant'Angelo."

From the journalistic point of view they could not have arrived at a more interesting moment. Cardinal Allen, the leading English Catholic of that time, had been summoned to Rome in 1575 to advise about the foundation of an English Catholic College. He had urged the establishment of an English seminary in Rome, on the lines of those he had already set up at Douai and Rheims. A suitable site was clearly the moribund English Hospice which we last encountered at the time of Sir Edward Carne's death, eighteen years previously. The Hospice possessed land and houses, but no money and practically no students. It was therefore expropriated by Pope Gregory XIII, at Christmas 1578, when Munday had left England but had not yet arrived in Rome. It was intended that the work of the new seminary should be controlled by the Jesuits. Mr Henshaw, the last Warden elected by the students of the old Hospice, was pensioned off. The first Rector of the new College, though he was never formally appointed as such, was Dr. Maurice Clenock, a Welshman and a former Warden, who was to have authority over the students, but not over the buildings and corporate property of the foundation, nor over the two Jesuit fathers who would be in charge of the teaching. The Bull founding the College was signed on 23 April 1579, but it was not published until 23 December 1580.

The arrival of visitors from England to the College was a welcome diversion for the forty students. Munday and Nowell "had a number about us quickly, to know what news in England, and how all matters went there." They presented their letters of introduction to Dr. Maurice Clenock (referred to by Munday as "Dr. Morris") and to Dr. Owen Lewis, Archdeacon of Cambrai (who conversed with them exclusively in Latin), and were told that they might stay in the hostel for eight days, the maximum time permitted to visitors from home.

It soon became clear that they would not be allowed to behave merely as tourists. Munday, buttonholed on his first evening by an enthusiastic priest, was asked by him why he had come to Rome.

"Only for the desire I had to see it", replied Munday innocently, "that when I came home again, I might say, once in my life I have been at Rome."

"Then", commented the priest shrewdly, "you come more upon pleasure than any devotion, more desirous to see the city, than to learn the virtues contained in it." Munday could hardly deny it, nor could he counter his interlocutor's next statement, that "there ought none to come hither, the place being so holy, ancient and famous, but only such as with earnest endeavour, seek and thirst after the Catholic faith."

Munday had been mistaken in Paris for a certain English Catholic's son, and had assumed this man's identity for the rest of his journey to Rome. But his *alias* was becoming difficult to keep up. In answer to a leading question he could only protest rather lamely that he had not been as good a Catholic as he might have been, having been led astray by "delightful pastimes". At this point the bell fortunately rang for supper, enabling Munday to escape.

Munday described the daily routine of the College in some detail in his book *The English Roman Life*. The students were roused every morning by a bell; then they made their beds and awaited the second bell (for morning prayers) and the third (for study). A fourth bell called them down to the refectory for breakfast – a glass of wine and a quarter of a manchet[4] each.

After breakfast the students went two by two to the Roman College for lectures, returning to their own college for dinner. There were more lectures in the afternoon, with recreation and private study to complete the day. In common with all students throughout history, they loved to "sit about a great fire talking" after supper, striving, as Munday put it, "who shall speak worst of Her Majesty, of some of her Council, of some Bishop here, or such like; so that the Jesuits themselves will often take up their hands and bless themselves, to hear what abominable tales they will tell them." Finally the lamps were lit in the students' rooms, and after evening prayers they awaited the bell that summoned them to bed.

Munday was at great pains to describe the ample fare provided for the English students. "They have feeding enough, four meals a day," he grumbled, though in fact three of these meals were of bread and wine only. Dinner, however, was a substantial Italian meal of *antipasti*, soup, two meat courses, and cheese, fruit or sweet:

> *Every man has his own trencher, his manchet, knife, spoon and fork laid by it, and then a fair white napkin covering it, with his glass and pot of wine set by him.[5] And the first mess, or antepast (as they call it) . . . is some fine meat to urge them to have an appetite: as sometimes the Spanish anchovies, and sometimes stewed prunes and raisins of the sun together . . . The second is a certain mess of pottage of that country manner, no meat sod in them but are made of divers things, whose proper names I do not remember; but methought they were both good and wholesome. The third is boiled meat, as kid, mutton, chicken and such like; every man a proper modicum of each thing. The fourth is roasted meat, of the daintiest provision that they can get, and sometimes stewed and baked meat . . . The first and last is sometimes cheese, sometimes preserved conceits, sometimes figs, almonds and raisins, a lemon and sugar, a pomegranate, or some such sweet gear; for they know that Englishmen loveth sweetmeats.*

So much for the agreeable side of student life. But penances of various kinds, and flagellations both public and private – sometimes with whips that had "crooked wires" through every knot, and tore the flesh unmercifully – were also part of the daily life of the College. Munday was persuaded to watch a Jesuit whip himself with wire cords for nearly half an hour, but refused to try it himself, and went away lamenting to see such a foolish spectacle. He was not able to escape the minor penances, however, such as deprivation of dinner, "since I was always apt to break one order or another."

In describing what he saw as he walked about the city, Munday was able to allow full play to his Protestant scepticism. Everywhere he came across "paltry relics" in the churches, "whereby the ignorant people are beguiled". Everywhere he saw the remains of saints which for all he knew might be "a company of rotten bones, God knows of what they be." He visited the catacombs, and mentioned the Jewish ghetto, "a dwelling place within themselves, being locked in their streets by gates on either side, and the Romans every night keepeth the keys." He went to the Carnival races, in which naked Jews were pursued down the Corso by horsemen carrying steel-pointed goads, and pelted by boys with oranges. At Easter time "the odd conceits and crafty jugglings of the Pope" reached their climax. Maundy Thursday was the occasion for a malediction by the Pope in person, in which he denounced Turks and Protestants alike, not forgetting "her Majesty, our most gracious Princess and Governess, affirming her to be far worse than the Turk, or the cruellest tyrant there is."

Munday was certainly gifted with news sense, but in other respects he would have been a disgrace to modern journalism. At best he was inaccurate, at worst a shameless liar – skilful in the omission of facts that did not support his case, equally skilful at manipulating that case so as to place himself in the most favourable light. Nowhere is this brought out more clearly than in his account of the events which, according to him, ended in his own admission to the College as a student, and in the discomfiture and disgrace of "Dr. Morris".

Munday's case, in brief, was that the Rector took a dislike to him personally ("he could not abide me in any case") and to the English students in general, showing favouritism to the small minority of students who, like the Rector and Dr. Lewis, were Welsh. The English students complained, and supported Munday in an agitation to get the Rector removed. The dissension reached the ears of the Pope, who eventually agreed to separate the English seminary from the English hostel. The Jesuits were given charge of the seminary, while the Rector found himself shelved in the relatively minor post of warden of the hostel. Thus, concluded Munday triumphantly, he himself came to be accepted as a seminary student "by the Pope's own consent."

Quite a different picture is presented in the well documented Roman Catholic account of this English-Welsh fracas. While admitting that Dr. Maurice Clenock was an unsatisfactory Rector who could not control his students and did unduly favour his own countrymen, this account does not even mention Munday as one of the four ringleaders in the English students' revolt. These students, after unsuccessfully petitioning for the dismissal of the Rector, left the college together in protest on Ash Wednesday, and prepared to leave Rome. Interviewed by the Pope, they were persuaded to remain, and the crisis ended by the pensioning off of Dr. Clenock and the transfer of all College authority to the Jesuits.

Soon after this, Munday, who had apparently convinced the authorities that he was a genuine if unconscientious Catholic, was sent back to England with messages and holy images for the Catholics in England. We can be pretty sure that these were never delivered, because after a prudent period of silence he turned anti-Catholic informer, and helped to betray Edmund Campion and other Jesuits who had come to England in disguise. In the meantime he had published his first extant work, *The Mirror of Mutability*, and in 1580 his *View of Sundry Examples*, a sort of crime thriller which reported all the "strange murders" and other sensations of the year. Then he wrote and published *The English Roman Life*, which was an immediate success and ran into a second edition eight years later. From that time onwards, until his death in 1633, Anthony Munday was never out of the public eye.

After 1587, when the execution of Mary, Queen of Scots, made open war between England and Spain inevitable, it became really dangerous for a Protestant Englishman to travel not only in the Papal States, but also in the parts of Italy then controlled by Spain – Milan, Naples, Sicily and Sardinia. Edward Webbe, ransomed from the Turkish galleys in 1588, was imprisoned by the Inquisition in Rome, as well as at Naples and Padua. A fanatic, Richard Atkins, who went to Rome with the idea of converting the Pope to Protestantism, was denounced to the Inquisition, tortured and executed. In 1582, an official report stated that:

There are not above twenty Englishmen in Italy, besides those that are of the seminaries. Without the capital there is inquisition for them everywhere, so that no man of what religion soever can set foot upon the mountain, but he is taken. Fifteen were taken about the end of May, and others since.[6]

Those who did not go to Rome expressly in search of trouble were safer. William Davis, an English sailor who fell ill in Rome in 1598, was given hospital treatment, with food and money when discharged, although it was known that he was a Protestant. Protestants who had come to Rome purely in order to see the "antiquities" often managed to secure a few days' grace for this purpose by applying to Cardinal Allen, who supervised the training of the priests of the English College who were to be sent to England to propagate their beliefs. The degree to which this favour was granted depended on the current Pope. Sixtus V (1585-1590) was more severe in this respect than Clement VIII (1592-1605). The defeat of the Spanish Armada in 1588 obviously had something to do with the change to a slightly more lenient policy.

However, Fynes Morison, who paid a brief visit to Rome in 1593, found it advisable to be very wary of any association with Catholic priests during Holy Week. The attention of the priests was "most dangerous about Easter time, when all men receive the Sacrament," he wrote. He arrived in Rome in March, having crossed the Apennines from Loreto, and left almost at once for Naples. On the return journey he stayed a week or so in Rome, in order to see the sights, sharing a lodging-house near the Vatican with two German Calvinists and, not without trepidation, disclosed his identity to Cardinal Allen. But he left Rome before Holy Week, and arrived in Florence on Easter Sunday. At this time the Grand Duchy of Tuscany was both independent and Anglophil. Tuscany was a safer part of Italy for the travelling Englishman than Rome, but not as safe as Savoy or Venice.

Sir Henry Wotton, later to become first English Ambassador to the Venetian Republic, was either in disguise or posing as a Catholic on each of the three occasions when he visited Rome during the papacy of Clement VIII. On his first visit, in 1592, when he was twenty-four, he travelled as a German, with a German companion, and boldly entered Rome wearing a conspicuous hat with a blue feather in it. This, he thought, would call people's attention to him in such a way that no one would take him for a convinced Protestant. Having successfully completed his visit he wrote to his friend Lord Zouche that "no Englishman, containing himself within his allegiance to her Majesty, hath seen more concerning the points of Rome that I have done; which I speak absolutely without exception."

The most frequented road to Rome in the later sixteenth century was still that over Mont Cenis. Most travellers left London by the Dover road, though some now crossed the Channel either via Rye and Dieppe, or Gravesend and Flushing. At Dover the traveller would still need to apply for his "licence to travel". Only authorized merchants were allowed to go abroad without a licence. All other travellers were granted a document specifying the length of time they might stay abroad – usually one year, sometimes three – and the places they might not visit – Rome nearly always, and sometimes St. Omer, then in Spanish Picardy, where there was an English Jesuit College. This passport[7] cost five shillings – ten shillings if the traveller took a horse with him – and the basic single fare across the Channel was also five shillings. But this did not include extras such as rowing-boats to take the traveller out to his ship, and porterage charges for his luggage. Nor was there any regular service to Calais or Boulogne; several days might pass before a suitable vessel had been chartered, and the weather and tides were right for the voyage.

France had as yet no real system of public transport. A few English travellers might obtain places on the *coche royale*, which was running between Amiens and Paris by 1584 and took passengers. But mostly they followed the post-road on horseback, noting with insular surprise that the French stages were of four or five miles instead of ten, as in England. They would have to pay to be guided along the road, which was never much better than a rutted track through mire or dried mud, was scarcely ever signposted, and might be impassable in bad weather. At the inns, the traveller usually slept on a table in his clothes, in order to escape the vermin. He ate two meals a day only, at midday and evening, and his breakfast would consist of a glass of wine and a piece of bread, coffee being known as yet only among the Turks, tea only in the Orient, and chocolate only to the Spaniards. But when he reached Paris he would be in civilization again, for Paris was now a large city; there were no less than five bridges across the Seine, two of them of stone, the others of wood.

From Paris onwards, it was quite usual to travel by canal or river boat to Italy, wherever this means of transport existed. It was cheaper to travel this way, and safer too; the travellers formed a compact party and were less likely to be attacked by thieves. The Alps were still a dreaded barrier which had to be endured. "The high and hideous Alps . . . those uncouth, huge, monstrous excrescences of Nature," as a seventeenth century writer described them, cut off Italy from the rest of Europe more effectively than we can realize today. Throughout the whole range, only one pass, the Brenner, was suitable for wheeled traffic, and this was much too far to the east to be often used by English travellers. Approaching Mont Cenis, the traveller would have to dismount from his horse and be carried over on a sledge by professional guides, who charged the equivalent of £4.50 for their services. The horses, specially shod to prevent their slipping, would

The English Road To Rome

follow riderless, and the baggage would come over separately. At the top of the pass the guides would not fail to point out the wayfarers' mortuary, which in March 1578 contained fifteen bodies.

In order to avoid crossing the Alps via Mont Cenis, some travellers continued down the Rhone to the Mediterranean, and then took a ship to Genoa. Even if the crossing over Mont Cenis was chosen, it was wise after 1587 to head for Genoa rather than Milan, the latter city being then under Spanish rule.

In Italy there was now a certain amount of public transport, mostly on the rivers. The traveller starting from Turin (capital of Savoy from 1559) could go to Ferrara by boat or by road, then by regular river transport to Venice. Or he would set out on the road journey from Ferrara to Bologna, which took half a day in summer, or a whole day in winter. If he did not travel by cart, or river barge, or by means of a litter carried by servants, he would, as in England and France, follow the post-road. In Italy, however, he could hire a horse in the morning and leave it at the stage where he spent the following night. The innkeeper would take care of the horse until a return fare was forthcoming. Those who had chosen to travel to Genoa could complete their journey to Rome by sea. There was a regular service of boats between Genoa and the coast near Rome in 1588. To travel this way made it possible to avoid Spanish-ruled Milan, but there was an alternative danger: the traveller might be captured by Turkish or Barbary pirates.

But it was not only the Protestant travellers to Rome who suffered discomfort and danger on their journeys and subsequently. Between 1579 and 1603, over three hundred and fifty Catholic Englishmen were admitted as students of the English College in Rome, and most in due course became priests. When they graduated, they went as Catholic missionaries to England. Few survived their perilous journey without being captured; they knew that imprisonment or execution must be their fate if they were caught. On the principal staircase of the present building of the Venerable English College is a memorial to the forty-one graduates of the College who died as martyrs to their faith.

The war with Spain lasted more than fifteen years, and would have gone on longer had James I not decided to call a halt to it. When it ended, the sixteenth century had given way to the seventeenth, Elizabethan to Jacobean England. The heroic age of the Elizabethans had flowed over into the rich bucolic interlude of the succeeding reign. England's national independence was now assured, the Church of England safely established, popery a much less dangerous threat. Fewer people now travelled in order to equip themselves for service to the State. But travel for educational reasons was still popular, and there began to be added a new reason for travel to Italy – to bring home objects of interest or of art, for the adornment of town houses or country mansions.

The restrictions on travelling to Rome were, however, only relaxed very gradually, and those who went there in the early seventeenth century still had to tread very warily. Thus we find that George Sandys, in 1612, stayed only four days in Rome ("as long as I durst") under the protection of a Catholic gentleman, Nicolas Fitzherbert, "who accompanied me in the surveying of all the antiquities and glories of that city." He then "departed to Siena."

William Lithgow, of Lanark, contrived to spend a month in Rome in 1610, but he appears to have had a very worrying time, being repeatedly recognized by Catholic fellow-countrymen who had come to Rome from Scotland and settled there. He was obliged to spend his last three Roman days in hiding, and finally "leapt the walls" and hurried off into the night.

In 1607 an active Protestant, John Mole, acting as "governor" to Lord Ross, had been persuaded against his better judgment to accompany his pupil who had been taken by a *Vagari* to visit Rome, was seized for interrogation as soon as they arrived there. Refusing to abjure his religion, he spent no less than thirty years in the prison of the Inquisition in Rome, dying there in 1639 at the age of eighty. As for Lord Ross, he was "daily feasted, favoured, entertained," made no effort, apparently, to get his tutor out, and became himself a Papist. But in 1614, Sir Edward Herbert frankly declared to the English College that he was a peaceable Protestant whose only reason for being in Rome was to visit the "antiquities". He was not molested, and spent a quiet month touring the ruins.

By this time there were quite a number of gentlemen prepared to make the tour to Rome, whatever the form of words on their travel licences. James I, writing to his Ambassador in Venice, Sir Henry Wotton, was obliged to remark that:

> ... *many of the Gentry, and others of Our Kingdom, under pretence of travel for their experience, do pass the Alps, and not contenting themselves to remain in Lombardy or Tuscany, to gain the language there, do daily flock to Rome, out of vanity and curiosity to see the "antiquities" of that City; where falling into the company of Priests and Jesuits . . . return again into their countries, both averse to religion and ill-affected to Our State and Government.*

In 1614 Wotton's predecessor, Sir Dudley Carleton, had reported with growing annoyance that Lord and Lady Arundel had been to Rome in defiance of the stipulation on their travel papers:

> *The common recourse of his Majesty's subjects to Rome, notwithstanding their direct inhibitions on their licences for travel, to the contrary, is continued with that freedom that both the Earl of Arundel and his Lady have spent many days in that place.*

The time had come when such orders were beginning to be ineffective, and we may be glad that this was so. Rome was about to re-enter English life, not as a religious centre, but as the climax and the turning-point of the Classical Tour.

The Earl of Arundel's journey to Italy in 1613-15 has an importance which deserves the utmost emphasis. He was the first of the English milords who travelled slowly and expensively down one side of the Italian peninsula as far as Naples, and then back up the other side. The route he followed – over the Alps and down to the Lombardy plain; to Verona, Vicenza and Venice; southwards through Bologna and Florence to Rome; an excursion to Naples and back, northwards through Pisa, Leghorn and Genoa and so by the road to France – was to be followed, with few variations, by thousands of travellers in the subsequent two centuries. Lord Arundel's object was neither religious nor political, but frankly that of an art connoisseur. He was the first Englishman who travelled in Italy as a picker-up of the unconsidered trifles that the Renaissance had left behind – though the phrase is hardly appropriate, for neither in weight, value nor number were the artistic treasures carefully shipped from Leghorn or Venice on the advice of his agents to be regarded as trifling. He was also the last Englishman – or one of the last – who travelled in Italy in the style of a feudal nobleman, accompanied by a considerable "family" or household.

And, not least among the circumstances that made this one of the most important English journeys to Rome in any century, Lord Arundel was accompanied by Inigo Jones as art commentator and guide. Arundel and his fellow-noblemen could visualize the "antiquities" embellishing their residences at home. Jones, pacing out distances, noting down details, studying "the arts of design", belongs to the modern world – he is the first English classical architect. As a result of this journey there came back to England, firmly in Inigo Jones' mind, the idea that the classical principles first enumerated by the Roman architectural writer Vitruvius, and resuscitated by the Italian architect Palladio, whose *Quattro Libri d'Architettura* had been first published in 1570, could be successfully and completely introduced into England.

Inigo Jones had been born in 1573, and after having been apprenticed to a joiner, had established a reputation as "a picture-maker", "a great traveller", and a designer of Court masques. In 1611 he became Surveyor to young Prince Henry, and two years later secured the reversion of the post of Surveyor-General to the King, which meant that he could take over this secure and responsible post as soon as it fell vacant. Since the incumbent, Simon Basill, was a very old man, he probably would not have long to wait. In the meantime, he could feel himself free to join Lord Arundel, and to see the two cities that most interested him – Vicenza and Rome.

Lord Arundel left England in April 1613, the main official purpose of his journey being to escort Princess Elizabeth, daughter of James I, to Heidelberg with her newly-married husband, the Elector Palatine. This duty completed, he proceeded with his own retinue to Milan, where he arrived in July. Sir Dudley Carleton, English Ambassador in Venice, reported that the Earl had with him Inigo Jones, "who will be of best use to him, by reason of his language and experience of these parts."[8] Inigo Jones made an entry in his copy of Palladio (the main source of information concerning his journey) at Vicenza on 23 September, but there is no other record of his movements until he arrived in Rome. Lord Arundel is known to have travelled to Bologna, then to Florence, then to Siena, where he wrote innocently that the air pleased him, and he proposed to settle there for the winter. In fact Lady Arundel and most of the "family" remained for some time in and around Siena and Lucca; but the Earl, probably accompanied by Inigo Jones, slipped away to Rome towards the end of 1613.

It is to be hoped that Inigo Jones first saw the city at sunset, the buildings rose-red in that astonishing clarity of light, with the church bells ringing across the valleys and the first lights of the night flickering on. Certainly in the early seventeenth century the reds and yellows of the Renaissance buildings would have been fresher. St. Peter's would have looked brand new, for although work had now been continuing on the great cathedral for nearly a hundred years, still it was not quite completed. There was no Corso Vittorio Emmanuele cutting through the maze of narrow streets between the Corso and the Tiber. This maze was, in 1613, the heart of the contemporary city's life. The Via Guilia, running parallel to the river on the south bank, was Rome's principal street. This whole district, busy with life and new buildings, would be the first that the traveller from the north would come upon as he entered the city. Further away, the antique Roman remains were scattered, half buried beneath the surface, and in ruins.

In the first note he had written in his Palladio since leaving Vicenza, he recorded:

> *In the name of God Amen.*
> *The 2 of January 1614 (new style) I being in Rome compared the designs following with the ruins themselves.*

Then follows a list of a score of buildings illustrated by Palladio on the subsequent pages. Alongside the text are many of Inigo's marginal comments.

He remained in Rome, visiting temples and antiquities, throughout the months of January and February. It was time enough to make a thorough study of the two schools of architecture which particularly interested him – the classical and the neo-classical. These were, in fact, the ancient and modern manifestations of the same school. He had never built in the Gothic or Tudor styles; he preferred the work of the earlier architects, whose vision of the classical idea was purer, to those of a later period; and he did not like either the baroque, or the "abundance" brought in by Michelangelo.

His field-work in Rome must therefore have been largely limited to two areas in particular – the Roman Forum and its surrounding ruins, and the district between the Tiber and the Corso. Indeed, many of the designs that appealed to him when he studied them *in situ* in these districts can be shown to have formed the basis for later work. We know that he studied the Forum, because he made a composite sketch of it for the masque *Coelum Britannicum*, and in this sketch the campanile of Sta. Francesca Romana was also included. This church, standing at the southern end of the Forum, was shining in its new white coat at the time of his visit; its façade had been rebuilt in 1613. Having also noted S. Lorenzo in Miranda, rebuilt in 1602, he would have passed on to the Arch of Constantine. This arch he greatly admired, and later used as a model for his design for the gate at Temple Bar, London,

The English Road To Rome

a project which was never carried out. Still in the same district, he noted sorrowfully that the Pope was having the last of the columns in the great hall of the Basilica of Maxentius pulled down, in order to set up this column in the square outside Sta. Maria Maggiore. And next to the Lateran Palace he would certainly have observed Fontana's north front to St. John Lateran, with its twin steepled campanile.

But especially in the contemporary city would he have seen the classical concept of architecture, not deserted and in ruins, but brought right up to date. Nearly all the streets and buildings in that district were new or nearly new in 1614; and in their midst stood the only building of Imperial Rome which has survived the centuries practically untouched – the Pantheon. Inigo Jones returned time after time to the Pantheon, measuring it, sketching it, walking about inside it, gazing up at the circle of sky at the top of the great dome. The portico of this temple appears several times in his later work; it formed the model for the portico design in his restoration of Old St. Paul's. He was working on this project from 1634 to 1643, declining to accept payment for "so good a work."

Could it have been while he was examining the Pantheon that Inigo Jones conceived the idea of introducing the Italian *piazza* into England? The design for Covent Garden *piazza*, the first of the London squares, is thought to be based on that of the *piazza* at Leghorn, which Inigo Jones certainly saw. But the idea itself may have taken root while he wandered through the remarkable agglomeration of little Roman squares round about the Pantheon. The streets and squares hereabouts form an intricate succession, opening into one another in a way that is geometrical yet unexpected, and is completely different from the topography of the crazily packed lanes and alleys of Tudor London. Inigo Jones could not have failed to observe the contrast, and the fact that the narrow streets and the broad streets all led into large or small squares, many of them with a fountain as the natural centre of children's games, lovers' meetings, conversation or sleep. From such a concept the architectural mind steps easily to the *piazza* at Leghorn, and then to its London version at Covent Garden, and then in due

76

course to the formal squares, crescents and circuses that gave a new concept of town living to London, Edinburgh and Bath.

Even on the outskirts of Rome it is possible to trace Inigo Jones' itinerary in his later work. Among the twenty-six temples that he noted in and around Rome, he was particularly impressed by Bramante's *tempietto* in S. Pietro in Montorio, and it has been suggested that this charming little building inspired the scheme for James I's funeral hearse in 1625. And as a result of studying the villa of Pope Julius III, outside the northern gate of Rome, he evolved all the preliminary designs and models for the Queen's House at Greenwich, whose Italian appearance was an absolute novelty in English domestic architecture.

Inigo Jones so nearly succeeded in bringing the concept of the Italian Piazza back to England. The colonnade of Covent Garden Piazza, which must have been impressive, is no longer there. The renovated market buildings now fill the whole of the square. But we do still have the church – St Paul's, Covent Garden.

(Photograph by Peter Barefoot, FCSD AA Dipl RIBA)

At the end of February or the beginning of March, 1614, Lord Arundel and Inigo Jones went down to Naples, examining the Appian Way en route, and enduring the extremely primitive conditions south of Rome. They encountered "vile hosterias", wrote the Earl to his Lady, "one blanket, one mattress, no bolster or anything else." The whole of March and April and the first week or two of May were spent on this expedition: much longer than became usual in the eighteenth century, when a short visit to Naples, returning again to Rome, was regarded as an essential part of the Grand Tour. The length of Lord Arundel's stay in Naples was partly determined by politico-religious considerations. Although he was a Roman Catholic, he had taken a political risk in going to Rome against the wishes of Authority at home, and clearly he desired to avoid any possible controversy during his visit. He is said to have displayed an "intimidating courtesy" in all his social dealings; and he judged it best to be out of Rome altogether during the whole of the Easter period. As for Inigo Jones, he was baptized and died a good Anglican, and was later entrusted with the restoration of St. Paul's Cathedral; but it is not recorded that he took any active interest in either religion or politics. And that in itself is something new.

At the end of May, Inigo Jones was back in Rome, witnessing the procession on the anniversary of the Pope's coronation, on the 29th, and once more studying the Pantheon:

> *This temple I observed exactly the last of May 1614, and have noted what I found, more than is in Palladio.*

He made an excursion to Tivoli, and another to Trevi. Sometime in June, he set off for home with the Arundel cavalcade, paying another visit to Vicenza before he left Italy. He reached England again at a very convenient time for his future career. He had only been home a few months when Simon Basill died, and Inigo Jones stepped into the vacant post that had been awaiting him.

It is not recorded that he ever went abroad again. Like Milton and

Gibbon, whose debt to Italy was equally great, he spent one winter only in Rome. It was sufficient. He remained in and around his native city of London until he died there, in 1652, at the age of eighty.

His influence on English architecture was very great. He was not England's first professional designer of residences, for his pupil John Webb filled that role. He was not the first to introduce the idea of *architettura* into England, for there had been a book, *The First and Chief Grounds of Architecture*, by John Shute, in 1563, as well as a work by Sir Henry Wotton. He had been preceded, too, by great master-builders such as John Abell, whose half-timbered town halls in Herefordshire were the final expression of the Tudor tradition, and were being completed at the time of Inigo Jones' journey to Italy.

The basic concept that he brought back was simplicity of design. He introduced into England, not the exotic embellishments that had failed to catch hold a century earlier, but the classical style itself. He remained very close to the classical ideal as laid down by Vitruvius and later expressed by Palladio. "To vary is good," he wrote, "but not to part from the precepts of the art."

Vitruvius' principles had been the following: order, arrangement, eurhythmy (i.e. beauty and fitness), symmetry, propriety and economy of embellishment. Palladio resurrected these principles; Jones went further, believing that external ornaments were inessential. He thought that such ornaments ought to be "solid, proportionable according to the rules, masculine and unaffected", that a building should be simple without and lavish within, and that any ornaments that were adopted should fit in with the general scheme, just as the parts of the human body must correspond with the proportions of the human figure as a whole.

These principles are seen in all Inigo Jones' surviving work, and in the work of those who learned from him. It does not matter that very little work undoubtedly of his design can be seen today – his influence on his successors is what counts. His Covent Garden Piazza was the forerunner of the English city square; his Palladian villas set a new standard for the English country house; his stairs – wide, geometrical, noble – were as much an abiding novelty in England as were his oval ceiling panels. Some of his theatrical inventions long outlived the Court masque, and are looked at every night by the modern playgoer. He was the first English stage producer to introduce a painted curtain which could be lowered on to the stage to form a fixed background to the play, and he established the proscenium arch as a permanent feature of the English theatre. This neat frame for both the scene and the action of the drama was as striking an improvement on the Elizabethan stage as his Palladian villas were on the half-timbered Tudor houses. In stage design, just as in architecture, he adapted the classical formula to the requirements of his own time – and ours.

After 1615, when Inigo Jones had begun to practise as the king's Surveyor-General, and the Earl of Arundel had begun to build up his art collection, we are no longer in an age when Rome, for Englishmen, is either loved or hated as the centre of the Roman Catholic world. It has become a place chiefly to be visited for the memories and remains of antiquity that it contains.

GIRO D'ITALIA AND GRAND TOUR

THE SEVENTEENTH AND EIGHTEENTH CENTURIES

The Grand Tour embraced other countries than Italy, other cities than Rome. One "limb" of the Tour even took the traveller first of all to Berlin, Potsdam and Dresden, only heading southwards where the road from Kassel led to the Rhine and on towards the Alps. Some Grand Tourists, indeed, never reached Italy at all, or never got beyond the Lombardy plain. Nevertheless, the thought of Italy was implicit in the Grand Tour. And who, being in Italy, could fail to be aware of Rome? To most travellers, Rome was the culmination of the Grand Tour.

Throughout these two centuries (from 1615 to 1814), the path to Italy and Rome was more and more crowded with intelligent, enquiring travellers who saw Rome from the typical standpoint of the Grand Tourist. At the lowest and most imitative level, they were merely interested in looking at "the "antiquities"" and being able to say that they had visited Rome; at the highest, they were able as a result of their experience to make a positive contribution to English (British, American) thought, literature and art.

The phrase "Giro d'Italia" originally meant the Italian section of the classical tour, while "Grand Tour" referred to the French section of it. Both names were used in English for the first time in 1670, by Richard Lassels, who referred to "the *Grand Tour* of France and the *Giro* of Italy". But since "Grand Tour" looked conveniently the same in both

French and English, and since, also, the whole tour through a number of countries soon began to be seen as a single entity, "Giro d'Italia" fell into disuse, and "Grand Tour" became equated with "classical tour". In the early seventeenth century it was still felt that one of the main purposes of travel was to acquire knowledge that could later be put to the service of the State. Sir R. Dallington, in *Method for Travel* (1606) had expressed this idea in much the same terms as an earlier writer, W. Bourne, *Treasure for Travellers* (1578). This view of travel hardly lasted into the eighteenth century, but the accepted view remained that travel without some definite educative purpose was a waste of time.

In a word, then, European travel was essentially educational, and educational journeys could only reach their full flowering in times of peace. Such times were comparatively rare in the seventeenth and eighteenth centuries. For a few years before the outbreak of the English Civil War in 1639, the road to Rome (through France, but not through Germany, then suffering the worst cruelties and famine of the Thirty Years War) could be ridden in peace. There were other brief interludes after the end of the Thirty Years War in 1648, before 1665, and before the start of the War of the Spanish Succession in 1698. During the eighteenth century there were three notable non-belligerent periods: between 1713 and 1733; between 1748 and 1756; and following the end of the Seven Years War in 1763.

National histories, concerned as they are with the enthroning and dethroning of kings, the execution of military campaigns, the endless sequence of declarations of war and conclusions of peace, have relatively little to say about these intervals between wars, which may even seem irrelevant to their main theme; but the social historian regards these intervals differently. For him it is a matter of regret that they were so short, and of surprise that so much was achieved despite the almost continual wars. At the same time it is fortunately the case that, in France and Italy, these dynastic struggles, waged by small bodies of professional soldiers and mercenaries, did not completely interrupt the pattern of civilian life nor entirely hinder the search for enlightenment. Even during the English Civil War, permission could be obtained to travel abroad for educational reasons. Even at the height of the Napoleonic Wars, it was possible for suitably introduced men of science or letters to pass through France without personal danger.

James I died in 1625 and gave place to Charles I, who was more favourably disposed towards the Papacy, though his people were not. Very soon it was possible for Protestants to live for prolonged periods in Rome without fear of molestation. One of the first of these was the painter William Smith. In 1632 he was a shocked witness of the removal from the Pantheon portico roof of two hundred tons of ancient bronze beams on the orders of Pope Urban VIII. The beams were destined for incorporation into the new cathedral of St. Peter's, though some of this bronze was turned into papal cannon. Two years later one Thomas Abdy came to Rome in November, and stayed until April 1635. In 1636 the increasing liberality of the papal regime made possible the exchange of ambassadors between Pope Urban VIII and Henrietta Maria, Charles I's queen. The envoy to the papal court in Rome was Sir William Hamilton; the Papal Agent in London was George Con.

Hamilton and Con, both Scots and both Catholics, were in other respects very different. Sir William Hamilton was a relative of King Charles, and well connected in Rome. He was friendly with the Pope's nephew, Cardinal Francesco Barberini, who went out of his way to make life easier for the English travellers, irrespective of their religion and social class. George Con was a middle-aged Aberdonian priest who had then lived abroad for twenty-four years. He had to contend with a King who was rapidly becoming unpopular, and with a people that remained implacably hostile to the Pope and all his works.

Friendly Anglo-Italian relations in the sphere of art were easy to foster in Rome at that time. However, in London there was little enthusiasm among the Puritans for the "gifts of pictures, antique idols and suchlike trumperies" which the King was anxious to add to his own art collection. The pro-Papal policy being so unpopular in England, discussions on the purchase of *objets d'art*, and their safe delivery to London, were used by the King and the Papal Agent as camouflage for other and more weighty discussions that finally failed, while the meetings succeeded in their ostensible purpose. The King's policy of rapprochement with the Pope was a failure. In due course he lost the Civil War and went to the scaffold, while George Con, having also failed, did not secure his coveted Cardinal's hat, and died in Rome, an embittered and disappointed man, in 1640.

Sir William Hamilton was succeeded in 1645 by Sir Kenelm Digby, who during his residence in Rome did his best to persuade the Pope that the Catholics were still numerous in England, and that money was needed to prevent the Parliamentary forces from winning the Civil War. Innocent XII finally decided to make a grant of £72,000 (at interest) in order to improve the position of the Catholics in England and Ireland. Charles I was never able to ratify this treaty, which came to nothing. Digby finally returned to England after the Restoration.

The Anglo-Roman cultural interchange, however, led to the establishment of the Carolean art collection, to the completion of Inigo Jones' design for the Queen's House at Greenwich, and to Bernini's commission to make a bust of the King. It also facilitated Milton's visit to Italy in 1638.

Bernini was fortunate in that his most productive period coincided with this lifting of the barriers that had for so long hindered artistic contact between Rome and London. He became better known in England than some greater artists who flourished in Rome about that time. The transportation overland from Rome to London, in 1637, of his bust of the King – a symbol as well as a work of art – was one of the minor triumphs of the day. Cardinal Barberini made the arrangements. His nephew, Bonifacio Olivieri, and a Scotsman, Thomas Chambers, were entrusted with the precious package. They travelled only by day, only in fine weather, and the journey took them three months, but at last the bust was delivered. It continued in existence for sixty years – then it was lost for ever in the fire that destroyed Whitehall Palace in 1697.

Among the English artists who met Bernini in Rome were the brothers Nicholas and Henry Stone, sons of Nicholas Stone the elder, the best English sculptor of his day. The father had served his own apprenticeship in the Netherlands, round about 1600, since he could not get permission to go to Rome to study. His sons were more fortunate; they were in Rome from October 1638 until May 1642. They rented an unfurnished house at Trinità dei Monti – the first hint that the district around Piazza di Spagna would be, henceforth, the new English centre in Rome. Nicholas Stone described his meetings with Bernini in his diary. At one of them, they discussed the Charles I bust; at another, Bernini praised the young sculptor's drawings that he had copied from Raphael, and advised him to continue drawing in chalk.

John Milton was in Rome at the same time – from October 1638 until March 1639. As one would expect of such an immensely talented, immensely serious young man, all of whose literary work arose from the depths of a prodigiously well-informed mind, Milton had worked out well in advance of his actual journey why he needed to go to Italy, what he might expect to find there that would assist him in his future work, and the route that it would be best for him to follow.

In the first place, he needed for the future development of his literary career a direct and living contact with the poetry of the Italian renaissance. He had spent six years in solitary study on his father's estate at Horton. He had completed, and seen produced, his masque *Comus*. He had also finished the last of the poems of his youth, *Lycidas*, with its oft-quoted final couplet:

> *At last he rose, and twitched his mantle blue,*
> *Tomorrow to fresh woods, and pastures new.*

He had already assimilated a considerable fund of technical information from the Italian poets during the latter part of his stay at Horton. He was influenced in particular by three Italians who are thought of today as prose writers, although to Milton it was their poetry that was chiefly of interest – Bembo, Della Casa and Tasso. All of them had one characteristic in common: they used words in an unusual order, developing complexities of structure and involved figures of speech – poetical devices which resulted in an unreal imagery and, at least to us today, a peculiar unreadability.

Milton, however, was able to assimilate this technique, using it as a skeleton on which to graft the flesh and blood of his own native tradition. Learning from Bembo the distinction between vocabulary and idiom, he was able to work familiar English words into an un-English structure. Imitating Della Casa's trick of breaking up verses and separating words that are normally placed together, he found he could simulate in English the word-order of Latin. Finally, he learnt from Tasso how to invent figures of speech of Virgilian complexity. His ultimate achievement was to help the classical style to be re-born in English literature. And he could do this not only because he had a profounder knowledge of the Greek and Latin classics than any English poet before or since, but also because he had an equally deep understanding of, and feeling for, the Italian language and Italian literature.

But he needed practical experience to reinforce this theoretical knowledge, and he knew he would have to spend time in Florence most of all, in order to learn from the tradition of critical analysis that flourished there. He hoped also to meet Manso in Rome or Naples – Manso, the only living man who could tell him from first-hand experience about Tasso, the Italian epic poet whom Milton most admired.

Secondly, he travelled, as the scholars a century earlier had travelled, in order to equip himself for service to the State. He may already have had a career as a civil servant in mind – he was later to become Secretary of State for Foreign Tongues under the Commonwealth – and he knew that it would be advantageous to him and to the State if he could master modern foreign languages as well as Latin and Greek. As a convinced Protestant he felt a strong desire to see for himself "the metropolis of Popery", as he called it; and as a political writer he would be gathering material that he would later put to good use in the *First Defence* and the *Second Defence of the English People*.

For information as to his route across Europe he sought the advice of Sir Henry Wotton, now retired from his diplomatic career and holding the office of Provost of Eton. No living Englishman knew more about Italy than Sir Henry. He had visited Rome (in disguise) as well as Naples, and had twice been English Ambassador to Venice (1604-1610 and 1616-1623). He also greatly admired Milton's *Comus*, although he had not previously known its author's name. He wrote Milton a letter in April 1638, praising *Comus* and confirming that the road through France to the Mediterranean would be the best one to follow:

> *I should think your best line will be through the whole length of France to Marseilles, and thence by sea to Genoa, whence the passage into Tuscany is as diurnal as a Gravesend barge.*

This road to Rome was the standard one in the early sixteenth century. It was quite impossible to travel with safety through the Netherlands and up the Rhine valley, because of the devastation, depopulation and general misery that was then being imposed on the civilians by the troops engaged in the Thirty Years War; and the route over the Mont Cenis pass was not in use, because there was also war in Savoy. So the alternative route through Genoa became popular, and retained its popularity into the succeeding century.

About a month after receiving Sir Henry Wotton's letter, Milton had completed the preparations for his journey, sought and obtained his father's permission to go, and was off. In all he was abroad fifteen months, of which four were spent in Rome and nearly as long in Florence. He was also some time in Geneva, Venice and Naples, and visited, among other places, Lucca (with its Protestant and republican tradition), Siena and Verona. He met the Dutch humanist Grotius in Paris, the astronomer Galileo in Florence, and Manso in Naples. It had been his intention to travel even further, to Sicily and Greece, but the imminence of the English Civil War caused him to abandon that plan, and return home.

In Florence, where he arrived about the end of July 1638, he sought acquaintance with poets and scholars, made excursions to Fiesole and Vallombrosa, and in September was present at a meeting of a literary society, the *Svogliati*:

> *The gentlemen of the Academy being met in sufficient numbers, various compositions were read, and in particular Mr John Milton, an Englishman, read a very learned Latin poem in hexameters.*

Having in a remarkably short space of time "contracted an intimacy with many persons of rank and learning," he left Florence for Rome.

It is not known for certain where Milton stayed in Rome, though it has been surmised that he lodged at the Albergo della Croce di Malta. It is shown by the records of the English College that he dined at the College together with three other Englishmen, on 30 October 1638. Sir Henry Wotton had advised him that the best motto for a traveller in Italy, or indeed anywhere, was *i pensieri stretti ed il viso sciolto* ("keep your thoughts to yourself and your face unconstrained"), and he had followed this advice. While in Rome he determined "never to be the first to begin any conversation on religion; but if any question were put to me concerning my faith, to declare it without any reserve or fear." At the same time he evidently took some pride in the fact that he had "openly defended the reformed religion in the very metropolis of popery."

This policy worked: he was not in any way molested. Manso, in Naples, considered that Milton only fell short of perfection in that he was an Anglican and not a Roman Catholic.

In Rome, Milton met Lukas Holsten, the Vatican Librarian, and was shown the library's collection of classical books and manuscripts. Holsten presented him with two copies of a volume that he had himself edited, and gave him an introduction to Cardinal Barberini. As a result,

Milton was enabled to be one of an audience of 3,500 people who were entertained to a performance of Rospigliosi's comic opera *Chi soffre spera*. This performance was one of the most spectacular events of the 1639 carnival. It was given in the Barberini theatre, at that time the only opera house in Rome, and one of only three in Italy. The stage design was by Bernini, and the audience did not merely watch the show; they were feasted and entertained during the *intermezzi* as well. The complete entertainment lasted five hours. Opera as an art form had not yet reached England, but it had affinities with the masque, of which Milton was a practised artificer. This performance would therefore have held the utmost interest for him.

Milton's poem *Mansus*, addressed to Manso in Latin hexameters, was the only one he actually wrote in Italy, but there are in his later work several passages that appear to have been inspired directly by his visit to Rome, including the description of Pandemonium in *Paradise Lost*, which strikingly resembles the new church of St. Peter's, completed about the time of his visit; and the description of Imperial Rome in *Paradise Regained*[1]. But what is more significant is that Milton's visit to Italy was vitally important both for his subsequent career and for the course of English literature. It may not be inappropriate to compare his achievement in conjunction with that of his contemporary Inigo Jones. Just as Inigo Jones sought in Vitruvius the classical principles of architecture, so Milton took Greek and Roman poets and enriched English poetry with their ways of thought and modes of expression. Just as Italy was the only country where Inigo Jones could find these classical principles reinterpreted in the contemporary idiom of Palladio, so Italian was the only modern language in which Milton could find, in Della Casa and Tasso, certain verbal and metrical devices.

The poet and the architect had another trait in common. Both were sufficiently sympathetic to the foreign idiom to be able to compose in it if need be. Milton's sonnets in Italian are a remarkable *tour de force*, but they are scarcely more. *Paradise Lost*, while owing much to classical originals, is essentially an achievement of English literature. Inigo Jones could imitate the work he had seen in Italy, but his greatest buildings

The English Road To Rome

were unquestionably English, yet cast in the classical mould. Furthermore, the achievement of both these two would have been impossible at any earlier stage of English history. The English way of living could not previously have accepted or assimilated either the Palladian villa or Milton's prose.

Milton hurried home when he realized that the Civil War was imminent, and did not go abroad again. But there were others, a little less quick off the mark, who found the way home barred to them. Among these was Robert Boyle, the future chemist, who was in Rome in 1641, at the age of fourteen. He had been sent by his father, the Earl of Cork, to make the Grand Tour with his elder brother; but it was 1644 before they were able to return home. Others again saw nothing reprehensible in applying for a travel licence during that time of conflict. The architect Sir Roger Pratt, for example, was glad to be able to avoid the entire war by means of an educative tour:

> *In this very nick of time comes on the Civil War, and then 'twas almost thought a crime to ask anyone for interest money; to avoid which storm, and give myself some convenient education, I then went out of England about April anno 1643 and continued travelling in France, Italy, Flanders, Holland, etc., till Aug. 1649 viz. about six years and a half, at which time I again returned after the end of the war and the death of the King.*

John Evelyn was in a very similar position. He thought of abandoning his estates and joining the king's forces, but reflected that he would probably be ruined if he did, without any great benefit to the Royalist cause. Instead, on 2 October 1643, he "obtained a licence of his Majesty, . . . to travel again." It was exactly four years later – on 2 October 1647, – that he returned to London at the end of his continental tour; and by that time the war was over and the King a prisoner.

Evelyn may be claimed as the first English tourist in Rome. He had no specialized interest in art, architecture, literature, religion or politics that could only be satisfied and enlarged by a visit to the city. All he wanted was to spend the greatest possible time gazing at the sights and "antiquities", having them explained to him by a "sights-man", and copying the information into his diary.

He certainly "did" Rome with a thoroughness which would have been impossible both to his predecessors half a century earlier, and to his successors of our own day. He remained in Rome from the beginning of November 1644, until the middle of May 1645. During those seven months he went everywhere: to the ruins on the Campo Vaccino, to all the churches and palaces that were open to inspection, to the Vatican library and gardens, to "rare music" at the Chiesa Nuova, to St. Peter's to kiss the toe of the Pope's embroidered slipper, to the Greek Orthodox church, to Frascati, to Tivoli, though not to Hadrian's Villa, since this was still regarded as "only a heap of ruins". He witnessed a Jewish circumcision ceremony, and an execution; he stood godfather to two Christian converts, a Turk and a Jew. He was invited to dinner at the English College on the peak night of their year – the *festa* of St. Thomas of Canterbury on 29 December. On Christmas Eve he did not go to bed at all, but "walked from church to church the whole night in admiration of the multitude of scenes and pageantry which the friars had with much industry and craft set out, to catch the devout women and superstitious sort of people." After the winter excursion to Naples, there were the Easter celebrations at St. Peter's, and finally the fireworks that greeted Cardinal Medici on his arrival from Florence.

During his stay in Rome, Evelyn lodged near Piazza di Spagna. He left the city in early summer partly in order to reach Venice in time for the great festival there, partly because high summer in Rome was held to be "very dangerous, by reason of the heats."

As might be expected of a tourist, Evelyn's opinions on the buildings and events that he saw, though they are clearly and interestingly described, are not particularly original. His views were those generally accepted at the time. Thus, the Capitol is "certainly one of the most renowned places in the world." The architecture of the Theatre of Marcellus "appears to be inferior to none." St. Peter's is "that most stupendous and incomparable Basilica." The ruins of the Baths of Diocletian "testify the vastness and magnificence of the original foundation." Often the "sights-man" seems to be speaking, rather than Evelyn. Still, Evelyn's careful and conscientious account of his time in Rome is none the less valuable for being conventional. He provides us with a complete picture of mid-seventeenth century travel as seen from the Englishman's point of view.

Evelyn obtained much of his factual information about Rome from John Raymond's "*An Itinerary Contayning a Voyage made through Italy in the Yeere 1646-47*" (1648), also known as *Il Mercurio Italico*. History has been a little unfair to John Raymond. Although he wrote quite copiously about Rome (forty pages of his book are devoted to it), and although the book was successful at the time it was published, it would hardly be known at all today had not Evelyn picked up so many of his facts from it. Yet Evelyn had no plagiaristic purpose; his diary was never intended for publication, and was not in fact discovered and published until 1818.

John Raymond was in Rome in 1647, three years after John Evelyn. In his book he listed the three "evitable dangers" inherent in making a journey to Italy: "the first is the heat of the climate; a second, that horrible (in report) Inquisition; the last, hazard of those merciless outlaws Banditas." "Moderation," he points out, "will save the traveller from the first of these dangers; discretion, from the second; while the third," he says, not very convincingly, "should be taken care of by "the defence of those states you pass through."

However, not all English-speaking visitors to Rome were rich, or even content with their lot in being there. The Irish priest and mediocre poet Richard Flecknoe, known to history primarily because of his misfortune in having been lampooned both by Marvell and by Dryden, complained that "when you have seen the Ruins, you have seen all here." This is perhaps a little surprising in a priest, whom one would expect to praise the churches and be indifferent to the ruins. But Flecknoe was not a tourist – he viewed Rome with the very different eyes of the semi-permanent resident, environed for two or three years by the "cramped lodgings, hunger, and shabby ancient clothes" that Marvell, in 1646, having taken him out to a much-needed dinner in Rome, later unfeelingly described.

During the brief period of peace after the Treaty of Westphalia, in 1648, which marked the formal end of the Thirty Years War, the records show that there was a marked increase in the number of Englishmen who visited Rome. Richard Lassels, originator of the phrase "Grand Tour", and by profession a gentleman's tutor, was in Rome a number of times in this capacity, and was eventually regarded as an authority on the place. He had been a lecturer at Douai, the Catholic exiles' college in what was left of the Spanish Netherlands. He used to advise parents to send their sons abroad at the age of 15 or 16, and the route recommended in his book (*An Italian Voyage, or a Compleat Journey through Italy*, published in 1670) soon became, if it was not already, the standard one. He advised: Mont Cenis pass – Turin – Genoa – Milan – Bologna – Florence – Pisa – Leghorn – Siena – Rome – Naples – Rome – Loreto – Ferrara – Padua – Venice – Padua – Vicenza – Verona – Milan – St. Gotthard pass. More than a third of his book (153 out of 434 pages) was about Rome: a city "where every Stone almost is a book: every Statue a Master; every Inscription a Lesson; every Anti-chamber an Academy."

Other visitors to Rome about this time were Sir George Savile and the second Earl of Chesterfield, in 1650, and Francis Mortoft and two friends. The three, in 1658-59, being unable to hire a boat from Marseilles to Genoa, were obliged to cover that section by road – "accounted by all travellers absolutely the worst in Europe" – but having once arrived in Rome, specially praised the "sweet and ravishing music" to be heard there, and attended Mass at St. Peter's chiefly in order to hear the singing of the *castrati*. John Bargrave, another Englishman who lived abroad during the Commonwealth and Protectorate, was in Rome at least four times, the last being in 1658-59.

Even some writers with no recent personal experience of Rome sought to profit from this augmented interest in the city. In 1654 there appeared in London a translation of Martinelli's *Roma Ricercata*, a guide-book which took the tourist round the sights of the city in a mere ten days. This translation, published in English as *Directions for Such as shall travel to Rome*, was carried out by an impoverished Royalist gentleman, Henry Cogan, who had once been secretary to Sir Henry Wotton in Venice, and was later to be one of the overseers of Inigo Jones' will. Thus he had connexions with Italy, but had not been there himself since he was a young man.

Among those Englishmen who remained abroad in voluntary exile before the accession of Charles II was William Sancroft, who happened to be in Rome when the news of the Restoration reached him. Later, in 1667 he became Archbishop of Canterbury – and was the last holder of that office, until modern times, to visit Rome either before becoming Archbishop, or during his tenure of the post.

The returning Court in 1660 had closer ties with France, Italy and the art world generally than the Parliamentarians. One of the consequences of this was a further increase in the numbers of English visitors to Rome. These included Robert Southwell, afterwards Secretary of State, in 1660-61, while in March 1661 Banister Maynard, son of Lord Maynard, rode northwards from Naples "in the company of at least twenty English gentlemen and their servants." In 1664-65 Edward Browne, eldest son of Sir Thomas Browne, the Norwich physician and essayist, was in Rome before settling down to a course of medical study at Padua.

An interesting visitor to Rome about this time was the Rev. John Ray, who lost his fellowship at Cambridge for refusing to conform to the Prayer Book. His interests were mainly scientific. The tour of the Continent that he embarked on, with two friends, in 1662, lasted three years. After the rather too often repeated lists of ruins, monuments and churches to be found in Rome, it is refreshing to read in Ray's book that Rome was then "noted for several commodities and manufactures, such as viol and lute-strings the best in Europe; perfumed gloves;

combs of buffles' horns, women's fans, vitriol, essences". Rome, he wrote, is "well served for all provisions of the belly". But he did not find it as cheap as Florence or Naples, nor so populous as either Venice, Milan or Naples. "They reckon the number of inhabitants to be about 120,000 souls, besides strangers, of which there are a great number always here." After visiting Naples, Ray climbed Mount Etna and penned lengthy descriptions of the plants he found there. His route northwards out of Italy was unconventional, too: he crossed the Alps by an eastern route – Trento – Bolzano – Chur – and then altered his course to the south-west, in order to visit Montpellier, in France, which was of interest to him because of its botanical garden and its importance as a centre of pharmaceutical studies.

In 1665, war broke out again between England and France. Louis XIV ordered all Englishmen to leave the country – and that was the end of the Grand Tour for another generation or so. Rome, however, was now rapidly becoming one of the best places in Europe for an artist to live and work. One such was Michael Wright, who was born probably in London but was later apprenticed to an Edinburgh tailor before he embarked on his career as a painter. He went to Italy in 1647 and was in Rome a year later, living and working abroad until 1656. He became a professional painter when he returned to England, was widely employed especially by Catholic patrons, and came to be considered second only to Lely as a portraitist. He visited Rome again in 1685-7, as Steward to the Household in Lord Castlemaine's embassy to the Pope, and wrote an account of this mission in Italian, which was translated into English and published in 1688. Wright was the only English artist in the seventeenth century who was enrolled a member of the Academy of St. Luke in Rome. To this academy were attached also Poussin and Velazquez. Michael Wright just outlived the seventeenth century, dying in London in 1700, at the age of 82.

Another English artist who spent some time in Rome at the beginning of the eighteenth century was William Kent, called "the father of modern gardening" by Walpole. He was successively a painter, sculptor, architect and landscape gardener. The educated Englishman of the seventeenth and eighteenth centuries was very thoroughly versed in the Latin classical writers. Consequently, a visit to Italy meant, most of all, a tour of the places associated with some of the most enduring memories of his schooldays. Robert Adam, for example, studied nothing else but the Latin classics and Latin grammar during his five years at Edinburgh High School, and felt completely at home in Rome from the moment he entered it.

This was even more true of Joseph Addison, who was primarily a classical scholar. He set out from Dover to Calais on the Grand Tour in 1699, having been allocated a grant of £200 by the Treasury for purposes of travel. He obtained two pupils – George Dashwood, son of the Lord Mayor of London, and Edward Montagu, his own patron's nephew – and took them on the standard tour of Italy. To Addison, every place he visited had a classical connotation. Mantua was where Virgil had been born; Padua was Livy's birthplace; near Lake Garda was Catullus' retreat. He crossed the Rubicon, like Julius Caesar; and in Rome every hill, every monument, recalled one or another of the classical authors. He rode out to Tivoli feeling like Horace, and sailed from Naples to Ostia feeling like Virgil, who had described Aeneas as following that coast. Yet he was not completely unaware of contemporary Italy: he attended a comic opera, and went out of his way to visit San Marino.

From about 1713 onwards, there were three groups of Englishmen for whom the idea of a journey to Rome had considerable appeal: the winter tourists, who came to see the "antiquities" and to complete their education; the Catholic exiles, soon to be reinforced by the *émigré* Court of the titular James III; and the practising or professional artists, who gradually changed their status from that of transients to that of residents, so that by the middle of the century they could be said to constitute a British artists' colony. We shall meet these three groups most of all during the periods of peace that occurred during the eighteenth century – after the Treaty of Utrecht in 1713 until 1733; after the Peace of Aix-la-Chapelle in 1748, which closed the War of the Austrian Succession, until 1756, when Prussia's advance into Saxony began the Seven Years War; and from 1763 until the loss of the American colonies and the renewal of the war between Britain on one side, and France, Spain and later the Netherlands on the other, again disrupted cultural contact between these nations. Between the Treaty of Versailles in 1783 and the outbreak of the French Revolution in 1789, the road to Rome was also fairly free from warlike interruptions.

It is notable that the three groups mentioned above were all, to some degree, minorities. The leading men in the intellectual life of England in the early eighteenth century – Pope, Defoe, Hogarth, Vanbrugh, Steele, Swift and Gay – never embarked on the tour to Italy, while Fielding, the only early eighteenth century English writer of importance who spent much time abroad, chose to go not to Italy but to Portugal – and that only for his health's sake. In Britain literature, if not art, was now closely associated with the rise of the commercial middle class, and one of its characteristics was a greater insularity. Writers did not feel the same need to travel to Italy for professional reasons. Those who had most to say, preferred to work in their native land.

Although James Edward Stuart – the Old Pretender to his enemies, James III and VIII to his friends, and officially recognized as such by the Pope and by the kings of France and Spain – was a Scotsman and spent almost the whole of his life outside the United Kingdom, he does just qualify for inclusion in the list of men who, born in England, later travelled to Rome, since he first exercised his lungs in St. James's Palace in 1688 – and was forthwith taken away, a babe in arms, into France and lifelong exile. Under the terms of the Treaty of Utrecht, he was not permitted to live any longer in French territory; so he accepted the invitation of Pope Clement XI to settle in Rome. The Muti Palace in the Piazza dei Santi Apostoli (now Palazzo Balestra) was leased by the Apostolic Chamber in 1718 for the residence of "the King of England". There James remained for the rest of his long, virtuous and harmless life, surrounded by his little Court and Jacobite hangers-on. He remained a constant source of interest both to the visiting Grand Tourists and to the Hanoverian secret agents (such as Philip von Stosch, who became a noted "antiquarian" in Rome and wrote despatches to London under his pseudonym John Walton) who were instructed to report on the doings of the Stuarts.

The Jacobites at first were somewhat more than an embarrassment to the reigning Hanoverians. Some of their adherents were apparently quite well placed to cause trouble – such as the Irishman Parker, who commanded the Papal Navy, though as the Pope's fleet consisted merely of three antiquated vessels, without a single properly equipped naval port that they could use, this was hardly a threat to be taken seriously. Equally flimsy were the powers, the normal prerogative of a sovereign state, that the titular king, through his secretary Murray (Lord Dunbar) and Murray's agent the Abbé Grant (who was a gregarious man and very popular among the visiting Grand Tourists), was permitted to wield. In theory he was entitled to appoint Consuls at the papal ports of Civita Vecchia and Ancona, though it does not appear that these functions were ever exercised. The threat that they *might* be was a constant source of irritation to the loyalist English, who had no diplomatic representation in Rome during most of the eighteenth century. The nearest Consul was at Leghorn, while more important matters were dealt with by Sir Horace Mann, appointed in 1738 as "Resident to the Great Duke of Tuscany" at Florence. He later became very well known to every Englishman and Scotsman who travelled south from Florence to Rome and back.

The Stuarts were sometimes in a position to sabotage the plans of Englishmen who wanted to visit Naples from Rome. For this purpose travellers had to have passports. Although these passports were issued by the Roman government, the Minister for Naples was quite likely to refuse the application unless it had been supported by the Jacobite secretary or the Abbé Grant. It also appears from a letter of Thomas Gray in 1740 that the Jacobites censored the English mail. "This letter", he wrote, "[like all those the English send, or receive] will pass through the hands of that family, before it comes to those it was intended for. They do it more honour than it deserves." And finally, the Royal Arms of England were placed above the door of James III's palace in the

Piazza dei Santi Apostoli. In that palace were born Prince Charles Edward, the Young Pretender, in 1720, and Henry, Duke of York, in 1725.

Socially, the presence of the Stuarts in Rome was extremely awkward to visitors accustomed to the protocol and civilities of Court life. The Marquis of Blandford, in Rome a few weeks after Prince Charles was born, was walking in the grounds of Villa Ludovici when he came "sudden face to face with the Pretender, his Princess, and Court." The Marquis was not a Jacobite; but there was nothing he could decently do but remove his hat. He was invited to attend the Pretender's Court that evening; and again felt that he could not properly refuse. He wrote:

> ... *there is every day a regular table of ten or twelve covers well served, unto which some of the qualified persons of his court or travellers are invited; it is supplied with English and French cookery, French and Italian wine, but I took notice that the Pretender ate only of the English dishes, and took his dinner of roast beef.*[2]

The two young princes grew up in this confined and pathetic society of exiles, with its jealousies and intrigues, which existed parallel to, but had very little contact with, that other world of the itinerant English who came to Rome in the autumn and left in the early summer. But the exiles had no contact at all with the vastly greater majority of the British people who had already rejected the Stuarts and would never visit Rome. Those who did go there, regarded the Jacobites as one of the sights of the city. According to the French observer Charles de Brosses, there were in 1739 "crowds" of English in Rome, all of them eager to set eyes on the titular king and more especially his sons.

How to see the Pretender, Prince Charles and Prince Henry without becoming involved in a difficult predicament was a social problem that worried the British visitor from 1717 until 1788, when Prince Charles died at the Palazzo Muti. During all that time there was a Jacobite claimant to the thrones of England and Scotland. Indeed, it was not until 1819, when Pius VII commissioned Canova to create the monument, in St. Peter's, to the last three legitimate members of the Stuart line, that the unfortunate dynasty was relegated to the safety and immobility of stone and past history.

Most visitors followed Lord Chesterfield's advice. Writing to his son in 1749, he recommended the young man never to meet a Stuart at all if he could help it, and if he must, "feign ignorance of him and his grievances. If he begins to talk politics, disavow any knowledge of events in England, and escape as soon as you can." As late as 1770, when the two surviving princes were among the established sights of Rome for the English tourist, this could still be a dilemma. In that year we read of Lady Anne Miller, suddenly and unavoidably in the presence of Prince Charles at a party, not wishing to snub the Prince but uncertain how to style him. Having rejected "Mon Prince" as disloyal, "Your Highness" as not proper, she was about to address him as "Monseigneur" when the Prince himself eased her difficulty by taking the initiative and speaking to her in English.

Among the English visitors who saw Prince Charles and his brother before the "Forty-five" rebellion were Horace Walpole and the poet Thomas Gray, who entered the gates of Rome together in the cold and belated spring of 1740. "Good fine boys," Gray thought them, but "especially the younger, who has the more spirit of the two."

Walpole and Gray, who had been friends since they were at Eton together, left for their Grand Tour in March 1739. Neither of them had ever been abroad before, and to them, as to so many English travellers, Calais represented the quintessence of "abroad". No place seen later in their travels seemed half so strange or more foreign. "Calais is an exceedingly old, but very pretty town," wrote Gray, "and we hardly saw anything there that was not so new and so different from England, that it surprized us agreeably." They stayed two months in Paris, one at Rheims, then travelled via Lyon and Geneva and over the Mont Cenis pass (where Walpole's dog Tory was seized and devoured by a wolf in broad daylight) and down to Turin. They reached Florence in December 1739, and stayed there until the end of March 1740. It was in Florence that the profound differences in temperament of the two men first began to make themselves felt. Walpole, a Prime Minister's son, well conversant with society, used to elegance and refinement, was delighted with Florence, and flung himself with gusto into the events of the Carnival season. "I have done nothing," he wrote, "but slip out of my domino into bed, and out of bed into my domino. The end of the Carnival is frantic, bacchanalian: all the morn one makes parties in masque to the shops and coffee-houses, and all the evening to the operas and balls". When the time came for them to go on to Rome, Walpole was fretting about the inclement weather, impatient with the "little society" of Rome, eagerly awaiting the day when he could get back to Florence and the whirl of Society.

Gray, on the other hand, wistful, poetic, *simpatico*, knew he would always be on the fringe of the world represented by Walpole, however much he might wish to be a part of it. In Florence he visited the art galleries, took copious notes and prepared for the experience of Rome. It took them four days from Florence, of which the first night was spent at Siena, "an agreeable, clean, old city, of no great magnificence or extent." The second night was spent at the "terrible black hill" of Mount Radicofani, where "after stopping up the windows with the quilts, we were obliged to lie upon the straw beds in our clothes." For their third night they were in Viterbo, where they dined on "the leg of an old hare and some broiled crows."

The entrance to Rome, which was a disappointment to other eighteenth century travellers such as Gibbon and Smollett, fulfilled all Gray's expectations:

> *The first entrance to Rome is prodigiously striking. It is by a noble gate, designed by Michel Angelo, and adorned with statues; this brings you into a large square, in the midst of which is a vast obelisk of granite, and in front you have at*

> one view two churches of a handsome architecture, and so much alike that they are called the twins; with three streets, the middlemost of which is one of the longest in Rome. As high as my expectation was raised, I confess, the magnificence of this city infinitely surpasses it. You cannot pass along a street but you have views of some palace, or church, or square, or fountain, the most picturesque and noble one can imagine. We have not yet set about considering its beauties, ancient and modern, with attention; but have already taken a slight transient view of some of the most remarkable. St. Peter's I saw the day after we arrived, and was struck dumb with wonder.

In his account, Gray captures, and records with a wonderful exactitude and simplicity, the sensation familiar to all who have been there that no one else's description of the sights of Rome can adequately prepare one for the first-hand marvellousness of it:

> I do assure you that everything one has heard say of Italy is a lie, and am firmly of opinion, that no mortal was ever here before us. I am writing to prove that there never was any such people as the Romans, that this was anciently a Colony of the Jews, and that the Coliseum was built on the model of Solomons temple.

And later:

> It is the most beautiful of Italian nights, which in truth are but just begun (so backward has the spring been here, and everywhere else, they say). There is a moon! There are stars for you! Do you not smell the orange flowers? That building yonder is the Convent of S. Isidore; and that eminence with the cypress trees and pines upon it, the top of M. Quirinal.

This is all true, and yet my prospect is not two hundred yards in length.

Gray also visited Tivoli, and wrote a long description of it which not only illustrates his literary style at its best, but is probably the best word-picture ever penned of this place:

She [Nature] has built here three or four little mountains, and laid them out in an irregular semi-circle; from certain others behind, at a greater distance, she has drawn a canal, into which she has put a little river of hers, called Anio; she has cut a huge cleft between the two innermost of her four hills, and there she has left it to its own disposal; which she has no sooner done, but, like a heedless chit, it tumbles headlong down a declivity fifty feet perpendicular, breaks itself all to shatters, and is converted into a shower of rain, where the sun forms many a bow, red, green, blue and yellow. To get out of our metaphors without any trouble, it is the most noble sight in the world. The weight of that quantity of waters, and the force they fall with, have worn the rocks they throw themselves among into a thousand irregular craggs, and to a vast depth. In this channel it goes boiling along with a mighty noise till it comes to another steep, where you see it a second time come roaring down (but first you must walk two miles farther) a greater height than before, but now with that quantity of waters; for by this time it has divided itself, being crossed and opposed by the rocks, into four several streams, each of which, in emulation of the great one, will tumble down too; and it does tumble down, but not from an equally elevated place; so that you have at one view all these cascades intermixed with groves of olive and little woods, the mountains rising behind them, and on the top of one (that which forms the extremity of one of the half-circle's horns) is seated the town itself. At the very

> extremity of that extremity, on the brink of the precipice, stands the Sibyls' temple, the remains of a little rotunda, surrounded with its portico, above half of whose Corinthian pillars are still standing entire; all this on one hand. On the other, the open Campagna of Rome, here and there a little castle on a hillock, and the city itself on the very brink of the horizon, indistinctly seen (being 18 miles off) except the dome of St. Peter's; which, if you look out of your window, wherever you are, I suppose, you can see.

No wonder that Gray and Walpole quarrelled. Temperamentally they were quite incompatible. Walpole had his way, and brought Gray back to Florence. But Gray was unwilling to leave, having written "the city itself I do not part with so easily, which alone has amusements for whole years." He was still wistful for Italy when, at last, they landed again in England.

Three and a half years later, on 11 January 1744, when he was aged nearly twenty-four, Prince Charles left Rome in secrecy, bearing a patent of Regency from his father, intending with French help to recover the three crowns of England, Scotland and Ireland for the Stuarts. France had sixteen thousand men and a fleet of twenty-two ships concentrated at Dunkirk, and seemed to be in earnest. When asked to expel Prince Charles from France, in accordance with the terms of the Treaty of Utrecht, Louis XV replied by declaring war on England, on 20 March.

In the meantime storms had driven half the troop transports ashore; the expedition was postponed, then finally abandoned. Despite the battle of Fontenoy the following year (in which the Scottish and Irish regiments of the King of France soundly defeated the English soldiers under their German general), the Jacobite cause was already practically lost. Prince Charles sailed for Scotland without his father's knowledge and without the support of the King of France, in two ships, one of which was so badly damaged by an English man-of-war that she had to turn back. He landed in the Highlands with seven men, a little money, and a modest armament of muskets and broad-swords. The rest of the story of the rebellion is well known.

It was not until 1766, when his father died, that Prince Charles returned to Rome. He lived in France until his cousin the King of France had him expelled, and then incognito in various European cities where he had no roots, but where it was safe for him to stay – Avignon (then still part of Papal territory), Strasbourg, Basle, Ghent – anywhere except Rome and the United Kingdom, though he did pay a brief visit to London in 1750, where, for obvious political reasons, he was received into the Church of England. He spent his time plotting, quarrelling, drinking, borrowing and spending money, but always concealing his intentions. He was determined not to heed his father's unasked-for advice, determined to remain in hiding and baffle the agents who were sent to keep an eye on him. He did that partly because he bore a grudge against anyone – his father, the King of France, the old Jacobites – who tried to tell him how his life should be organized; partly because his sense of political reality told him that so long as he stayed an enigma, he still had some slight chance of being restored to the English throne as Charles III. This chance would vanish entirely if he returned to Rome.

Meanwhile, in Rome, the English artists were entering an unusually prolific period. The ground had been prepared for them in 1722, when the first English account of Italian art based on personal observation was published. *An Account of some of the statues, bas reliefs, drawings, and pictures in Italy, etc., with Remarks* was written by the two Jonathan Richardsons, father and son. Richardson senior edited the work at home from fieldwork material supplied by his son, who successfully carried out what was, in the context of the eighteenth century, a lightning tour of Italy. With only a month or so available for the journey, Richardson junior raced round the galleries, churches and palaces, assimilated the essential facts and even found time to pronounce one or two independent judgments. Two-thirds of the book was devoted to the art treasures of Rome, which to Richardson junior was the place he most wanted in the world to see. Richardson senior, in his preface to the book, defended the unorthodox rapidity of his son's tour in words that were true enough:

> *He may have been long in Italy who spends but a few months there; or come home too soon after having liv'd there half an Age.*

The book was successful; though it was only after another long period of European war (1733-1748) that the learning it imparted could be fully assimilated.

We saw in earlier centuries that improved facilities for travel to and from Rome, sometimes promoted by the Church, made their appearance at the time of the Holy Years. Such facilities were, not surprisingly, often made use of by persons who professed no religious reasons for going to Rome. This applied also to the Holy Year of 1750 which, for a wonder, occurred during the middle of a period entirely uninterrupted by war. Artists, as well as their prospective patrons, were very numerous in Rome in 1750 and the immediately preceding and succeeding years.

For a city to become an art centre, indeed, it is not sufficient that artists should like being there, and find there plenty of suitable subjects to portray. It is also necessary that art patrons should like the place, and return to it in ever larger numbers. Otherwise the artist will not sell his work at all, and will either die of poverty, or move on somewhere else. In either case, the place in question will cease to be an art centre.

From 1750 onwards, if not before, there was never any danger of Rome suffering that fate. The patrons of art were coming there every autumn, and staying in most cases until the spring. Many artists found that they could make a living by copying the work of the masters in the Vatican art galleries, and selling their copies to tourists. This was no doubt, as Joshua Reynolds called it, "a delusive kind of industry", but it helped to perfect the painter's technique and it enabled him to live in Rome.

Other artists found it much more lucrative to follow the trade of antiquary, that is, they acted as middlemen between producer and consumer, discovering an artist's work and introducing it to a potential purchaser. All the antiquaries had originally been artists of one kind of another. They came to Rome to study, found that selling art to the visitors brought in far more money, and remained in Rome to earn a very satisfactory income in this way. In the seventeenth century, Michael Wright had been as much an antiquary as a painter. In the 1750s two more British painters entered this field: Thomas Jenkins, who had arrived in Rome in 1752 with Richard Wilson and stayed there until obliged to leave in 1798 because of the Napoleonic Wars; and James Russel, who helped to sell several pictures by Wilson and Thomas Patch. After Russel died in Rome in 1763, his place as leading guide and antiquary was taken by Gavin Hamilton and James Byers. Gavin Hamilton was a painter, dealer and excavator who spent more than fifty years of his life in Rome, first between 1740 and 1750, and then from 1756 until his death, also in Rome, in 1797. James Byers, originally an architect, is remembered as the man who guided Gibbon round the sights of Rome. He lived in Rome from 1750 to 1790.

In the Holy Year of 1750 some of the British artists working in Rome were Thomas Patch and Richard Dalton, who had arrived in 1747; John Astley, who came to Rome in 1750; Nathaniel Hone; and Joshua Reynolds. Reynolds' journey to Rome was a highly unconventional one: he first obtained a passage to Minorca (then a British possession) in a naval vessel, was delayed as a result of his horse falling over a precipice and breaking its rider's leg, finally went by ship to Leghorn and from there by road to Rome, in 1750. In that year Astley was 20, Hone 32, and Reynolds 27.

Thomas Patch was an engraver and etcher, whose eccentric behaviour later antagonized the Church authorities, and obliged him in 1756 to leave Rome and settle for the rest of his life in Florence, where he made a red chalk drawing of Edward Gibbon, in 1764. John Astley shared lodgings with Reynolds and returned to England with him in 1752. Nathaniel Hone was an Irish artist who specialized in miniatures; he figures in one of Reynolds' caricatures of English visitors to Rome.

Joshua Reynolds' two years in Rome were spent "with measureless content." He met there his future friends and patrons, Lord Charlemont, Sir William Lowther, Lord Downe and Lord Bruce. When he came back to England, he brought with him one fifteen year old Italian pupil, Giuseppe Marchi. Within two or three years of his return he was a successful and famous artist in London, with over one hundred sitters in 1755. Yet while he was actually in Rome he painted very little. Almost the only original work he did there consisted of caricatures of visiting Englishmen. It cannot be doubted that in Rome he was learning rather than executing; determining in which direction his style would later develop.

A few months before Reynolds left the city, Richard Wilson arrived. Of his patrons in Rome, the most important was William Legge, second Earl of Dartmouth. Wilson went with him on an excursion to Naples. It was Wilson's *View of Rome from the Villa Madama*, commissioned by Dartmouth and exhibited in London in 1765, that established Wilson's reputation as the leading landscape artist of his day.

Richard Wilson also painted comparatively little while he was in Rome. Most of his paintings of Italian subjects were completed in England, and some of them were not even derived from sketches made in Italy. Among his works that can definitely be named as having been painted in Rome, however, were *Rome and the Ponte Molle* (1752), *Shepherds in the Campagna* (1755), *Outskirts of Rome under Snow* (1756) and *Banks of the Tiber* (1757). Wilson was one of the first of British painters who explored the Campagna, that strange, half deserted, at that time still malaria-ridden region to the south of the city, where the ruined aqueducts straddled the plains bounded by the Alban Hills and the sea, where wild flowers of an infinite variety illuminated the ground, where the only human beings likely to be encountered were the sun-tanned shepherds, with their flocks. Wilson worked in many places in the Campagna, at Tivoli and at Lake Albano. His own pupils William Marlow and Thomas Jones, who were in Rome towards the end of the century, developed this trend.

Reynolds and Wilson, though contemporaries, were otherwise as different as it is possible for two artists to be. Reynolds was a city man, fond of society, as much a man of letters as a painter, who cultivated the intellectual and fashionable world for its own sake. Wilson was an open-air man, a pure landscape artist, who wished only to draw the trees, the parkland, the lakes, the crumbling ruins and the occasional distant individuals that figure in his most characteristic work. But both of them brought back from Rome something vital for the subsequent development of English art: Reynolds the seed of the English school of portraiture, Wilson the seed of the English school of landscape painting.

All these artists lived in the neighbourhood of Piazza di Spagna while they were in Rome. Wilson and Jenkins lived in the Piazza itself; Reynolds, Gavin Hamilton and Joseph Wilton in the nearby Palazzo Zuccari, which served as a kind of hostel for foreign art students. In the same neighbourhood was their social centre, the Caffè degli Inglesi, just off Piazza di Spagna. In 1766 this cafe was unflatteringly described by the painter Thomas Jones, in words that probably hold good also for the years around 1750:

> *The English coffee house, a filthy vaulted room, the walls of which were painted with Sphinxes, Obelisks and Pyramids, from capricious designs of Piranesi, and fitter to adorn the inside of an Egyptian Sepulchre, than a room of social conversation. Here – seated round a Brazier of hot embers placed in the Center, we endeavoured to amuse ourselves for an hour or two over a Cup of Coffee or glass of Punch, and then grope out our way home darkling, in Solitude and Silence.*[3]

Two years before the outbreak of the Seven Years War, in October 1754, Robert Adam set out from Edinburgh on the Grand Tour. One of

The English Road To Rome

the ten children of William Adam, who was already Scotland's leading architect and had been nicknamed "The Scottish Vitruvius", he was both born great and inherited greatness. He had had the Grand Tour in mind for some years, and had amassed a capital of £5000 in order to pay for it. But his tour abroad turned out very differently from what he had imagined.

He began it in the company of the Hon. Charles Hope, younger brother of the Earl of Hopetoun. With his own prosperous and enlightened family background, together with that precious £5000, there seemed no reason why he should not be accepted as the social equal of the Earl's brother, and even as his friend. At first their journey was entirely conventional within the context of the Grand Tour. They were three weeks in Paris, where Robert Adam cultivated the social round and indulged his somewhat extravagant taste in clothes at the establishments of the French gentlemen's tailors. They went on to Lyon, down the Rhone valley, by felucca from Nice to Genoa, and then by way of Leghorn and Pisa to Florence, arriving in time for the Carnival. Robert Adam threw himself into the gaieties of this round of events with the same enthusiasm that Robert Walpole had displayed, fifteen years previously. At the final ball of the carnival he claimed to have "danced no fewer than two hundred minuets and three hundred country dances," and to have mixed "with all the greatest Quality and with some of the greatest Whores and with the handsomest of both kinds whenever I could get at them."[4]

An introduction that he sought in Florence altered not only the pattern of his visit to Italy, but the whole course of his future life and, it is not too much to say, the future development of British architecture. He had been keen to meet the French *avant-garde* architect Charles Louis Clérisseau, who had won a Prix de Rome and had lived at the French Academy there. After they had met, Clérisseau offered, in return for the cost of his board and lodging, to be Robert Adam's guide and antiquarian during his stay in Rome. He would introduce him to the artistic and architectural world, would tutor him in perspective and drawing, and give him copies of his own work to study. He did not in any case intend to have anything more to do with the French Academy, and would be happy to share a rented house with his prospective pupil.

Robert Adam was quick to realize the implications of this offer. It was exactly what he wanted to do in Rome, but he could not do it and still remain within the conventional limits set by the Grand Tour. It was not only that he would need to stay in Rome for at least a year in order to profit from Clérisseau's tuition; it also meant that socially speaking he would have to step out of the Grand Tour ambit, and down in the social scale. Artists were simply not regarded as members of fashionable society. "If I am known in Rome to be an architect," he wrote, "if I am seen drawing or with a pencil in my hand, I cannot enter into genteel company who will not admit an artist or, if they do admit him, will very probably rub affronts on him in order to prevent his appearing at their card-playing, balls or concerts."

In point of fact he did not have to make quite such a complete break with the world of Society as he had imagined. He found later that he could present himself to Roman society, during the seasons of 1755/56 and 1756/57, as a *dilettante* knowledgeable about art, a buyer of pictures, who dressed well, was as prepared as any other Scotsman to embark upon a "sea of liquor" on St. Andrew's Day, gave parties "in the French style, putting on the table about twenty little plates, some hot and some cold, with fruits &ca., all at a time, so that the whole ceremony was conducted with vast decency, yet splendid and showy," had Italian friends, and was always willing to give "a twirl in my coach" to any of his acquaintances' handsome daughters. He became even more the eligible bachelor after he had had the luck to acquire for £35 a second-hand carriage which could be adapted to a post-chaise, "one of the handsomest little chariots I ever saw: painted green and gold, well lined and as good as new."

Nevertheless, he had weighed up the two alternatives and had decided to accept Clérisseau's offer. The face he presented to the world was very different from the one Clérisseau and the artistic circle saw. He rented rooms at the Casa Guarnieri, near the Villa di Malta, facing the present Via Sistina and Via Francesco Crispi. In other words he was not too close to the distractions of Piazza di Spagna, and had a peaceful atmosphere in which to work. "I am enabled to seclude myself a good deal," he wrote home to Edinburgh, "from the English travellers without falling out with any of them, and to preserve the greater part of my time for painting, drawing and reading, which, were I living in their neighbourhood, would be altogether spent in dinners, suppers and jaunts." The house contained a bedroom for himself and one for Clérisseau, "a hall in which to have two or three tables for draughtsmen and other myrmidons of art whom we employ," as well as a dining room, and a chamber for the valet. He reckoned that they would be able to live in Rome on twelve shillings a day. This would include the wages of their cook, valet, valet-de-place ("servant for going errands or behind the coach") and the coach itself, which would cost four shillings for the whole day, coachman included.

He knew very well what he wanted to do: to become the leading architect in Britain. He also knew how he could begin to achieve this aim: by cultivating possible patrons, all of whom would be on the Grand Tour, and by a thorough study of Roman architecture at its *fons et origo*. In fact, he proposed nothing less than to "measure and record afresh every important example of Roman architecture" and thereby "to be able to reach out towards a more thorough understanding of the principles of proportion on which the secret of the classical style was thought to depend." To this end he was up every morning at seven o'clock and working at his drawing-board, wearing a "green silk short coat and waistcoat, with a pair of thin breeches and my stockings ungartered." He spent all his mornings like this, in study and drawing. After dinner he would do his field-work in the Roman sunlight, sketching palaces and ""antiquities"". That left only the evenings for relaxation and the social life that he never entirely relinquished.

Thousands of English tourists at this period bought the work of Piranesi, the artist who had published in 1750 his volume of engravings of scenes in Italian prisons, *Le Carceri*, which immediately made his fame, and in 1756 the still more sought-after *Le Antichità Romane*. Robert Adam became a friend of Piranesi. The Italian master was, he thought, "the most extraordinary fellow I ever saw," who became "quite distracted" on seeing Robert's sketches, and claimed that he had "more genius for the true noble architecture than any Englishman ever was in Italy." Soon they were going on sketching expeditions together, Piranesi always "brisk" and "un peu sauvage" in his enormous hat and short hunting jacket.

However, to be exposed to Piranesi for any length of time was somewhat of a trial, and Robert Adam soon found that a quarter of an hour was ample. Still, he was surprised and flattered to learn that Piranesi proposed to dedicate one of his engravings to him, with an appropriate inscription. But he was not quite so flattered on discovering that he would be expected to buy 80 or 100 copies of the engraving, in return for the compliment. Robert Adam he was not a hard-headed Scot for nothing. He calculated that he would probably be able to dispose of the surplus copies, at a profit, to a friend of his who was a bookseller in London.

Robert Adam was just two years in Rome – from May 1755 to May 1757 – after he returned from the excursion to Naples and settled down in the Casa Guarnieri. Much as he was impressed by the liveliness of Naples, he infinitely preferred Rome either to that city or to Florence. He declared uncompromisingly:

> *Rome is the most glorious place in the universal world. A grandeur and tranquillity reigns in it, everywhere noble and striking remains of antiquity appear in it, which are so many that one who has spent a dozen years in seeing is still surprised with something new. The hills it stands on give you everywhere elevated prospects of town and country – the town rich with domes, spires and lofty buildings, ancient and modern; the country near Rome uneven, hilly, woody and adorned with villas, villages and churches, so that had*

one there friends, nothing could persuade one to quit it for any other part I ever saw. In fine, for a man of taste the day is too short, as you never tire of the agreeable, grand and picturesque walks.

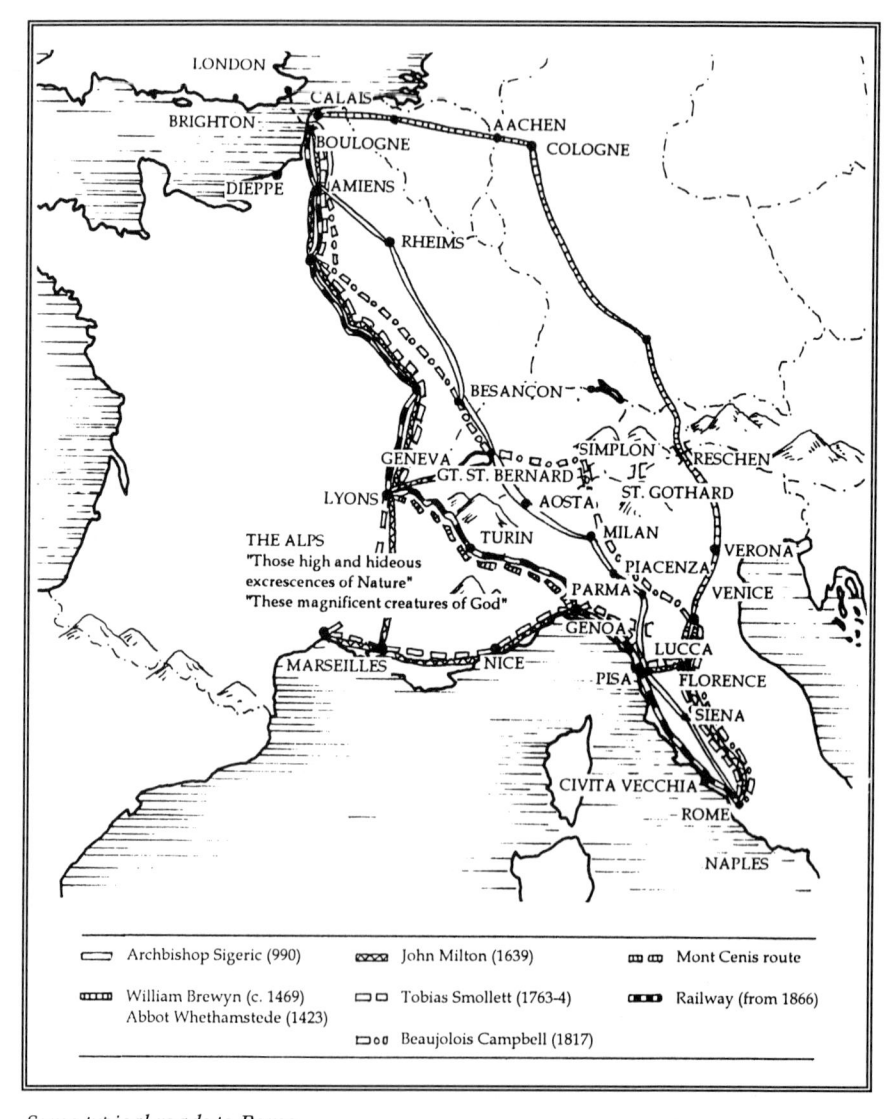

Some typical roads to Rome

The outbreak of the Seven Years War in 1756 made no difference to his plans. He was not going to follow the example of the Grand Tourists and make quick tracks for home. He knew very well that architects are not much in demand in war time, but he was also aware that the Adam family had a long-standing contract with the Board of Ordnance in connexion with Fort George, near Inverness. When the time came for him to go home, there would be no difficulty in replenishing his spent capital. So he continued with his studies of Roman architecture. He made a tour of the "Hadriatick Shoar" with Clérisseau. He produced a grandiose but unacceptable plan for rebuilding Lisbon after its destruction by earthquake in 1755. Piranesi mentioned him in one of the frontispieces to *Le Antichità Romane*. But, inevitably, the time came when the £5000 had been almost spent. He discarded the "unpracticable advice" of John MacGowan, who suggested he would do well to spend another two years abroad. He planned his last expeditions – to Civita Vecchia, Nettuno and Ostia – and finally despatched his roomful of "antique ornaments" to Leghorn, "by oxen-cart".

Just before he left Rome for the last time, that "most changeable, interested madman", Piranesi, completed his promised dedication to Robert Adam. The dedicatory plate, which referred in Latin to "Robert Adam Architect, Member of the Academy of St. Luke in Rome and of Florence and of the Institute of Bologna", was included in Piranesi's *Campus Martius*, published in 1762.

The only other of the Adam brothers who visited Rome was James, who was on the Grand Tour between 1760 and 1762. Since England was still at war with France and Spain, he had to be smuggled out to Venice in the guise of a Jacobite officer. He reached Rome in February 1761, and stayed at first at the Albergo Londra, "an extravagant inn". He liked to describe himself as the *Cavalieri Inglese*. Indeed, it soon became clear that he was more interested in appearing to good advantage in Roman society than studying Roman architecture. He was a great buyer of pictures; he travelled abroad in grander style than his brother and was in Italy longer; but he accomplished very little there, and in due course took up his proper place as his brother's assistant. The Adam style had been formed, chiefly as a result of Robert Adam's two years in Rome, before James ever went abroad.

It is inevitable that a comparison should be drawn between Robert Adam's stay in Rome from 1755 and 1757, and that of Inigo Jones a hundred and thirty years previously. Both of them come well out of the comparison. Both were great architects, who in different ways successfully achieved a period of serious study in Rome. Both sought their inspiration in classical Roman architecture, though Inigo Jones' ideal, Palladio, was considered out-dated by Robert Adam. Very little was known about their personal lives until the discovery of letters Ronert Adam wrote from Rome. The chief difference between them is perhaps that Robert Adam was already imbued with the classical literary tradition, both in his family environment and at school. He originated, too, not from London like Inigo Jones, but from Edinburgh – and from an Edinburgh which was no longer the small capital of an unruly, poverty-stricken, northern nation, but was now the second cultural centre of a United Kingdom, a city which from that time henceforward would (not least because of the Adam family's architectural enrichment of it) remain within the mainstream of European life. Smollett, a few years later, may well have been thinking of Robert Adam and his brothers when he referred to Edinburgh as "a hot-bed of genius".

There were still quite a number of British visitors to Rome during the Seven Years War. Some were very transient. One of them was Patrick Sarsfield, who escaped from a British man-of-war in Naples, went to Rome, and appealed to the Stuart Pretender for "cloaks and victuals to carry me to Leghorn". There were also two unnamed Irish sailors, who the following year similarly escaped from a British warship at Ancona and petitioned the titular king for help. "We neither have," they wrote, "Shirt nor Shoes or Stockings only Bear Naked."[5] They did not appeal in vain.

In 1760 the eccentric English sculptor, Joseph Nollekens, appeared in Rome despite the difficulties of travelling in war time, and remained there despite the even more formidable difficulties of making ends meet in the face of an insufficiency of patrons. Nollekens was twenty-three when he came to Rome, an unknown artist without either money or connexions. If we are to believe Nollekens' somewhat hostile and resentful biographer, J.T. Smith, who had no first hand knowledge of the sculptor's life in Rome, Nollekens existed chiefly on melons and what he called "Roman cuttings": "bits of skin, bits of gristle, and bits of fat", which he bought from the butcher twopence a portion, and which his Roman housekeeper peppered and salted for him, serving them up with "a slice of bread and sometimes a bit of vegetable."

Nollekens earned a living at first by piecing together fragments of antique statues and selling them to tourists. The tribulations of these lean years were alleviated by the two substantial prizes that Nollekens won in 1760 and 1762 for bas-reliefs that he sent to England. After 1764 he amassed a considerable fortune, though he seems never to have given up, in prosperity, the parsimonious habits that he had perforce learnt when he was poor. By the time he was 33 he was a sculptor of some renown, well known to the fashionable society that frequented Rome, and indeed owing to Rome the start he needed for a successful career. The first bust he ever modelled was of David Garrick, which he made in Rome during the actor-manager's visit. He was paid £12 for it.

Lady Mary Wortley Montagu wrote that Rome was "crammed with Britons" in 1758, but in the circumstances of war time this statement may perhaps be taken with a pinch of salt. There is no doubt at all, however, that foreign visitors crammed themselves into Rome after peace was concluded in 1763. In terms of foreign travel, that year was like 1814 or 1945. The urge to go abroad had become irresistible. Not only impecunious artists and young men of quality set out on the Grand Tour, but also upper class and middle class people of all kinds. Gibbon related (though with scepticism) that at this peak period of the Grand Tour, no less than forty thousand Englishmen were travelling on the Continent. During the two seasons 1763-64 and 1764-65 alone. James Boswell, Garrick, Smollett, Sterne and Wilkes were all in Rome independently. When Gibbon returned from his tour, he became a member of a club, "The Romans", whose membership was confined to those who had made the Tour as far as Rome. The club expired in 1773, and no wonder, for by that time there was nothing at all remarkable in having been to Rome.

Boswell's visit was entirely characteristic of him. He "entered Rome with full classical enthusiasm," but soon found that "the streets of Rome . . . are very little different from those of any other city." He duly occupied himself with "the study of antiquities, of pictures, of architecture, and of the other arts which are found in such great perfection in Rome." As for relaxation, he rather liked the idea of strolling through a city "where there are prostitutes licensed by the Cardinal Vicar." Nor was his interest in this matter merely theoretical. He met Wilkes, as he entered Rome, in the Custom House. They often met during the subsequent weeks, though they had little in common. Boswell was presented to the Pope, and attended *conversazioni* in the palaces of Roman nobles.[6]

At first sight, David Garrick was disappointed with Rome; the crooked streets, dismal houses and mud-yellow Tiber did not appeal to him. But was captivated as soon as he had entered the Pantheon, had seen the Colosseum and had toured the ruins. He was there for a fortnight in December 1763, before going on to Naples, and for about three months on his return, giving most of his time to the "antiquities".

Edward Gibbon was twenty-six when he visited Rome; he stayed there 18 weeks. With his friend William Guise, he set out from Lausanne, and visited Turin, Milan, Genoa, Parma, Modena, Bologna and Florence. Then, having "compared the solitude of Pisa with the industry of Lucca and Leghorn," he continued his journey through Siena to Rome. Throughout this journey he kept his Journal in French, with which language he was, as a young man, more familiar than with his native tongue. The last entry in the Journal records his entry into Rome; on 2 October 1764:

Nous sommes arrivés à Rome à cinq heures du soir. Depuis le Pons Milvius, j'ai été dans un songe d'antiquité qui n'a été interrompu que par les Commis de la Douane, Gens très modernes qui nous ont forcé d'aller à pied chercher un logement, car il n'y a point d'auberges, pendant qu'ils conduisoient notre Chaise de poste à la Douane. L'Abord de Rome n'est pas gracieux.[7]

The "dream of antiquity" enveloped him so completely that there was no time thereafter to keep up the journal. He only wrote a few pages of description, in English and undated, of the paintings and "antiquities" that he had seen and nothing at all about his daily life in Rome. He wrote to his father a week later:

I am now, Dear Sir, at Rome. If it was difficult before to give you or Mrs Gibbon any account of what I saw, it is impossible here. I have already such a fund of entertainment for a mind somewhat prepared for it by an acquaintance with the Romans, that I am really almost in a dream. Whatever ideas books may have given us of the greatness of that people, their accounts of the most flourishing state of Rome falls infinitely short of the picture of its ruins. I am convinced that there never, never existed such a nation, and I hope for the happiness of mankind there never will again.

The actual moment of inspiration, when the idea of "The Decline and Fall of the Roman Empire" was born, was recorded a week after that letter, in words which, though familiar, cannot be omitted from any history of the English in Rome:

It was on the fifteenth of October, in the gloom of evening, as I sat musing on the Capitol, while the barefooted friars were chanting their litanies in the temple of Jupiter,[8] *that I conceived the first thought of my history. My original plan*

> *was confined to the decay of the City; my reading and reflection pointed to that aim; but several years elapsed, and several avocations supervened; before I grappled with the decline and fall of the Roman Empire.*

He then embarked on the standard course on the Roman "antiquities", confessing that his "powers of attention were somewhat fatigued" as the instruction proceeded. James Byers acted as his banker, art dealer and guide; an Irishman, Meighan, was his tailor.

He never needed to visit Rome again. He did not start work on the "Decline and Fall" until 1773, when he was thirty-six, and completed the first volume three years after that. He finished the last volume in 1788, when he was fifty-one, almost a quarter of a century since his visit to Rome. He died six years later, at the age of fifty-six.

Most of the British travellers who set out for Rome after 1763, however, did so with very different preconceptions from those of their predecessors. They were aware that their country had become the most powerful empire on earth. They came to Italy not to seek information, but out of a desire to do the fashionable thing. They duly followed the courses on the "antiquities" – three hours each morning over a period of six weeks – but they were constantly drawing invidious comparisons between their own country and those they happened to be visiting. They were, in fact, far more insular than the British had ever been before.

This new trend is well typified by the journey of Tobias Smollett to France and Italy, between 1763 and 1765. Smollett was a travelling companion whom few would choose to have, and any sensitive innkeeper must have trembled at his approach. Irascible, cantankerous, xenophobic, he almost prided himself on making enemies wherever he went. His trail was littered with the insults he heaped on the ostlers, postilions, boatmen and other servants who had the misfortune to run across him. Yet his journey was a fairly typical one, and his account of it gives us a vivid insight into the actual conditions of mid-eighteenth century travel.

Coaches at this period usually took one day – and five changes of horses – from Charing Cross to Dover. The first change was at The Bull, Shooters Hill. People often had to stay a week at Dover waiting for a ship or for a change in the weather. Smollett considered the Dover road the worst in England:

> *The chambers are in general cold and comfortless, the beds paltry, the cooking execrable, the wine poison, the attendance bad, the publicans insolent, and the bills extortionate; there is not a drop of tolerable malt liquor to be had from London to Dover.*

In 1715 it had still been possible to get a seat in the cross-Channel packet for five shillings, but now the minimum charge had risen to half a guinea, only servants being carried for five shillings. The basic charge was doubled if the passenger had the use of the master's cabin. The clerks of the passage, the searchers, the water bailiffs and the landing boatmen all expected their additional payment, and were no doubt "insolent" if this was not forthcoming. Smollett chose the most expensive procedure of all – he hired a cutter to take him across to Boulogne, which cost him six guineas, plus another guinea for a boat to take him ashore at Boulogne, as well as ruinous tips to porters.

Smollett settled at Boulogne for three months, arranging for the customs clearance of his heavy luggage, including his books, which to his extreme annoyance had to be specially examined by the *chambre syndicale* in case they contained anything subversive. He spent the three months nursing his health, venturing on the "desperate remedy" of curing a fever by plunging daily into the sea; penning contemptuous descriptions of the *noblesse, bourgeoisie* and *canaille* of Boulogne; and preparing for his long journey across France to the Mediterranean. He found that his "great chests" could be shipped to Bordeaux, at the rate of one guinea per 1000 lbs. weight of baggage. They would then be forwarded by canal boat (the Canal du Midi had been opened in 1681) to Montpellier, where he would be able to collect them.

Around 1763 it was possible to cross France by public conveyance – stage-coach or river-boat – at a minimum charge of sixpence a mile. Or a private coach could be purchased or hired at Boulogne or Calais. If the coach was bought, it would have to be re-sold, probably at an enormous loss, on completing the return journey a year or two later. Again Smollett chose the most expensive way of travelling. Disdaining to travel in the stage-coach to Paris, of which he said, "a vehicle no man would use, who has any regard to his own ease and convenience; and it travels at the pace of an English waggon," he set out in a costly hired carriage, finding good inns only at Montreuil-sur-mer and Amiens. Everywhere else he found, "abundance of dirt, and the most flagrant imposition."

From Paris to Lyon there were three modes of travel: the stage-coach, the diligence and the post-chaise. A seat in the diligence, together with food and lodging along the read, was relatively cheap, but with "indifferent company". Thomas Gray had described the post-chaise in detail in a letter written in 1739:

> *A strange sort of conveyance, of much greater use than beauty, resembling an ill-shaped chariot, only with the door opening before instead of the side; three horses draw it, one between the shafts, and the other two on each side, on one of which the postillion rides, and drives too. This vehicle will, upon occasion, go fourscore miles a day.*

This vehicle had not then been introduced into England. Smollett decided in favour of the post-chaise, but he still had plenty to grumble about. The post system was well organized in England by this time, with fixed stages and an adequate supply of horses; in France, it was primarily a system of royal revenue. He wrote:

The postmaster finds nothing but horses and guides. The carriage you yourself must provide. If there are four persons within the carriage, you are obliged to have six horses, and two postillions; and if your servant sits on the outside, either before or behind, you must pay for a seventh. You pay double for the first stage from Paris, and twice double for passing through Fontainebleau when the court is there, as well as at coming to Lyons, and leaving this city. These are called royal posts, and are undoubtedly a scandalous imposition.

There was a choice of two routes to Lyon – via Nevers and Moulins or via Dijon. The former was once the Roman road, and is now the N7. In the eighteenth century it had sixty-five post stages. The route via Dijon had fifty-nine post stages. Smollett chose the latter in order to see the Burgundy wine harvest, setting out with a team of six horses, two postilions and his own servant on horseback. They had stocked up with tea, chocolate and sausages before leaving Paris, stopped every morning at a wayside inn for a breakfast of bread, butter and milk, and took their picnic luncheon about two or three in the afternoon, while the servants were changing the horses.

Beyond Lyon, Smollett travelled very slowly, in a berline drawn by three mules; but the weather was sunny and the views of the Rhône delightful. He made a detour south-westward to Montpellier, which he described as "one of the dearest places in the south of France." There he collected his heavy luggage, and expensively and unsatisfactorily consulted a local physician about his continuing ill-health. Then on to Tarascon, Aix-en-Provence, Cannes, Antibes and Nice. The journey from Boulogne had taken almost two months.

It was still usual to cross the Gulf of Genoa by sea rather than by land. Smollett did this nearly a year later in a gondola, rowed by four men and steered by the owner of the vessel. They put ashore for the night at San Remo, at an inn that "would disgrace the worst hedge alehouse in England", and at Noli, where there were bugs. Having obtained letters of credit for Florence and Rome, Smollett hired the same vessel to take him to Lerici. From there he travelled by post-chaise to Pisa. But the Italian post-chaise was "a wretched machine with two wheels, as uneasy as a common cart, being indeed no other than what we should call in England a very ill-contrived one-horse chair; narrow, naked, shattered and shabby."

The solitude and elegance of Pisa impressed Smollett, as they did Gibbon. However, the barren countryside and indifferent inns of Radicofani and Viterbo conveyed an unfavourable impression, as they had to Walpole and Gray. The final approach to Rome was characterized by a jarring contrast between the august memories of the past and the noisy materialism of the present. Just as Gibbon, Wilkes and Boswell had done the previous autumn, Smollett dismounted at Porta del Popolo in order to pass the customs. Importunate *servitori* were still clinging to Smollett's coach when it trundled into Piazza di Spagna. Here, where "most of the English reside," he rented a furnished apartment. His purpose in Rome was the conventional one: "to view the remains of antiquity by which this metropolis is distinguished, and to contemplate the originals of many pictures and statues, which I had admired in prints and descriptions." He was not going to waste money on hiring an "antiquary", however; it would be much less costly and just as satisfactory merely to buy a number of guide-books and maps, and to take into his service "a sober, intelligent fellow" as his personal servant.

In Rome, he met Sterne, sat to the sculptor Nollekens, and noted that the abundance of fine fountains in the city bore no relation to the cleanliness of the people. He also made typically xenophobic pronouncements, such as that St. James's Park would have afforded more room for chariot races than did the Circus Maximus, and that "half a dozen English frigates" could have routed both the fleets engaged at the battle of Actium.

He saw little of his compatriots; indeed, they did not seem very keen to see him.

> *When you arrive at Rome, you receive cards from all your country-folks in that city; they expect to have the visit returned next day, when they give orders not to be at home; and you never speak to one another in the sequel.*

English society was certainly not to be encountered in the coffee-houses. Such places were frequented by "no Englishman above the degree of a painter or cicerone."

At the end of his stay, Smollett got back to Nice as quickly as he could, and a few months later set out for England, whose nostalgically imagined "plenty, cleanliness and convenience" now seemed of all things the most desirable. Nevertheless, he returned again to Italy, and in 1771 died at Leghorn, where his tomb may still be seen in the English cemetery.

When Boswell, Gibbon, Smollett and their contemporaries were in Rome, the Old Pretender still inhabited the Palazzo Muti in the Piazza SS. Apostoli, the Royal Arms were still fixed above the main door, and the Pope's soldiers stood on guard before it. But James was now old, deaf and bed-ridden. He had given up all hope of restoration either for himself or for his disobedient son, whom he had not seen for twenty years. He died on 1 January 1766. His body lay in state for five days, crowned and sceptred. When it was carried in funeral procession, twenty cardinals supported the pall.

It was the last occasion upon which royal pageantry attended the doings of the House of Stuart. The Pope, Clement XIII, who was probably glad to be at last rid of the embarrassing Stuarts whom his predecessor Clement XI had invited to Rome half a century before, very quickly made it clear that Prince Charles would not be recognized as Charles III of England, Scotland and Ireland. It was equally clear that France and Spain would not recognize him as such either. Nevertheless, Prince Charles chose this moment to emerge from his incognito and return to his birthplace and, he appears to have hoped, his birthright. In so doing he merely killed his own legend and made himself a curiosity, to be observed as such in Rome for the remaining twenty-two years of his life. His brother, "Cardinal York", drove two stages out of Rome to meet him. But there was no one else to welcome him or to give him the royal reception that he considered was his due. The Cardinal caused great offence by driving his brother about Rome, seating him in the coach on his right hand, a compliment that a Cardinal might only pay to a crowned head, with the result that the Pope was obliged to reiterate his policy concerning the Stuarts. In March 1766, the Royal Arms of England were removed from the door of the Palazzo Muti "in the night time". The "Hunters after "antiquities"," commented the Secretary at Madrid, "will be no longer in danger of meeting with a Pageant King."[9]

As for Prince Charles, no one could take him seriously any more. But no one could forget that he existed. Although he was now old, bad-tempered, a notorious drunkard whose wife deserted him for an Italian poet, he still had a noble presence and a graceful manner. Those who met him could never be unaware that he had once held the letters patent of a Prince Regent. In his last years he was cared for and dominated by his illegitimate daughter Charlotte, whom he legitimized in 1783 by virtue of his *de jure* royal prerogative, and created Duchess of Albany. He died in Rome on 23 January 1788, three weeks after his sixty-eighth birthday, and only eighteen months before the outbreak of the French Revolution, which dethroned so many dynasties besides the Stuarts. The Duchess of Albany survived him by only a year. His wife, Louise de Stolberg, who was styled Countess of Albany, became prominent in Florentine society, and was often encountered by British travellers who went to Rome in the early nineteenth century.

Long before this, however, the Papacy had accepted the Hanoverians. In 1764 there were actually, for a few weeks, two Dukes of York in Rome: the Hanoverian Duke, a brother of George III, and the Stuart Duke, younger son of the Pretender. The Hanoverian Duke of York came to Rome incognito, but was given a splendid reception. In 1772 another brother of George III, the Duke of Gloucester, visited Rome. And finally, in 1774, the Duke of Cumberland, perhaps of all men the one whom Prince Charles would least have liked to meet, came to Rome and was received in the manner befitting a Royal Duke.

During the last twenty years of the eighteenth century, before the French Revolution and the Napoleonic Wars so drastically altered the face of Europe, the patrons of art were wealthier and more influential than they had ever been before. One such was Sir William Hamilton, who was George III's ambassador to the Kingdom of the Two Sicilies. He had a celebrated collection of "antiquities" at Naples, which he used to show the Grand Tourists on their traditional spring-time excursions. But he also frequently visited and excavated around Rome. He was responsible for the restoration of a vase discovered in 1770 near Hadrian's Villa at Tivoli. Piranesi made an engraving of the vase and its pedestal, with an inscription in commemoration of Sir William. A form of flood-lighting, by means of a wax torch, was also used by Sir William Hamilton to accentuate the beauty of classical monuments in Rome. The "attitudes" struck by his wife Emma on these occasions achieved great celebrity.[10]

Lady Hamilton, or Emma Hart as she was then, was frequently painted about this time by George Romney, who studied in Italy (mainly in Rome) between 1773 and 1775. His best work was done during the five years after he returned from Rome, i.e. between 1775 and 1780.

The most generous, most flamboyant and most eccentric of all the patrons of the artists of Rome – perhaps *the* most generous, most flamboyant and most eccentric art patron there has ever been anywhere – now appears. Had history taken a different course, he might have been remembered as the creator of one of the most spectacular collections of art to have been assembled in England. He was Frederick Hervey, fourth Earl of Bristol, Bishop of Derry in Ireland, sometime Colonel of the Irish Volunteers, Doctor of Divinity of the Universities of Oxford and Dublin, Fellow of the Royal Society. A man wealthy even by the standards of the landed aristocracy of the eighteenth century, he was immensely popular not only among the artists who had so much to gain from his patronage, but also among Protestants, Nonconformists

The English Road To Rome

and Catholics alike in Ulster, even though after 1779, when he succeeded to the Earldom, he was more and more frequently, and ultimately continuously, absent from his diocese. His generosity seems to have been a natural characteristic; it was not entirely a consequence of his wealth. His flamboyance and eccentricity extended beyond the accepted meaning of these words, and bordered on feudal *panache*. He was the first Earl-Bishop in English history since Odo, Earl of Kent and Bishop of Bayeux in the eleventh century. He was a great traveller, and the Hotels Bristol which are scattered all over the Continent were originally named after him.

But in Government circles and in polite society he was widely regarded with a fascinated horror. To Sir Robert Walpole he was "that mitred Proteus the Count-Bishop". To Sir Horace Mann, British Minister to Tuscany, he was "that curious being . . . the Episcopal Earl of Bristol." The Countess of Albany (who spoke no English) referred to him simply, and repeatedly, as "*le fou* Bristol". An excellent example of his special type of flamboyance occurred in 1779, when he attended the Maundy Thursday service in the Sistine Chapel in Rome, wearing the dress of an Irish bishop. "For this piece of absurdity", wrote an Irish politician who also happened to be present, "he was obliged to go to the lowest part of the chapel among the common people." The politician himself, more conventionally garbed, found himself placed alongside the scarlet Cardinals. The Earl Bishop was not at all deterred by this minor snub. In later years he used to ride through the streets of Rome in red plush breeches and a broad-brimmed white, or straw, hat. This bizarre costume was thought by many innocents to be the canonical dress of an Irish bishop.

The Earl Bishop owed his spectacular wealth to a combination, hardly possible save in the eighteenth century, of family inheritance, nepotism, luck and business acumen. He was born in 1730, the third son of John, Lord Hervey. His mother, a celebrated Court beauty, was of German origin. He went to Lincoln's Inn and then to Cambridge, coming down without a degree, but availing himself three years later of the right of a nobleman's son to take one without the formality of passing an examination. He married, gave up Law for the Church, held an appointment as Chaplain to George III ("a position more dignified than remunerative"), and visited the Continent for the first time, with his wife, in the post-war season of 1765-66. His brother George, now the second Earl of Bristol, had been appointed Lord Lieutenant of Ireland, and the King had promised him that Frederick should have the first Irish see that fell vacant. This was expected to be that of Derry, the richest in Ireland. Athough it was actually the Bishop of Cloyne who died first, so that Frederick had to be content with that for a year, he succeeded in 1768 to the vacant see of Derry, and to the six thousand pounds that constituted the annual income of that office.

From that year onwards he never, financially speaking, looked back. Yet he was never tight-fisted. He spent a considerable part of his income on schemes designed to benefit, not only his own flock, but all the inhabitants of the diocese. He promoted a bridge over the River Foyle at Londonderry, and a colliery. In 1771 he travelled to Rome, partly in order to persuade the Pope to approve of one of his favourite, though unsuccessful, schemes, that in return for an oath of allegiance to the English throne on the part of the Roman Catholics in Ireland, he would obtain for them the legal right to practise their religion, and would help them to build and maintain their own places of worship.

At the same time he was skilfully augmenting his own income. In 1773 he was writing to his sister about a scheme, "as profitable as it is simple," to purchase the expired leases of the Church lands in Derry from their impoverished tenants. He needed only, he wrote, £4000 to be lent by his sister's husband, Lord Mulgrave, which sum he could "easily replace" after two or three years. Since Lord Mulgrave did not feel disposed to risk this sum, nothing came of the scheme. But others were successful, and the income from the diocese soon rose to considerably more than £6000 per annum. In a public speech made in Derry in 1790, the Bishop referred with evident satisfaction to "the splendid rent-roll attached to this office."

In the meantime he had inherited an even larger fortune. George Hervey died in 1775 and his brother Augustus became the third Earl.

Augustus himself died only four years later, and since both brothers had been without issue, Frederick now became the fourth Earl of Bristol – with a landed estate worth £20,000 a year.

For the next thirteen years he divided his time fairly equally between Ireland, his Suffolk estate at Ickworth, and the Continent of Europe. The people of Derry, who saw him no more after 1791, do not seem to have resented being pushed somewhat into the background. Their Bishop, after all, was a famous man and a character, who had made the name of Derry familiar in all the hotels and drawing-rooms of Europe. They do not even appear to have objected to the Bishop's far too friendly association, in his later years, with ladies of such doubtful antecedents as Emma, Lady Hamilton, and Countess Lichtenau, mistress of King Frederick William of Prussia. He was, clearly, a man who enjoyed feminine company, and was entirely indifferent to whatever the gossips chose to make of this. His wife, from whom he had been estranged since 1782, was, in the Bishop's own words, now only "a majestic ruin".

It was in Rome, and also in Florence, that the Earl Bishop's wealth, his originality, his enthusiasm and his apparently genuine love of art coincided in the last of his phases, that of art patron. It seems to have been during the winter season of 1777-78 that he started this career. The leading Roman antiquary at that time was Thomas Jenkins, who twenty-five years previously had come to Rome with Richard Wilson. The Earl Bishop considered him "the most intelligent antiquarian", as well as "the most prosperous. He is possessed of the most elegant remains in every kind, and in my opinion, sets the most reasonable price upon them."

He also bought from the painter Thomas Jones a view of Lake Albano, for £40, a figure his banker considered excessive. When he succeeded to his earldom in 1779, he was already popular among the artists of Rome. They held a party to celebrate the event, fully aware of its monetary significance for them too.

The Earl Bishop was in Rome again in 1796, commissioning artists to paint landscapes for him, himself choosing the subjects. In 1797 he was toying with an ambitious scheme: he intended to sponsor and personally lead an expedition into Egypt, followed by a large party of artists, authors, scientists, and even his "*divine Comtesse*" suitably placed in the retinue. The Countess, however, would have nothing to do with it, and the plan fell through.

The Earl Bishop's art collection in Rome, which he valued in 1798 at the then stupendous figure of £20,000, did not consist entirely of contemporary works. Among the more important, artistically speaking, of his purchases were Old Masters, and he was one of the first, if not the first, to buy Italian Primitives, though all these seem to have disappeared. This great collection was not intended to remain permanently in Rome. It was to be housed at Ickworth, in a building designed specially for that purpose, a building of which the Bishop's first country mansion in Ireland, Ballyscullion, had been the prototype. For some years he had been briefing architects to work on the house, and the work of construction began in 1796. Ickworth was to be, wrote C.H. Totham in 1794, "a Villa to be built in Suffolk, extending nearly 500 feet, including offices. The distribution of this plan is very singular, the House being oval according to his desire."

Unfortunately the Earl Bishop had reckoned without one vital factor – the consequences of the French Revolution. In 1798 the French invaded Rome. As elsewhere in Italy, they seized the art collections. The Bishop's pictures were taken and dispersed. Three hundred and forty-three of the artists then working in Rome signed a petition to the Administrator of Finances of the Army of Italy, protesting against the confiscation of this collection "of the most choice works of the first painters and sculptors of our time," brought together by "this generous Irishman", neither of these statements being strictly accurate. But it was all to no avail. The Bishop did not help matters by his outspoken criticisms of the French revolutionaries: "the damned Blackguard, pilfering, plundering, pillaging Republicans". His innocent proposal to the authorities at home, that he should be appointed "Minister to congratulate the Roman people on their emancipation", which would enable him to salvage at least part of his looted possessions, could hardly be taken seriously. In April 1798 he was himself arrested by the French and imprisoned, though not very closely, at Milan for nine months.

After his release he seems to have centred himself mainly upon Rome, where he occupied the Villa Mellini, on the Monte Mario, though he was also often seen in Florence and was, according to his custom, for ever on the move. He got part of his collection back, saw it confiscated again, but was still regarded as "the patron of all modern artists". After 1801 he was banned from remaining in Tuscany as a result of an unfortunate incident at Siena. Irritated by a tinkling of bells in the street, as he sat at dinner, he seized a tureen of *pasta* and emptied it out of the window, on to a procession of the Host that happened to be passing at the time. He never could abide bells. Aided by "an ample distribution of gold", he was enabled to retreat rapidly from the hotel and from Siena. The incident became magnified by hostile gossip until many people firmly believed that it was not *pasta*, but unspecified refuse that the Bishop had deliberately and maliciously poured over the innocent Roman Catholic heads.

In July 1803, on the road from Albano to Rome, the Earl Bishop was seized with what his contemporaries described as "gout in the stomach". He was carried to a nearby cottage, or rather to an outhouse, since the peasants would not admit the heretic bishop under their own roof. And there he died. The body was given a temporary resting-place in Rome, where eight hundred artists of all nationalities are said to have attended the obsequies. Months later, it was packed and shipped to England, labelled (final irony!) as an "antique statue" in order to disarm the sailors' superstitions, and was buried at Ickworth in April 1804.

By this time the curious house had begun to take shape and grow, more or less at the point where its originator's part in history was completed. The rotunda, inspired probably by the Pantheon in Rome and intended in the Earl Bishop's plan to serve as living quarters, had reached a considerable height. The east and west wings, designed to house respectively the paintings and sculpture, were only a few feet above the ground. No more work was done on the house for more than twenty years, but between 1826 and 1830 the east wing was completed, serving thereafter as the Bristol family residence. After 1907 many improvements were made to it and to the central rotunda, which now contains the Bristol family portraits and furniture. The west wing has never been finished.

Ickworth today rears its unexpected rotunda, portico and wings amid the enveloping, and so un-Italian, parkland of rural Suffolk – the most enduring of the Earl Bishop's extravagant schemes. In 1796 he had written to his daughter, Lady Elizabeth Foster, rejecting the suggestion that the house should be built of white stone brick.

> *What! Child, build my house of a brick that looks like a sick, pale,* jaundiced *red brick, that would be red brick if it could, and to which I am certain our posterity will give a little rouge as essential to its health and beauty?*
>
> *. . . I shall follow dear impeccable Palladio's rule, and as nothing ought to be without a covering in our raw, damp climate, I shall cover house pillars and pillasters with Palladio's stucco which has now lasted 270 years.*

Ickworth has now lasted nearly two hundred years in "our raw, damp climate." One of the last English houses in the classical Palladian tradition, it suitably recalls the great days of the Hervey family in the eighteenth century, wherein their *panache* reached, in the Earl Bishop, its most exuberant fruition.

Ickworth House
(Credit: The National Trust / Alan Blair)

TO ROME FOR THE WINTER

FROM THE NAPOLEONIC WARS TO 1870

In 1797, the French, under Bonaparte, defeated the Austrians in northern Italy. As a result Italian territory was annexed to France for the first time. The French rule lasted until 1814, when the Treaty of Paris was signed at the end of May, thus enabling the Roman winter season to be prepared for and enjoyed during a time of peace. The turmoil of these seventeen years finally demolished the eighteenth century pattern of the Grand Tour – aristocratic in origin and form, educational in purpose.

The invasion of Italy by the French resulted in much more than the looting of the art treasures and the transfer of many of them to the Louvre: it also sowed the seed of the future unification of the Italian nation. It established the Napoleonic Civil Code and the metric system over most of Europe. Travellers to Rome would henceforward have to calculate in kilometres rather than leagues or miles. There were more considerable factors: the Industrial Revolution, the altered balance of international power, the vastly increased populations of western Europe[1], the shift of power and financial resources away from the aristocracy and towards the middle class. It all ensured that when the roads across Europe were open again, travel to Italy would take place in a very different atmosphere from that which had prevailed during the earlier post-war period.

The English Road To Rome

The French Army captured Rome in 1798, set up the Roman Republic and removed Pope Pius VI to Florence and then to Valence. Apart from seizing the art collections, the French also closed the ecclesiastical colleges – including that most resilient of English institutions in Rome, the English College, which practically ceased to function for two decades. The next year, when the French were retreating from Italy, an odd incident occurred: a British naval force sailed up the Tiber and put a landing party ashore. A young naval officer, who later became Sir Thomas Louis, ran up the British flag on the Capitol in Rome – perhaps the only time this has ever been done[2].

From that time until 1814, there was only one autumn when it seemed that the wars had ceased, and a normal Roman winter season could be planned. This was after the Treaty of Amiens, in March 1802. But the English tourists who optimistically set off on the Tour in the autumn of that year were soon to regret that they had ever left Dover. Napoleon was elected President of the new Italian Republic, and in May 1803 war broke out again. A thousand Grand Tourists were caught in France, and a number of them were interned at Verdun until 1814. At the time, this seizure of innocent civilians seemed an act of unheard-of barbarity; but in terms of war the event brings us into the modern world. War was on the way to becoming total.

Between 1803 and 1814, only American citizens could travel freely in Europe, so that Englishmen were forced to rely on American descriptions for up to date information about Italy. Similarly the seaways of Europe were freely open to American ships, whereas British merchant vessels sailing close to the war zone – arriving in Malta from Sicily, for example – were liable to be put in quarantine until they and their crews had been examined. It is against this background that we need to consider the visit of one of the few Englishmen who managed to visit Rome during this period – that tragi-comic character, S.T. Coleridge.

Coleridge had for some years been contemplating a journey abroad, mainly, it seems, for his health's sake. He had convinced himself that he was suffering from "Atonic Gout", which only a warm dry climate would cure. But in war time it was not so easy to attain such a climate. When even poets were in uniform (Wordsworth had joined the Volunteers), it was difficult to go abroad unless one had some quasi-official post. Determined to take a chance, but uncertain about the means, Coleridge eventually secured a passage to Malta aboard the merchant brig *Speedwell*, which sailed from Portsmouth in April 1804, one of a convoy of thirty-five vessels. He was well set up for the voyage, with a good stock of wines and spirits, a portable escritoire and two separate loans of £100. Soon after his arrival in Malta he had made such a good impression on the Civil Commissioner that he found himself appointed that dignitary's Public Secretary, with an excellent salary, all found, and limitless opportunities for his dazzling table talk, and his *conversazioni* which were really one-man entertainments.

But the more superficially satisfying his public life, the greater grew his inner misery and homesickness. His health was better, but he had not achieved physical happiness. Already enslaved to opium, the margin in his mind between dreams and hallucinations was slender. He never seemed to be able to send enough money home to his loved children and not-so-loved wife. Early in 1806 he suddenly resigned his post, went to Sicily, thence to Naples and thence to Rome.

In Rome he acquired, he later wrote, "more insight into the Fine Arts in three months than I could have done in England in twenty years." But meantime his friends were worried because they had no idea where he was. The Prussian Ambassador in Rome, Baron von Humboldt, was puzzled by him, because he seemed to be clever and talented, and not a gentleman. These were qualities that the Baron had found conspicuously absent in the British diplomatic world of the day; and he concluded that the British government must on this occasion have been a little more *rusé* than he had given them credit for. Obviously, Coleridge was a British secret agent. Coleridge seemed half convinced of this himself; he was sure that Napoleon was about to imprison him because of articles that he had written, some years before, in the London *Morning Post*. The Baron was able to pass on to Coleridge the news that an order for his arrest had in fact been made.

The English Road To Rome

Coleridge left Rome, and five hours after his escape all the remaining English visitors in Rome were arrested. Coleridge safely reached Leghorn and sailed in an American ship to England, where he landed, in a Medway creek, in August 1806.

In 1808, the French again sent their troops into Rome, and the next year they annexed the city and the Papal States to the French Empire. The English College, like its predecessor the English Hospice in 1527, was sacked, and its buildings were used as a French barracks. Pius VII replied by excommunicating Napoleon. Napoleon's reply to that was to arrest Pius VII. For the remaining years of the Napoleonic Wars there were virtually no British visitors to Rome.

The Treaty of Paris was signed at the end of May, 1814 – which had the consequence that 1814/15, and not 1815/16, was the first post-war Roman season. The escape of Napoleon from Elba, and the battle of Waterloo, occurred at a time of year when there were few tourists in Italy – between seasons, in fact.

The urge to travel abroad in 1814 was far greater than it had been in 1763. The frontiers had been closed for longer, and much more effectively closed as well. Since the population was larger, and since wealth was beginning to be distributed more evenly within the population, there were more potential travellers. There were more varied things to see, and more reasons for going to see them. J.R. Hale has instanced some of the motives for journeying abroad at this period, in his account of travel in Italy between 1814 and 1821, *The Italian Journal of Samuel Rogers*. There was the desire for the warm and sunny climate of the Mediterranean – by which the 1814 traveller meant that objects seemed more beautiful in that clear and vivid light: he was not concerned with bathing either in the sun or the sea, nor was light clothing envisaged. There was the need to escape from the high cost of living at home. As always in war time, the price of consumer goods had risen enormously in England, but prices in Italy were relatively low. It was possible to live well in Florence, perhaps even in Rome, on an income that would have permitted no luxuries at all in London. Those who pursued society and fashion knew they would be perfectly content in Rome – during the years after Waterloo it was the most fashionable city in the whole of Europe. Those who knew a little about the "antiquities" and archaeology generally were particularly interested in the prospect of going to Rome, because the French had been excavating strenuously there between 1810 and 1814, and almost no Englishman had seen the result of the excavations. Those whose interest lay in fine art were extremely keen to know more about Canova, who was now working in Rome and whose influence on this generation was to be as great as that of Piranesi sixty years or Bernini 180 years previously. Finally, those whose interests were political wanted to take a good look at certain well-known ex-enemies who were to be seen in Italy, in particular, members of the Bonaparte family in Rome.

It cannot be said that the journey to Rome was very much easier or more comfortable than it had been in 1763. It is true that there were now three cross-Channel routes to France: from Dover to Calais (where the standard fare was now one guinea per passenger), from Brighton to Dieppe and from Southampton to Le Havre (two guineas on each of these routes).

On the Dover – Calais crossing it was now possible to have one's own coach ferried over – either secured on deck, or partly dismantled and stowed below. The cost of this was six guineas, and the travellers who chose this method of conveyance would also need to bear in mind that the French customs duty amounted to one-third of the value of the temporarily imported coach, of which sum only two-thirds would be returned to the traveller when he left France. Even so, it was probably less expensive than buying a coach at Calais, and selling it again there a year or so later. The Brighton to Dieppe packet was supposed to take eight to ten hours, but Samuel Rogers was aboard the Dieppe boat for thirty hours, on a rolling sea. The Dieppe packet, of course, could not await her passengers in harbour at Brighton; sailors carried them through the breakers to a small rowing boat, which went out to sea to join the packet.

The first steamer crossing was made in 1816; the first regular steamer service between Dover and Calais, run by a French company, began in 1821. Hazlitt was one of the first to cross from Brighton to Dieppe by steamer, in 1824. That was the year the Brighton packet blew up.

The diligence, which covered 80 miles a day, was now the best means of crossing France, but these coaches only ran on the most frequented roads, and in northern Italy. Smaller vehicles – a four-seater cabriolet, for example – could be hired for moderately long journeys, from Calais to Paris or from Paris to Lyon.

In Italy, a *vetturino* was usually engaged. This operator would strike a bargain with the traveller for conveying him from one place to another, including transport, supper, bed and breakfast en route, for an agreed price. Thus the "gentleman's gentleman" from Yorkshire, Matthew Todd, who accompanied his master, Anthony Barlow, to Rome in 1815, contracted with a Rome *vetturino* to take them to Naples and back for 40 Spanish dollars, equivalent to about £8. This package deal was for a return journey of 300 miles altogether, lasting four days on the outward trip, but only three days back to Rome. The same negotiator got several quotations for their next journey, from Rome to Florence, and finally settled for a *vetturino* who offered to arrange the 183-mile trip (five and a half days) for 24 Spanish dollars.

Although the pattern of these journeys was still in the tradition of the Grand Tour, everywhere the settled habits of the eighteenth century were being infiltrated or overthrown by the totally different attitudes of the nineteenth. Most people, however, were still unwilling to calculate in kilometres rather than leagues. Similarly, the decimal currencies did not find adherents everywhere. The traveller found that while the 100-centime franc was now generally accepted, and the Roman unit was now 1 *scudo* of 10 *paoli* or 100 *bajocchi*, many of the older currencies were still firm favourites, and post-house keepers usually preferred to be paid in the Spanish dollar or "piece of eight".

Politically, Europe had in theory been unified and centralized, with Paris as its capital. But the Treaty of Paris had restored, at least temporarily, all the old frontiers and independent states that existed before the Revolution. Passports still had to be endorsed for travel to a particular country or place. Thus Matthew Todd, arriving at Civita Vecchia in the Papal States, had to wait half a day before he could get his and his master's passports to Rome, from the Minister of Marine. In Rome they needed another passport to get to Naples, and at Naples a third document to enable them to return to Rome. A journey from Paris to Milan involved obtaining a passport from the British Embassy, which had to be *visé* by the Ministry of the Interior, the Prefecture, the Austrian Ambassador, the Swiss Minister and the Sardinian Minister – and the traveller had to appear in person at all the offices concerned. As J.R. Hale says: "All this was no more than exasperating for the tourist, but for the native this was the Italy of the *Chartreuse de Parme*, where a flaw in one's papers could lead to imprisonment or death."[3]

When the 1814 travellers finally reached Rome, they found that it was more expensive than it had ever been. Everyone still wanted to stay near Piazza di Spagna, which was still unpaved, with an uneven surface over which the goatherds every morning drove their flocks from door to door, selling fresh milk. At one of the lodging houses in Piazza di Spagna which regularly accepted English boarders (no. 26, where seven years later Keats was to die), John Mayne in 1814 paid seven pounds six shillings a month for six rooms. This included a servant's wages and was considered reasonable for this fashionable district. Three years later, Henry Matthews was paying fifteen pounds a month, again for six rooms (two sitting rooms, three bedrooms and a kitchen) together with one room for the servant. Rome at that time was more costly than either Naples, Florence or Venice. Even in 1815 Matthew Todd had written:

> *The people ask such uncommon high prices for everything; there is no dealing with them. I returned disgusted with their system, which is to ask about 10 times as much as the article is worth, and the only plan to be adopted is to barter them down, which is neither pleasant nor easy.*[4]

Matthew Todd did not have a very high opinion of Roman streets either:

> *[They were] mostly without flagging, and extremely disagreeable to walk in, particularly as the coachmen never observe foot passengers. The mode of calling your attention is by hissing, something like a large serpent, which is extremely unpleasant.*[5]

He was not the only traveller who experienced disillusion in Rome. Those who had little money were dismayed to find that the Italians still stubbornly believed all English visitors to be rich "milords" and raised their prices accordingly. There was almost universal disappointment with the squalid modern streets through which one had to pass when entering Rome from the north. The arrival at Piazza di Spagna, with its parked coaches and milling crowds of English tourists and Italian servants and touts, must have been the early nineteenth century equivalent of arrival at a twentieth century Mediterranean seaside resort at the height of summer. Those travellers who had not the benefit of a classical education, found themselves at a loss to understand the significance of the monumental remains that they were shown. Meanwhile, those who had inherited the eighteenth century attitude were upset to discover that the French excavations in the Forum and elsewhere had been so thorough that Piranesi's engravings were completely out-dated; they no longer represented what the travellers actually saw. The fact that the real structure of the old buildings was exposed to view for the first time for hundreds of years was vitally interesting to the scientific archaeologist, and indeed to the architect; but it was a great disappointment to the classically-minded ordinary visitor, who preferred his ruins to look like ruins.

Still, there were other visitors who had eagerly looked forward to the day when they would be able to see Rome, and who were not disillusioned by the reality. Of these, the poet, conversationalist and literary patron Samuel Rogers was one of the most influential. The poem *Italy* that he wrote as a result of his 1814 visit, came out in an illustrated edition in 1830 and was not only read but was bought in such numbers that it soon began to show a profit, despite the fact that the edition had cost over seven thousand pounds to publish. As J.R. Hale says:

> *In a short time it had become, like Rogers himself, an institution; known to all and read at least by a few. For two generations it remained the ideal present for those about to leave for Italy or who had just come back. It appeared in edition after edition, simple and elaborate. Nor was it valued for the plates alone. Ruskin, as is well known, claimed that he owed to his first sight of Turner's plates the whole subsequent course of his life; but the numerous references to the poem scattered through his work show that he cared for the verse as well.*[6]

Samuel Rogers' Italian Journal was a sketchbook, the raw material that he later worked up into his poem. Reading it, we not only obtain a vivid picture of Rome in 1814, we can also not fail to realize that Rogers saw the city with a poet's eye, and that for all his admiration of ancient Rome he had a strong awareness of the living present.

> *Of Antient Rome its roads, & aqueducts its walls & watchtowers, its seven hills its campagna, & the mountains that skirt it, the river that crosses it & the sea that opens beyond it, still remain to us. Many of these things are not only unchanged but unchangeable.*

But at the same time:

> *Saw the sun set for the first time in the Mediterranean, the*

> *sky afterwards red as a ruby, & immediately the distant tinklings of the ave-maria died away in the air.*

As he walked through Rome, he saw and recorded sights that the Grand Tourist would never have deigned to notice, sights that, in the way he recorded them, are themselves a poem or a picture – the living fowls on the poulterer's shelves, "side by side as if they were roosting"; the supper of "a fricassée of frogs and porcupine in sweet sauce"; the "snow mountains sun-gilt" seen from the Villa Pamphili Doria in January, with the green lizards peeping out and the fresh fragrance of the purple crocuses; and the "Roman girl of low condition elegantly drest, with scarlet sleeves and bright green bodice and yellow petticoat. The men of the country with white hats, and very high tapering crowns."

In December 1814 he described in his journal the uninhabited, almost uncultivated campagna with its ruined aqueducts, the "far from unpleasing stillness and melancholy of the Protestant cemetery," and wrote that he had repeated, from the hill of the Janiculum, Milton's lines on Rome:

> *The City which thou seest, no other deem*
> *Than great and glorious Rome, Queen of the Earth*
> *There the Capitol*
> *On the Tarpeian Rock – & there Mount Palatine*
> *The Imperial Palace,*
> *With gilded battlements, conspicuous far*
> *Turrets and terrasses, & glittering spires.*
> *Many a fair edifice besides, more like*
> *Houses of Gods –* [7]

Before Christmas he heard bagpipes being played in the streets "like our Waites", and on New Year's Day he sauntered about in the bright, cold weather, finding "the streets full of walkers, an unusual thing in Rome, and nothing could be more quiet and silent than the happiness of the people."

The range of Samuel Rogers' acquaintance in Rome during the 1814 season included patrons of the arts, such as Jane Fane, subsequently Countess of Westmorland; writers, such as William Stewart Rose, who lived many years in Italy and translated Ariosto into metrical verse, and J.C. Eustace, whose *Classical Tour* was then the most successful guide to Italy; public men such as John Allen, Warden of Dulwich College, and John Russell, sixth Duke of Bedford; and scientists, such as Sir Humphrey Davy, who had previously experimented in Italy on ancient pigments and on the combustion of diamonds. He introduced Rogers to Canova, and told him that vermilion was the "most expensive colour of the Ancients". The breadth of interest and experience represented by this small sample is an indication both of Samuel Rogers' position in the intellectual world of the day, and of the great appeal that Rome then had for that world.

Rogers was in Naples when the news came through that Napoleon had left Elba and was marching on Paris. The poet returned to Rome and then northwards, following a roundabout route home, through Innsbruck, Cologne, Antwerp and Ostend. Other travellers were said to be running "like startled hares" towards Genoa; but Matthew Todd and his master, northward bound to Florence that same month (March 1814) reported meeting several English carriages on their way to Rome.

Just how many Englishmen there were in Rome in the years following the Napoleonic Wars seems never to have been accurately estimated. In 1814 there are said to have been about a thousand. An authority gives the number in 1818 as two thousand, but the "Gentleman's Magazine" (1817) says there were five hundred English in Rome that year. Joseph Severn, in 1821, judged that his compatriots numbered "about a thousand". Obviously there must have been many transient visitors, who did not stay for the full season. As J.C. Eustace wrote:

> *Many drive through the country with the rapidity of couriers; content themselves with a hasty inspection of what they term its curiosities, visit the Opera-house, perhaps intrigue with an actress; then return home, and write a Tour through Italy.*[8]

Indeed, between 1815 and 1821 nearly fifty books describing contemporary Italy emerged from the printing presses and publishers' houses of London, Edinburgh and New York. They bore titles such as *Hints to Travellers in Italy* (Richard Colt Hoare, 1815), *A Picture of Italy* (Henry Coxe, 1815), *A Journey to Rome and Naples* (Henry Sass, 1818), *Travels in Italy* (H.W. Wilkins, 1820); and they have mostly now retired into a deserved obscurity. Eustace's own book, however, merits attention, since it was the leader in its field and has thus at least a prototypical importance.

The Rev. J.C. Eustace was an English Catholic priest who had managed to complete the Tour himself in 1802-03, though he did not publish his book until 1813. It was thus very opportunely first in the field when travel to Italy again became possible. It was in its fourth edition by 1817, and was republished for the eighth time in 1841. Eustace himself did not live to see these later successes. He was in Italy again in 1814, but in 1815 he died in Naples, of malaria.

He was a thoroughly conservative traditionalist. This is shown in the usual route that he followed, in its timing, in the buildings that he admired, in the opinions that he expressed, and not least in his habit of quoting extensively from the Greek and Latin authors without ever considering it necessary to supply English translations. He despised the new tendency to rapid travelling, and was one of the first English writers to use the word "tourist" in a derogatory sense:

> *Tours succeeding each other, with little or no interval of repose, harass the body, and new objects crowding on each*

other too rapidly leave nothing in the mind but confused images and shadowy recollections.

At Paestum he gazed wistfully towards "the southern provinces, which have never yet been visited by travellers, and scarcely noticed by geographers". But since the itinerary demanded that he should be back in Rome for the *festa* of St. Peter, it was the itinerary that retained his allegiance. So back he came, through the "desolate campagna" whose "exhalations" of humid air must at all costs be avoided in summer, to Rome, finding the approach through the Lateran Gate every whit as magnificent as the more frequently described approach from the north:

As we approached, the beams of the rising sun darted full on the portico of the Basilica Laterana, *in itself from its elevation and magnitude, a grand object, and now rendered unusually splendid and majestic by the blaze of glory that seemed to play around it. The groves of deep verdure that arose on each side, and the dark arches of the ruined aqueducts bending above the trees, formed a striking contrast, and gave the approach a magnificence and solemnity highly conformable to the character and destinies of the Eternal City.*

This kind of thing could have been written at almost any time during the seventeenth or eighteenth century, but Eustace brought his book right up to date by including in it the anti-French diatribes that his contemporaries liked to hear. The French language, habits of dress, customs and civilization were all affected or ludicrous; the French were vandals, looters of the artistic treasures of Italy. If French influence, he thought, "should extend to many years, it will half dispeople Rome, open its deserted palaces and temples to the rains and tempests, and bequeath the Vatican itself, shaken and dismantled, to the wonder and the regret of posterity."

Frascati, View from the Belvedere Villa – JAMES HAKEWILL, 1817.

This "elevated and airy situation" (J.C.Eustace) of Frascati, with the Campagna stretching out below it, was very evocative for the travellers from the North.

One traveller who relied particularly on the work of J.C. Eustace was the English architect James Hakewill, who left Dover in 1816 at the age of 38, to begin a Grand Tour which lasted eighteen months. He himself is rather a shadowy figure – none of his building work survives. He did exhibit some architectural drawings at the Royal Academy, and he was among the ninety-seven architects who entered the competition for the rebuilding of the Houses of Parliament. Having made his reputation with the illustrated volume *The History of Windsor and its Neighbourhood*, in 1813, he planned his journey to Italy. According to Luke Herrmann in his essay in the British School at Rome's catalogue of Hakewill's drawings (1992), Hakewill must have used the most recent editions of Addison (1767), Eustace (1815 or 1817) and Forsyth (1817), in preparing for the journey.

Villa of Maecenas and Cascatelle, Tivoli – JAMES HAKEWILL, 1816

The Grand Tourists enjoyed visiting the peaceful environs of Rome in addition to viewing the sights of the city. Tivoli and Frascati particularly appealed to them.

In the preface to his best known work, *A Picturesque Tour of Italy*, published in 1820, Hakewill pointed out that the plates in his book (which according to then current practice had already appeared in separate parts) were "arranged according to the line of the route traced in Eustace's Tour, as being a popular work, and one in general circulation."

Although *A Picturesque Tour of Italy* was a financial failure, it was much praised and prized, and rightly so, for the 300 or so drawings comprised in it really constitute a line-drawing illustration of Eustace's recommended route from Calais to Naples and back, via Boulogne, Paris, Dijon, the Jura, Geneva, the Simplon or Sempione Pass, Milan, Turin, Genoa, Pisa, Florence, Perugia, Rome, the environs of Rome (Tivoli, Frascati), Naples and Paestum; then back via Ancona, Bologna, Vicenza, Venice and over the Brenner Pass to Insbruck. The drawings are nearly all of buildings and rural or mountain landscapes, with few human figures in the quiet streets, but that was what the Grand Tourists came to see. There is one engaging glimpse of the coach loaded for the journey, from which it is easy to visualise the trials and difficulty inherent to the immense distance it was to travel.

James Hakewill published several other volumes of plates with extended captions, but it is only by the *Picturesque Tour of Italy* that he is remembered today. 314 of his original drawings were presented to the British School at Rome in the 1920s, in six portfolios neatly stored "in a beautifully made mahogany box, with lock and key, resembling a coin cabinet," where they remained for another sixty years. The work of remounting and restoring them has only recently been completed, 175 years after they were drawn. A selection of the drawings, together with the magnificently illustrated catalogue, was exhibited in London for the first time in 1993.

A characteristic journey of the post-1815 period was that undertaken by Lady Charlotte Campbell who, finding that she was "unable to afford the enormously high cost of living" in England after the war, set out for Florence from London in July 1817, in two carriages with her five daughters, a governess and a maid. They spent the first night at Sittingbourne, and the second at a friend's cottage at Upper Hardres, a small village south of Canterbury, off the main road. Beaujolois, Lady Charlotte's fourteen year old daughter, wrote:

> *There being not room in mamma's carriage I went upon the Dickey and indeed I seldom remember having gone upon such bad roads or to have been so dreadfully shook about. Add to this it poured of rain incessantly and with a high wind it was with difficulty I could keep myself tolerably sheltered. The road was up hill all the way, and all in turns and angles. The postilions did not at all know the way and we went at a foot's pace. After continuing in this state of uncertainty for about an hour and a half we met Mr*

Sandys who rode before and we at length reached the cottage.[9]

The next morning they rose at dead of night and set out at four, reaching Dover not until ten o'clock, where they met the rest of their party, including the governess. But as it was blowing hard, they did not embark on the *King George* for Calais until the following morning. The carriage was apparently secured on deck, for Beaujolois wrote that such was the motion of the ship that she "quickly put away all writing implements and shutting myself up in the carriage resigned myself to all the horrors of my fate."

The Coach for Rome – JAMES HAKEWILL, circa 1817
These two untitled sketches vividly illustrate some of the discomforts of Continental travel. As Beaujolois Campbell wrote: "The postilions did not at all know the way and we went at a foot's pace . . . "

From Calais, where the French customs and passport officials, so recently defeated in war, took full and malicious advantage of their petty power over the English travellers, the party set off via Boulogne,

Amiens and St. Denis. With a view to economy they skirted Paris, and proceeded through Charenton, Sens, Besançon and Pontarlier to Lausanne, which they reached twelve days after leaving Calais. Along the road Beaujolois noted that:

> *It is curious to see how in every town and village they endeavour to appear Englishified. At every petty shop or alehouse they hang out a large sign with the French above and the English translation under, not always quite correct being the literal translation of the original . . . All these marks of civility to the English were not practised when we left the Continent last year.*

From Lausanne, where they spent three pleasant weeks, they began their journey again at the beginning of September. The most popular way across the Alps was now over the Simplon pass, due chiefly to the military road constructed through this pass on Napoleon's orders between 1800 and 1805. Now that the wars were over, the road could very conveniently be used for civilian traffic. They stopped at Martigny, where the road for the Great St. Bernard pass begins, for a few hours:

> *It is a little spot very beautifully situated entirely surrounded by high mountains, which though worthy of admiration for mere travellers must be dreadful as a place of abode. Most of the people have goitres and there is an unwholesome feel in the air.*

After overnight stops at Sion and Brig, they crossed the Simplon. To Beaujolois Campbell it was an experience as clear and sharp as the note of a silver bell:

> *We were called at three in the morning and in the carriages at five to mount the Simplon. The air was fresh and cold*

> *and many of the stars were still shining bright. We had five hired horses to our berline and 4 to mamma's carriage, guided by four men all excellent figures and speaking German the language of the place, whilst our voiturier horses went on before us to meet us at la Barrière.*

It took them eight hours to reach the top of the pass, and the road on the southern side of the mountain was beautiful beyond description. That night they slept in Italy:

> *. . . at Domodossola where I heard everyone talking Italian and where everything looked Italian. Large high rooms painted in gaudy colours, brick floors, etc., but little furniture. The beds were large but dirty. The people looked like rogues and when I said we are now in the country of the Italians I could not help thinking at the same moment yes and in that* dei Furbi *[of the thieves].*

They spent a year in a Florentine furnished house rented for £200, and the cook they engaged asked the equivalent of eighteen pence a day to cater for the family of eight. They then moved on to Rome, where Beaujolois Campbell met her future husband, Lord Tullamoore, in 1820.

More and more English visitors poured into Rome and stayed for the winter season. In 1817 Byron wrote tetchily from Venice:

> *I wished to have gone to Rome; but at present it is pestilent with English – a parcel of staring boobies, who go about gaping and wishing to be at once cheap and magnificent. A man is a fool who travels now in France and Italy, till this tribe of wretches is swept home again.*

Overcoming his repugnance to the masses, however, Byron arrived in Rome that same year. He emphasized his apartness from the vulgar mob by arriving, unfashionably, in April. He rode on horseback about the city and in the Campagna, he sat to Thorwaldsen for his statue and at his favourite table in the Caffè Greco, and he witnessed a series of executions. To this entertainment he took an opera glass, though this was hardly necessary, since he had a ringside seat. He was upset by the first death: "quite hot and thirsty". However, he regarded the second and third with relative indifference: "which shows how dreadfully soon things grow indifferent." The guillotine seemed merciful compared with an English public hanging, which he had also seen. Byron wrote that he was "delighted with Rome as a whole, ancient and modern; it beats Greece, Constantinople, *everything*, at least, that I have ever seen."

Ruins of the Palace of the Caesars on the Palatine Hill – JAMES HAKEWILL, 1817.
The setting for this and a companion view by Hakewill was "on a picturesque eminence amidst the gardens with which this part of Rome is entirely occupied." Every traveller, including Byron, who visited the Palatine in those times was impressed by the interplay of weeds and ruins.

Byron stayed only twenty-three days in Rome, but his reputation as a poet has always been so much higher on the Continent than in England that we should not be surprised to learn that this brief visit, purely in the guise of a tourist, was eventually commemorated by the erection of a marble statue of the poet (the head being a copy of Thorwaldsen's portrait bust) in the Borghese Gardens.

Percy Bysshe Shelley and his wife arrived in Rome in March 1819. He wrote *Prometheus* and *The Cenci* while in Rome, in lodgings that he occupied at the Palazzo Verospi, in the Via del Corso. In June 1818 their son William died and was buried in the Protestant cemetery, where Shelley's own ashes were later buried. This cemetery had first been used as such in the mid-eighteenth century – Sir James Macdonald, who died in 1766, was buried there, beneath a tomb erected by Piranesi. Samuel Rogers, in 1814, had found "the melancholy stillness and character of the scene far from unpleasing." "Some withered elms," he noted, "skirt the ground."

In the same year, Stendhal visited St. Peter's in order to see the Pope distributing blessings. He reported that:

> . . . *the seat I had procured lay at the foot of a stand or amphitheatre built of planks, rising up at the spectator's right hand, and occupied by some two hundred ladies. This number included two fair creatures from Rome itself, five from Germany and one hundred and ninety from England. In all the remaining area of the church, there was not a soul to be seen, save only some five or six score peasants, of horrifying aspect. I am indeed making an* English Journey, *without ever setting foot beyond the bounds of Italy.*[10]

Rome being now such a fashionable place to spend the winter, whether or not for reasons of health, the British colony had inevitably acquired a resident British doctor. This was Dr. James Clark, who had graduated from Edinburgh soon after the war, having previously been an Army

155

surgeon. He practised in Rome for seven years before moving to London, where he had a fashionable practice and achieved a knighthood, as well as an unfortunate notoriety as a result of two serious errors in diagnosis; but he remains in history only because, while he was in Rome in 1820-21, one of his patients was a young English poet dying of phthisis – John Keats.

Keats' journey to Rome was in some respects a typical one, which could even have been predicted. Rome was one of the places to which, according to the medical opinion of the day, a tubercular patient might beneficially be sent. Though little enough was known about the disease, and such treatment as there was (one thinks, for example, of the routine blood-letting) probably harmed the patients more than it helped them, it was at least understood that recovery was more likely in a country with a predominantly mild, sunny winter climate. Rome in particular was favoured since it was both a fashionable and, supposedly, a healthy place.

So in the summer of 1820 Dr. Darling, Keats' physician, and Dr. Lambe, a consultant, agreed that only the journey to Italy could save his life. Very gradually and reluctantly, Keats himself came to share this view:

> *This journey to Italy wakes me at daylight every morning, and haunts me horribly. I shall endeavour to go, though it be with the sensation of marching up against a Battery.*

He was, however, not only a very sick man but also a poor one. It was out of the question for him to hire a coach; and if he had tried to get to Rome by means of *diligence* and *vettura*, he would probably have died before he ever completed the journey. The last-minute unconventional alternative to this – a berth in the brig *Maria Crowther*, bound from Gravesend (ominous name!) to Naples, must have seemed to the organizers of his journey a providential opportunity. Keats could rest quietly throughout the voyage, and benefit from the sea air, and it would be less costly. The chance was seized, but Joseph Severn, the only one of Keats' friends who was willing at such short notice to accompany him, had only five days to make his arrangements to travel.

It turned out to be an appalling voyage. The brig, buffeted by gales, had to beat up and down the Channel for ten days, and finally put into Portsmouth for shelter. When they put to sea again, the four passengers, who shared the only cabin with the captain (with a mere "side-scene" for the ladies to retire to), had to endure another four weeks of squalls, high seas and bad food before they finally anchored in the Bay of Naples. Here the brig was put in quarantine, and the passengers were obliged to stay on board, "shut in a tier of ships," for ten more days. Severn was delighted with the bay, but Keats was utterly depressed, and felt in another world from the noisy Neapolitan trippers who came out in boats to peer at the foreign ships in the quarantine area.

When they finally landed, on 1 November, they found, as other travellers have done, that the romantic appearance of the bay was sadly different from the clamorous squalor of the city itself. After an uncomfortable week in Naples, they set off for Rome on a road that had had a reputation for discomfort and slowness ever since Lord Arundel passed that way two centuries earlier. Severn could usually walk alongside the coach, picking flowers. It was not until 17 November that they entered Rome by the Lateran Gate, and made their way to Piazza di Spagna. Here, in a reddish-brown building run as a boarding house by a niece of the guide-book publisher Vasi, John Keats spent the last three months of his life.

During those three months, it was only rarely that Keats or Severn emerged from the two small rooms they occupied. It is to Dr. Clark's credit that he contrived now and then to get Keats out of the closed room and on to a horse in the Pincio, and to Mrs Clark's that she cooked for both the young men. Dr. Clark also helped Severn financially. There was little more that anyone could do. Severn soon lost his delight in being in Rome:

> *These wretched Romans have no idea of comfort . . . this wilderness of a place (for an invalid).*

And indeed the Roman winter, whose days slowly lengthen after the December equinox under floods of rain, vertically deluging gutters and cobbles for hours at a time, is very far from the romantic daydreams of Arcady. In midwinter the streets are either running wet with rain from the western seas, or blown bone dry and bitterly cold by the *tramontana* from the Apennines. It must have been the final disillusionment for Keats that Italy was not a land of perpetual sunshine after all.

At 11 p.m. on the night[11] of 23/24 February 1821, Keats died. Three days later, after an autopsy had revealed complete wasting of the lungs, his funeral procession, with eight mourners, left Piazza di Spagna before daybreak and arrived at the non-Catholic burial ground, near Caius Cestius' pyramid. Keats knew that he would be buried there, and had had the place described to him several times by Severn. It had been his dying wish that his tombstone should bear only the simple inscription "Here lies one whose name was writ in water." Perhaps, had history played no further part, a plain stone might have stood in a lonely field to this day, carrying nothing but this deceptive phrase. But even a year later there was no chance of that. More non-Catholics had died in Rome, so that it had become necessary to extend their burial ground southwards, on the inner side of the Aurelian Wall. Meantime, in both England and Italy, the theory was being put about that the real cause of Keats' death was not tuberculosis, poverty or frustrated love, but the attacks of heartless reviewers. Shelley and Armitage Brown believed this firmly. It was Brown who wrote the inscription which finally appeared on the tombstone that was ordered and paid for by Severn, executed by the English sculptor John Gibson, then living in Rome, and erected over the grave in May 1823. It ran:

> *This grave*
> *contains all that is mortal of*
> *a*
> YOUNG ENGLISH POET
> *who*
> *on his Death Bed*
> *in the Bitterness of his Heart*
> *at the Malicious Power of his Enemies*
> *desired*
> *these words to be engraven on his Tomb Stone*
> *"Here lies One*
> *Whose Name was writ in Water"*
> *February 24th, 1821*

This wording has never been amended, and must be a little puzzling to anyone not familiar with the long-dead controversy. In fact Keats' self-epitaph, and Brown's attempt to elucidate it, were both rendered obsolete in 1848, when Lord Houghton's biography of Keats appeared, and vindicated him both as a man and as a poet. But we shall see later that history had by no means yet finished with Keats' grave and the anonymity he had desired for it.

During the post-war years from 1813 to 1821, travellers were more concerned to follow the well-worn routes of the Grand Tour, and to study the remains of classical Rome, than to look directly at contemporary Italy. This began to change as the Romantic movement in literature and art gained force, and between 1821 and 1828 there was a certain enthusiasm for all things Italian, since Italy was one of the sources of Romanticism. It recalled the similar Italianate enthusiasm that had prevailed in England during the sixteenth century. This new interest in Italy, however, was shallower and more restricted than the earlier interest had been. Although, for example, Italian influence can be seen in the lyric poetry of Shelley, Wordsworth and Leigh Hunt, and although Keats' poem *Isabella* was written in the Italian octave rhyme, there is no English literary masterpiece that owes its inception to its author's visit to Italy in the 1820s, nothing that recalls Milton's systematic study of the Italian renaissance poets.

The Palladian style which had so profoundly influenced English architecture for more than two hundred years was now falling out of favour. But its successor in architectural fashion, the Italian Renaissance style, was less significant and had a briefer popularity after its adoption about 1830. By 1860 this style was petering out in the debased porticos of provincial town halls. There was no Inigo Jones of the nineteenth century.

Rossini's romantic operas enjoyed a brief vogue in England. But this too diminished when, after 1830, German opera and German concert music captured the English imagination.

This Romantic interest in Italy and Italian culture did not extend to the Italian people themselves. The English travellers remained obstinately contemptuous of all foreigners, and of Latin foreigners most of all. Rarely indeed does any individual Italian appear in the pages of their journals, except in the capacity of innkeeper, postilion, waiter, landlord or artist's model. Italian was still, after French, the modern foreign language most often known by Englishmen, but it was learnt for social rather than for academic purposes, and after 1830 it dropped to third place, beneath German.

Italy was felt by the Romantics to be a place "where every prospect pleases, and only man is vile." Thus Mrs Anna Jameson, Dublin-born, who wrote a number of books of art criticism, found that the "sublime and heart-stirring beauty" of the traditional visit to the Colosseum by moonlight was somewhat spoilt for her by the "empty & tasteless & misplaced flippancy" of certain un-romantic members of the party who affected "a well-bred *nonchalance*, a fashionable disdain for all romance and enthusiasm". She was also disconcerted to find that all visitors to the Colosseum after dusk had to be followed by a guard of two soldiers.[12]

A little later, in 1839, Lord Macaulay had no scruples about bribing a customs officer of the Papal States not to search his baggage, but was highly incensed when the same officer asked for a lift in his carriage:

Precious fellow to think that a public functionary to whom a little silver is a bribe is fit society for an English gentleman![13]

In 1852, Catherine Sinclair wrote in her *Popish Legends*:

The life of the Italian is little more than an animal one, and he is not much better than an ape endowed with speech.

Italian art, however, remained immensely popular in England, and every English artist who could afford to go to Italy to study continued to do so. There was one place that no nineteenth century artist could leave out of his itinerary, and that place of course was Rome.

It was Rome which attracted the majority of travellers to Italy, because Rome was the home, first of the masterpieces of Michael Angelo and Raphael, then of the relics of classical antiquity, then of St. Peter's and the great Renaissance palazzi; also because the scenery around the city was pleasant and picturesque, and finally because Rome was at this time the meeting-place of artists of all nationalities, English, French, German, Danish, etc., who spent their mornings painting in the churches or the Vatican or the Colosseum, and their evenings in the cafés debating artistic problems. The English painter in Rome felt a new inspiration. One of them wrote: "Of an artist it may be said with the greatest truth and propriety, whoever has not seen Rome, has seen nothing. For myself I never had a conception of the dignity of the art till I entered the Vatican."[14]

The English Road To Rome

Joseph Severn stayed on in Rome after his harrowing experiences at John Keats' deathbed, and soon settled happily into this *vie de Bohème*. He began in the usual way by copying the old masters in the Vatican galleries, then started to paint pictures of his own. One of the first he did in Rome portrays Shelley writing *Prometheus Unbound* in the Baths of Caracalla, which was one of the poet's favourite spots. The picture is now in the Keats-Shelley Memorial there. Severn soon found himself taken up by the art patroness Lady Westmorland. To her dismay, and despite her unrelenting opposition, he courted and married her ward, Lady Elizabeth Montgomerie, in 1828, and thus moved across the dubious borderline that separates Art from Society. Severn had six children in Rome, of whom three grew up to be artists. He was still in Rome in 1840, and was one of the few people for whom Ruskin had nothing but praise. Joseph Severn was then "a rather short, rubicund, serenely beaming person," wrote Ruskin, who had a letter of introduction to him.

> *There is nothing in any circle that ever I saw or heard of, like what Mr Joseph Severn was then in Rome. He understood everybody, native and foreign, civil and ecclesiastic . . . He forgave the Pope his papacy, reverenced the beggar's beard, and felt that alike the steps of the Pincian, and the Aracoeli, and the Lateran, and the Capitol, led to heaven, and everybody was going up, somehow; but might be happy where they were in the meantime. Lightly sagacious, lovingly humorous, daintily sentimental, he was in council with the cardinals today, and at picnic with the brightest English belles tomorrow; and caught the hearts of all in the golden net of his goodwill and good understanding.*[15]

Among other artists whose Roman experience was significant for the development of their talent were the sculptor John Gibson, who came to Rome in 1817, took lessons from Canova, made the tombstone for

Keats' grave, spent all his working life in Rome, and died in 1866, leaving a fortune of £32,000; Richard Westmacott, another sculptor who trained in Canova's studio and was later Professor of Sculpture at the Royal Academy in London; Sir Charles Eastlake, who worked as an artist in Rome between 1816 and 1830, and was later Keeper of the National Gallery in London; and Turner, who visited Italy four times, and whose plates in the illustrated edition of Samuel Rogers' *Italy* were a popular success.

But not every visitor during the Romantic period was delighted with Rome. Hazlitt, who came on a short visit in 1825, loved Florence at first sight, but Rome was a great disappointment to him. It had neither, he thought, the beautiful environs of Florence nor the background of Turin, nor even (still odder comparison) "does it present any highly picturesque or commanding points of view like Edinburgh." This was not, he decided, the Rome he had expected to see. It was not so much the contrast between old and new, between magnificence and squalor, that he complained of, so much as:

> *... the want of any such striking contrast, but an almost uninterrupted succession of narrow, vulgar-looking streets, where the smell of garlic prevails over the odour of antiquity, with the dingy, melancholy flat fronts of modern-built houses, that seem in search of an owner. A dunghill, an outhouse, the weeds growing under an imperial arch offend me not; but what has a greengrocer's stall, a stupid English china warehouse, a putrid* trattoria, *a barber's sign, an old clothes or old picture shop or a Gothic palace, with two or three lacqueys in modern liveries lounging at the gate, to do with ancient Rome? No! This is not the wall that Romulus leaped over; this is not the Capitol where Julius Caesar fell: instead of standing on seven hills, it is situated in a low valley; the golden Tiber is a muddy stream: St. Peter's is not equal to St. Paul's: the Vatican falls short of the Louvre ... Rome is great only in ruins.*

The English Road To Rome

It seems, indeed, that British visitors to Rome now expected too much, and were disappointed. Or they did not know what to expect, and were overwhelmed. In this respect, Anna Jameson was unusually level-headed:

> [I] expected that the general appearance of modern Rome would be mean; and that the impressions of the ancient city would be melancholy; and I had been, unfortunately, too well prepared by previous reading, for all I see, to be astonished by anything except the Museum of the Vatican.

One of those who expressed no opinions worth mentioning was Sir Walter Scott, who was in Rome in the spring of 1832. He had come to Naples for the sake of his health, but was completely exhausted physically and mentally. It is reported that the only things he saw that could arouse a flicker of interest in him were those associated in some way with Scotland. In Rome, the only monument that seemed to impress him was Canova's monument to the Stuarts in St. Peter's. Later that same year, he died at Abbotsford.

By 1830 the post-war rush to Italy was over, the surge of Romantic enthusiasm had somewhat diminished, and the tradition of the Grand Tour had quietly wilted away. Most of the British private art collections had been completed, and the material out of which such collections might be formed was more or less exhausted. The interest of archaeologists was beginning to shift away from the Roman to the Greek "antiquities"; visits to Rome during the winter were tending to become shorter.

It is impossible to assign any precise date for the end of the Grand Tour – some would say the tradition continued at least until the coming of the railway. Even today, travel operators who organize coach tours through Italy are fond of calling them "Grand Tours". However, it has been said with some justification that Lord Macaulay's visit to Italy, in 1838/39, was "the last Grand Tour in the Augustan spirit, to observe not nature but the memorials and policies of man".[16] But Macaulay was untypical in that he preferred Naples to any of the other cities on his route, including Rome:

> *It is the only place in Italy that has seemed to me to have the same sort of vitality which you find in all the great English ports and cities. Rome and Pisa are dead and gone; Florence is not dead, but sleepeth; while Naples overflows with life.*

The British in Rome could still be subdivided into the three main categories that had come into being in the seventeenth century. There were the winter visitors, who might stay a few weeks or the whole winter, and whose opinions about Rome ran the whole gamut of violent emotion, from starry-eyed enthusiasm to disillusioned contempt. There were the artists and a few writers who, if they liked Rome at all, tended to settle down there for years, if not decades, and to some extent were assimilated into Italian life. And there were those for whom Catholic Rome was the only Rome they wished to know. This last group, which since the disappearance of the Stuarts had been of relatively small importance in Anglo-Rome, began in the mid-nineteenth century to become much more influential as a result of the Catholic revival in England.

The English College, which had remained empty after it had been seized and used by the French Army during the Napoleonic Wars, was reopened in 1818, under a new Rector, the Rev. Robert Gradwell. In that year, ten students arrived from England and took up their quarters at the College. They included the future Cardinal Wiseman, who in 1850 was to become the first Archbishop of Westminster. England granted Catholic emancipation in 1829, and this was followed in the 1830s and 1840s by a great revival of Catholicism in England.

One of the central figures in that revival, J.H. Newman, paid his first visit to Rome in 1833, when he was 32. He was then still an Anglican, but the deep impression that the city of Rome made upon him may have had something to do with his later allegiance to the Church of Rome. He arrived from Naples, passing through the Campagna:

> *The flat waste goes on and on; you think it will never have done; miles on miles the ruins continue. At length the walls of Rome appear; you pass through them; you find the city shrunk up into a third of the space enclosed. In the twilight you pass buildings about which you cannot guess wrongly. This must be the Coliseum; there is the arch of Constantine. You are landed at your inn . . .*

Rome was the only city outside England that Newman praised. He thought it was a "wonderful place", where ". . . the effect of every part is so vast and overpowering – there is such an air of greatness and repose cast over the whole", as well as "traces of long sorrow and humiliation, suffering, punishment and decay". In one sense it seemed dead, as it had done to Macaulay: and yet in another sense, the spirit of the place was very much alive.

Those who travelled to Rome for the winter in the mid-nineteenth century still went by road, and those who could afford to do so preferred to travel in their own coach. But the coach had now evolved into a vehicle of dinosaur-like proportions. It was then the travelling-carriage, into which a Victorian family could climb at the start of their journey, and remain comfortably incubated, protected from the outside world by the massiveness of the vehicle and the attentiveness of their servants, until journey's end was reached.

The travelling-carriage in which Dickens and his family went to Italy in 1845 came "fresh from the shady halls of the Pantechnicon near Belgrave Square." The Dickens party travelled across France in it as far as Marseilles. There the four-horse carriage was transferred to a barge, and was towed by the vessel that carried the passengers on their eighteen-hour voyage to Genoa. From Genoa the coach again took the road, through Leghorn, Pisa and Siena to Rome.

The Ruskin family also went by travelling-carriage through Italy, in 1840. John Ruskin was a boy then. Much later he wrote a nostalgic description of the travelling-carriage, that he so much preferred to the railway which, to him, seemed more appropriate for the transport of "cattle, or felled timber". The travelling-carriage, he pointed out, had three particularly commendable qualities:

> *[first] strength – easy rolling – steady and safe poise of persons and luggage . . . [second] stateliness of effect . . . for the abashing of plebian beholders . . . [third] cunning design and distribution of store-cellars under the seats, secret drawers under front windows, invisible pockets under padded lining, safe from dust, and accessible only by insidious slits, or necromantic valves like Aladdin's trap-door; the fitting of cushions where they would not slip, the rounding of corners for more delicate repose; the prudent attachments and springs of blinds; the perfect fitting of windows, on which one-half the comfort of a travelling-carriage really depends.*

This monster required four horses to draw it, a postilion to drive it, and a courier whose job it was to manage the journey and pay all the bills, "so as to save the family unbecoming cares and mean anxieties, besides the trouble and disgrace of trying to speak French or any other language."

Ruskin had no patience with the unworthy inhabitants of the matchless land of Italy:

> *I detest the Italians beyond measure. I have some vengeance against the French, but there is something in them that is at least energetic, however bad its principle may be, but these*

> *Italians – pah! they are Yorick's skull with the worms in it, nothing of humanity left but the smell.*

Nor was his view of Rome much more charitable:

> *St. Peter's I expected to be disappointed in. I was disgusted . . . As a whole, St. Peter's is fit for nothing but a ballroom, and it is a little too gaudy even for that . . . The Capitol is a melancholy rubbishy square of average Palladian-modern; the Forum, a good group of smashed columns . . . the Coliseum I had always considered a public nuisance . . . It is all like a vast churchyard, with a diseased and dying population living in the shade of its tombstones.*

Dickens, also, was unromantic about Rome. His descriptions of the Roman scene were admittedly superficial. He was there between Carnival time and Easter, and toured the sights as conscientiously as, but far more rapidly than John Evelyn two hundred years before. The incidents that stick most firmly in the reader's memory are precisely those that the Romantic writers would never have thought worth mentioning: the pickpockets who sought to rifle Dickens' empty pockets while he was watching a public execution; the fainting women in the crowd of sightseers that overflowed from the Sistine Chapel; the monotonous, dreary chanting in the dark churches; the busy, hard-bargaining ghetto; the sulky Romans and the gay peasants on holiday in the clear air. Although Dickens was half ashamed to admit it, yet it seems a typically 'Dickensian' thought, Rome at first sight reminded him of London: the smoke rising from the distant roofs, and the dome of St. Peter's so easily recognizable among them. To reach the Vatican on Easter Day he had to drive through "miles of miserable streets", but the colour was magnificent, all the fountains were "running diamonds", and:

> *The common people came out in their gayest dresses; the richer people in their smartest vehicles; Cardinals rattled to the church of the Poor Fisherman in their state carriages; shabby magnificence flaunted its threadbare liveries and tarnished cocked hats, in the sun; and every coach in Rome was put in requisition for the Great Piazza of St. Peter's.*

In the same year that Queen Victoria came to the British throne, the year that first saw Dickens' *Posthumous Papers of the Pickwick Club* as well as Carlyle's *French Revolution*, the English artistic colony in Rome acquired a new member – an aspiring landscape artist who was to remain in Rome almost uninterruptedly for the next ten years, but whose greatest fame was achieved not in the realm of landscape but in that of nonsense rhyming.

Edward Lear in 1837, when he first set out for Rome, was twenty-five years old and probably the best zoological illustrator in England. He had decided to abandon this somewhat restricted occupation in order to follow what he considered to be the healthier, more independent and more remunerative profession of landscape painter. The twenty-first and youngest child of a Highgate stockbroker who had gone bankrupt, he had been obliged to earn his living as a draughtsman from the age of fifteen. He started by doing "shop-sketches", colouring prints, making medical illustrations, then went to the London Zoological Gardens, where he completed and published his unsurpassed drawings of the parrot family, the *Psittacidae*, and was finally at Knowsley Hall, the Lancashire home of the Earls of Derby, where on a number of occasions between 1832 and 1836 he was commissioned to draw the contents of the menagerie and aviary. He also wrote, for the benefit of the small children of the household, his first nonsense limericks.

In 1835 he went on a sketching tour of Ireland. It was after returning from this tour – perhaps at least a year after – that he resolved to become a landscape painter and to travel abroad in search of subjects.

The conscious motives that prompted him to do this were reasonable. Although he had proved himself an outstanding illustrator of zoological subjects, both as regards his technique and industry, and in his successful exploitation of unknown fields – *The Family of the Psittacidae* was the first attempt at illustration of a complete family of animals – there was very little money in it. Lear had already had an unfortunate experience when he was working for John Gould, who used Lear's talent, and even his actual drawings, to further his own reputation. Landscape painting, on the other hand, though still a novel way of earning a living, offered the prospect of a more nomadic way of life and the advantages of being his own employer. It was certainly feasible as a stable source of income, in those days before photography had become a trade or profession. It is noteworthy that Lear's interpretations of precipices, ruins and trees (his favourite subjects) are often almost photographic in their technique. Furthermore, Lear's work for the Earl of Derby had already brought him into contact with the world of what he called "lofty society" – the world that has always been the young artist's best patron. His contacts with the scientific world, through his work in natural history, do not seem to have been nearly as extensive.

There was yet another motive, one that had prompted so many other English painters and writers to seek the warmth, sharp sunlight and clear air of the Mediterranean: the state of his health. The zoological work, he thought, would make his already weak eyesight worse. His asthma and bronchitis should certainly not be subjected to the rain, mist and cold that he had already experienced to the full in Lancashire and Ireland, and never ceased to lament whenever he came back to England and became a victim of it. On the sunny shores of the Mediterranean he would surely find innumerable subjects suited to the architectural precision of his art. At the same time he would be healthy enough to do justice to it.

Inevitably, he decided first of all to make his base in Rome, the only place where he could be sure of finding a sufficiency of patrons, a sufficiency of subjects, and the right conditions for his health. However, he was in no hurry to get there, and so chose the less popular Rhineland route. Starting in July or August 1837, he was delayed by illness in Frankfurt, though he recovered sufficiently to make drawings of the ghetto. He proceeded to Milan, then through Bologna to Florence, where he arrived in November, and was impressed by the number of English people then resident there. There were three hundred English at church one Sunday, he exclaimed, not counting the servants. At the end of November he set out over the Sienese hills to Rome, a journey that took five days. He started every morning before sunrise, and the coach jolted along until dusk. There were the usual rumours of bandits and disease. Lear, who hated being confined in a narrow space, was infinitely relieved when he finally reached Rome and was able to rent a studio and bedroom in Via del Babuino, near Piazza di Spagna.

Later in his Roman stay Lear had rooms in Via Felice, a street in the same district which has not survived to our own day. The lawyer James Whiteside, who also stayed in Via Felice in 1856-57, wrote:

> *The whole of this district is the favoured resort of sculptors and artists, whose studies are numerous around the piazza, and in the neighbouring streets and lanes.*

The artists' social centre was now the Caffè Greco, in Via Condotti. It was described by H. Noel Humphries as being, in the late 1830s, crammed full of painters and German tobacco. The Germans were the most numerous nation in the foreign artist colony, according to Humphries, then came the French, then the English, who made up for their inferiority in numbers by being "more presentable". The English painters, wrote Humphries, did not exhibit much in Rome. They were, he claimed, mostly established artists who did not need to sell their work until they had returned home to England.

Although the more famous ruins on the Palatine and in the Forum had been excavated, the city still remained supremely paintable. Away from the beaten tourist track, and away too from the crowded mean streets, there were scores of picturesque ruins covered in grass and flowering weeds, standing in solitude amid vineyards and peaceful gardens. Some idea of the rustic appearance of much of Rome at that time can be gained not only from the calm serenity of Lear's lithographed *Views in Rome and its Environs* – in which six of the twenty-five plates depict scenes in Rome, and the remaining nineteen are of the environs – but also from the little book published not long afterwards by Richard Deakin, an English doctor living in Rome, on the 420 species of plants then growing "spontaneously" on the six acres covered by the ruins of the Colosseum. These plants included not only common weeds and wild flowers, and fifty-six different species of grasses, but many others which anyone might be pleased to find growing "spontaneously" in his own garden: cherry, pear and olive trees, roses, the wild vine, chrysanthemums and orchids, candytuft, chicory and lettuce, broom (used by the Campagna shepherds to thatch their huts) and fennel ("frequently masticated by the country people, when drinking their wine, in order to bring out the flavour of the wine"), onions, garlic and leeks.

During the months from October to May the routine of Lear's life in Rome was much the same as that of any other artist. He frequented society life, more from professional necessity than personal desire; he had pupils to whom he taught drawing – he had seven, mostly titled ladies, before he had been in Rome very long; he worked up his own drawings and paintings for eventual sale; and when the weather was suitable he took his sketchbook out around Rome, or into the Campagna, or to well known places in the vicinity such as Tivoli, Frascati, Albano and Subiaco. He was, it seems, soon reasonably prosperous, and respected by the British colony. When there seemed a possibility that his sister Ann might come out and stay with him for the 1844-45 season, he advised her not to be "too dowdy" if she did come, since: "I am very much known here, and live in the 'highest respectability'."

Perhaps put off by this remark, Ann decided not to join her brother in Rome.

Part of the Colossium (sic), Rome – JAMES HAKEWILL
The tremendous ruins of the Colosseum have always excited the wonder of travellers.
　　So, too, did the flowering plants and weeds growing on the six acres of ruined site. Dr Richard Deakin described 420 of them.

During the summer months, Lear made longer excursions into the field, sketching rapidly in pencil the scenes that attracted him, and 'penning' them over in the evenings. He chose to visit regions in which few travellers, even Italians, had toured before, and which at that date were singularly ill-equipped to receive strangers of any sort – let alone an eccentric foreign artist who was rarely in the best of health, had no money other than what he earned, and usually travelled on foot, alone or with a single companion. He went up into the wild Abruzzi mountains, and on past Naples into Calabria and Sicily. In 1838, his first summer in Italy, he went alone and on foot to Naples and Amalfi; in 1842 to Sicily; in 1843 to the Abruzzi; in 1844 again to Naples and Amalfi; in 1847, accompanied by John Proby, again to Sicily and through Southern Calabria.

All these journeys he recorded in innumerable sketches and watercolours, and in due course he published some of them in further volumes. His *Illustrated Excursions in Italy* appeared in two volumes in 1846. The first illustrated his three tours through the Abruzzi provinces, and had a detailed journal in addition to the plates; the second was concerned with the Papal States, and had plates only, with brief topographical notes. The other book, the *Journal of a Landscape Painter in Southern Calabria*, which consisted of both text and illustrations, was not published until 1852, after Lear had left Rome.[17]

During his Roman decade Lear came twice to England, to sell his work, see his friends and supervise the publication of his books. The *Views of Rome* was published during his first visit in 1841; the *Illustrated Excursions*, as well as the first *Book of Nonsense*, in 1845-46. It was during this second visit that, as a result of the publication of the *Illustrated Excursions in Italy*, he gave a course of twelve drawing lessons to Queen Victoria, who was just seven years younger than he was.

Although Lear, with his restless temperament, never could remain in one place for very long, he might have centred his life upon Rome for many more years but for the revolutions of 1848. Like most artists, Lear, whose advancement in his career and indeed whose whole livelihood depended upon his contacts among the nobility and gentry, was a moderate traditionalist in so far as he had any political views at all. He personally had never been concerned with the political situation in the Papal States – although he was aware of the backwardness of the far from benevolent tyranny of Pope Gregory XIV. In the 1840s, censorship of liberal opinion was drastically enforced in Rome. English newspapers were often confiscated, and the Pope's own subjects were practically forbidden to travel. Street lighting and sanitation were conspicuously absent; ignorance and squalor festered in the slums. The lawyer James Whiteside was able to contrast Rome under Gregory XIV in 1845-46 with the more enlightened regime of Pius IX in 1846-7. In the crowded slums between the Corso and the Tiber, where the *piazze* resembled rubbish dumps, the street surfaces were broken, and the streets themselves cheerless, the inefficiency of the papal government was evident in 1845-46. At night there was neither street lighting nor police; a walk from the centre of the city to St. John Lateran would involve "profound silence, utter darkness, a solitude so universal as to make one doubt his presence in a great city." Other hazards of the night were sudden downpours of rain – against which the Romans would put up tent-like umbrellas consisting of "a mass of oiled calico . . . attached to a stout pole" – and still more unwelcome downpours of garbage which the inhabitants were apt to tip into the street from the windows above. Whiteside advised anyone walking in Rome to arm himself with a stout stick, and to keep well into the middle of the road.

The atmosphere when Pius IX became Pope was one of relief and hope. Whiteside wrote:

> *Joy beamed on every countenance, there was an unusual hilarity evinced by the people; the light of freedom had dawned amongst them."*

Lear commented that the new Pope was "a real good man, & a wonder". In consequence, the 1847-48 season was, for the visitors, "full of fuss and froth . . . a propitious season, & the rumours of distraction prevented a many nasty vulgar people from coming, and there is really room to move."

But it soon appeared that the new Pope was not as liberal as the initial contrast with his predecessor had made him seem to be. As the spiritual leader of Roman Catholicism, he could not declare war on the other Catholic state, Austria, whose occupation of part of Italy was most galling to the patriots; in consequence, the Roman people began to lose faith in him. Lear, who the previous summer had been in Calabria when it was seething with revolt, could see by the spring of 1848 that the "rumours of distraction" were after all going to increase, to the point perhaps where English society people simply would not come to Rome. He decided therefore to leave the city himself in the spring of 1848, and go to Corfu, which at that time was under British protection. His foresight was vindicated: in November 1848 came the Roman revolution, which led to the flight of the Pope to Gaeta, the establishment of the Roman Republic, and its eventual suppression, the following June, by the French army.

It was ten years before Lear was in Rome again, and by that time both he and Rome had changed. The important, formative years for him were those between 1837, when he came to Rome as a bright young man, and 1848, when he decided to leave as a mature and successful artist. During that Roman decade he painted some of his best pictures, established himself as a landscape artist, explored central and southern Italy, met for the first time his lifelong friends Chichester Fortescue and Thomas George Baring (later Viceroy of India), and enjoyed material prosperity. As for the nonsense rhymes that made him famous, they too came into existence during the Roman decade or earlier. In 1845 Chichester Fortescue described Lear as "a delightful companion, full of *nonsense*, puns, riddles, everything in the shape of fun, and *brimming* with intense appreciation of nature as well as history." *The Book of Nonsense* was then nearly ready for publication. It had brimmed up to the point where it had to be perpetuated as a book – and to its author's intense astonishment was an immediate success.

The years between 1848-49 and 1860-61 constituted a clearly defined period in Roman history. It was the last decade before the proclamation of the Kingdom of Italy, the last decade but one of the temporal rule of the Popes. It was a peaceful decade as far as Rome itself was concerned, but the peace was ensured by the presence in Rome of a garrison of French troops, who were there to guarantee the territorial rights of the Pope. It was a decade that began with the defection of J.H. Newman from the Anglican to the Roman Catholic Church, and ended with the publication of Darwin's *Origin of Species* and Marx's *Critique of Political Economy*. At its beginning, the coach and the diligence were still the recognized means of getting to Rome from the Channel coast. At its end, the railway carried passengers from London to Marseilles, and the steamer carried them from Marseilles to Civita Vecchia. It was clear that before many more years had elapsed, there would be railways on the Italian side of the Alps as well.

The three English Catholic Cardinals with their oddly similar names – Wiseman, Newman and Manning – burst upon the scene nearly simultaneously, between 1845 and 1851. *Burst* is an appropriate word in the circumstances, though it refers less to the character of the the prelates themselves than to the effect of their shared beliefs on the English theologians and churchgoers of the day.

It is hard for us today to realize how profound and widespread was the hold of the Anglican church upon ordinary thinking people everywhere in England at the mid-point of the nineteenth century, when practically everyone still firmly believed that God had created the world in 4004 B.C., and the deep sense of shock that therefore resulted when first Newman, and then Manning, both leading Anglican theologians, went over to the Roman Catholic Church (Wiseman, of course, had always been a Catholic). W.E. Gladstone was a life-long friend of Manning, and was himself instrumental in removing the restriction which, until 1871, prevented Catholics from taking degrees at Oxford, Cambridge and Durham Universities. But Gladstone regarded Manning's change of religious allegiance quite simply as "a death" which did not so much suspend or alter their friendship, but cut it clean short. When, in 1850, Cardinal Wiseman came to England as the first Cardinal Archbishop of Westminster, and wrote somewhat recklessly in a pastoral letter that "Catholic England has been restored to its orbit in the ecclesiastical firmament", an immediate outcry resulted. The Pope and Cardinal Wiseman were burned in effigy all over England (Guy Fawkes' Day conveniently occurring about the same time), there were public meetings, petitions to the Queen, thundering articles in *The Times*, anti-Catholic diatribes and cartoons in *Punch*, which was fond of featuring two characters called "Mr Newboy and Mr Wiseboy".

Wiseman had lived almost all his life abroad and can hardly have been aware of the opposition to Catholicism that still existed in England. He had been born in Seville, brought up in Ireland and at the age of only 16 he went to study at the newly reopened English College in Rome, becoming its vice-rector in 1824 and its rector from 1828 to 1840. Before becoming Cardinal Archbishop, he was in England only in 1835-36 and again in 1848, when he was the diplomatic envoy sent by Pius IX to Palmerston. He was Archbishop for fifteen years and became well known as a lecturer on a variety of topics.

J.H. Newman, who before he was received into the Roman Church in 1845 had established his reputation as a preacher and theologian at Oxford, was one of the chief supporters of the Anglo-Catholic movement (or Oxford Movement) in the 1840's. But he finally repudiated Anglicanism entirely. In 1846 he was advised to go to the College of Propaganda in Rome in order to study. It was the first time he had been out of England since 1833, and it was difficult at first, in France, to get used to drinking "cold wine instead of hot tea". He reached Rome at the end of October, 1846, by diligence from Pisa. The College of Propaganda hardly came up to the standards to which he had been accustomed at Oxford. It was dirty: "the carpet is a nest of fleas and they have milk pans for slop pails." The clothes he had to wear seemed absurd: "Buckles at the knees, buckles on the shoes, a dress coat with a sort of undergraduate's gown hanging behind, black stockings which must be without a wrinkle, and a large cocked hat; that I should have lived so long to be so dressed up!". However, he persevered, and in due course contrived to antagonize the English social world in Rome by telling them (at a funeral oration) that "Rome was not the place for them, but the very place in the whole world where Michael and the Dragon may almost be seen in combat". Such remarks did not go down at all well among the wealthy and fashionable people who had come to spend the winter in Rome; one of them, at a party, expressed the opinion that Newman ought to be thrown into the Tiber.

Manning had first visited Rome in the winter of 1838-39 when Wiseman was still at the English College as its rector. On St. Agnes' Day the latter took Manning to see the blessing of the lambs out of whose wool the archbishops' pallia are made. "How little we thought" wrote Manning in his memoirs, "that he and I should have the first two palliums in the new hierarchy of England!"

He was in Rome for a second visit in 1848 – there is a slightly incongruous glimpse of him touring the city accompanied by Sidney Herbert, the Minister for War, and Florence Nightingale – and again in 1851, after he had followed Newman into the Roman Catholic Church. He returned to England the following year, and succeeded Wiseman as Archbishop in 1875.

Most of the artists who came to Rome in the nineteenth century did so when they were still relatively unknown young men. There they perfected their individual styles, and returned home more or less established artists. On the other hand, most of the writers who went there made the trip after their reputations had been made. The fact that they could afford to winter in Rome was the measure of their success, and what they wrote as a result of their journey was not of any great literary importance. Dickens and Thackeray, otherwise so different, were alike in this. Thackeray had paid a first visit to Rome in 1844-45. His second visit, in 1853-54, was undertaken with two objects in view: he wanted to study the life of the Roman artist colony with a view to incorporating it in *The Newcomes,* and he wanted to present to his daughters, sixteen year old Anne and thirteen year old Harriet, the pleasures of a Roman season.

The two aims were incompatible. Thackeray soon discovered – he was neither the first nor the last writer to do so – that the literary life cannot easily be combined with the duties of a family man. Thackeray was notably unselfish, kind and devoted to his daughters, always willing to place others' interests in front of his own. But he was also lonely, insecure, harassed by painful recurring illnesses and the thought of his wife shut away in an asylum. On this particular journey he had no governess to take the strain off his shoulders; and he *had* to work.

The consequence was that he saw almost nothing of Rome. He was ill, he was concerned for his daughters: "O for the governess to take them in charge", he wrote in a moment of exasperation unusual for him, "and teach them a little order." He worked whenever he had a spare moment, and if he did get out at all, it was either at sunset to admire the scarlet sky over St. Peter's, or at night to attend "some of the tea parties which abound here." As for the life of the artist colony, that could not be observed at all:

> *I did not see one pennyworth of the jolly artist-life which I went expressly to look for. Having to be with ladies is very moral, right, paternal and so forth; but, having to dine with my little women at home, I couldn't go to Bohemia.*

All he managed to complete was something of *The Newcomes*, and his "Christmas play", as he called it, *The Rose and the Ring*, which owes nothing to the fact of having been begun in Rome and might as well, as its author was the first to admit, have been written "in Jericho or Islington."

Of course it was not only his daughters' welfare and his illnesses that kept Thackeray from the free and easy Bohemian life. There was the insularity that he shared with other materially successful men of the period, which made contact with ordinary Italians impossible for him. Still, it is sympathy that we most feel for Thackeray in Italy. Already ill when he reached Rome, he caught what was probably tertian malaria while he was there; and in Naples both the girls fell ill with scarlet fever. "O how I wish I was well back!" wrote the lonely despondent father from that lively city, "and how beset I am by these constant family cares! – To be father and mother too is too much work for anyone: let alone such a lazy fellow as me."

"This Italy has been a failure," was his final, reluctant admission.

The degree to which Piazza di Spagna had become the English centre in Rome by the mid-nineteenth century may be judged by this extract from a description by an American, George Hillard, who saw it in 1853:

> *English speech is the predominating sound, and sturdy English forms and rosy English faces the predominating sight. Here are English shops, an English livery stable, and an English reading-room, where elderly gentlemen in drab gaiters read* The Times *newspaper with an air of grim intensity. Here English grooms flirt with English nursery-maids, and English children present to Italian eyes the living types of the cherub heads of Correggio and Albani. It is, in short, a piece of England dropped upon the soil of Italy . . . So many are the occasions that bring the foreign residents to the Piazza di Spagna, that an Englishman or American, who should station himself in the midst of it on a fine day, would, in the course of a few hours be able to speak with nearly all his acquaintances without stirring from the spot.*

In the same year, one of the artists prominent in that artistic Bohemia which Thackeray so signally failed to encounter was Frederick Lord Leighton, whose stylized nudes seem to have supplied a real need in that corseted Victorian world. Leighton first took drawing lessons in Rome at the age of ten, and decided at fourteen that he would become an artist. "He is one already," commented his father, a doctor who himself took little interest in art, and made arrangements for his son's apprenticeship. Leighton returned to Rome in 1852, spent three years there, and in 1855 sold his *Cimabue's Madonna* to Queen Victoria for £600. Thereafter he knew only success. He settled in London, lived and painted there until his death in 1896.

Of the writers who spent some time in Rome in the 1850 decade, the best known are Robert and Elizabeth Barrett Browning. Their Roman stay is associated especially with the flat in the Via Bocca di Leone (near Piazza di Spagna) that they occupied in 1853, 1858, 1859 and finally 1860. Although Anglo-Roman intellectual life was largely dominated in the later years of this decade by the two poets, the effect of this on English literature was slight. The two were not nearly so *molto d'accordo* as they had been in the earlier, romantic days: Robert was irked (though unwilling to admit it) by the chores of caring for an invalid wife, and jealous of her interest in spiritualism. He pleaded lack of inspiration as an excuse for not working; but the plain fact is that most romantic poets write fewer and worse poems as they grow older. Robert Browning must sometimes have looked back nostalgically to his first visit to Rome in 1834 when, at a children's party given by the American sculptor and poet, William Wetmore Story, he had read *The Pied Piper* to the children, who were also entertained by a reading by Hans Andersen of *The Ugly Duckling*.

As for Elizabeth Barrett Browning, her home, both actual and spiritual, was Florence. She only came to Rome for the sake of her health. On her first visit, she wrote that she had "lost several letters in Rome besides a great deal of illusion." On the later visits she became increasingly frail and infirm. Indeed, she had not then long to live. She died in Florence in 1861.

By 1858 the journey to Rome could be almost completely covered by means of mechanical transport. Nathaniel Hawthorne, who had been United States Consul in Liverpool, set out in January of that year from London Bridge station, holding through tickets to Paris via Folkestone and Boulogne. They left London Bridge at 8.30 in the morning and were on board the steamer at Folkestone by about 1 p.m. The crossing took two hours (hardly more than it does today), and another three or four hours took them to Amiens, where they spent the night. From Amiens to Paris was a journey of three and a half hours. Hawthorne spent a week in Paris, and then went on by rail to Marseilles. From there a Neapolitan steamer took him to Genoa, Leghorn and Civita Vecchia, which left a mere 45 miles that still had to be completed by *vettura*.

Hawthorne's first view of Rome was not a pleasant one, though it must be remembered that he arrived at midnight, in midwinter, and that his first few days were spent in a "cold and cheerless hotel, where we shivered during 2 or 3 days, meanwhile seeking lodgings among the sunless, dreary alleys which are called streets in Rome." His first impressions, contained in the two volumes of his *French and Italian Notebooks*, included:

> *. . . sour bread, pavements most uncomfortable to the feet, enormous prices for poor living; beggars, pickpockets, ancient temples, and broken monuments, and clothes hanging to dry about them; French soldiers, monks, and priests of every degree; a shabby population smoking bad cigars . . .*

It was two months before the weather improved, and with it his spirits. In the meantime he toured Rome thoroughly, though leisurely. He went to St. Peter's four or five times; to the Sistine Chapel on Ash Wednesday; to Sta. Maria Maggiore, which he entered without knowing which church it was; and out along the Appian Way. He was gratified, at the end of March, by a glimpse of the Pope:

> *. . . a stout old man, with a white skull-cap, a scarlet gold-embroidered cape falling over his shoulders, and a white silk robe, the train of which was borne by an attendant . . .*

> *His face was kindly and venerable, but not particularly impressive.*

He also wrote, a little naively:

> *I am glad to have seen the Pope, because now he may be crossed out of the list of sights to be seen.*

After four months in Rome Hawthorne made a contract with a *vetturino* to take them to Florence for 95 *scudi* inclusive. Everything to be provided was set down in the contract, even to "milk, butter, bread, eggs and coffee" for breakfast. In the autumn they returned to Rome for a second winter, and this time had a furnished house at Piazza Poli (near the Trevi fountain) all ready to receive them.

Nathaniel Hawthorne's novel *The Marble Faun* was directly inspired by his stay in Rome, and we can see some of the process of inspiration taking place as we read the entries in the *French and Italian Notebooks*. After describing the statue of the faun that gave him the idea, " . . . it seems to me that a story . . . might be contrived on the idea of their species having become intermingled with the human race," he goes on, a page or two later, to describe the Trevi fountain:

> *Just round the corner of the street, leading out of our piazza, is the Fountain of Trevi, of which I can hear the plash in the evening, when other sounds are hushed.*

In *The Marble Faun*, his character Miriam visits the Trevi at night, and says:

> *I shall sip as much of this water as the hollow of my hand will hold . . . I am leaving Rome in a few days; and the tradition goes, that a parting draught at the Fountain of Trevi ensures the traveller's return.*

According to H.V. Morton[18], this is the earliest reference to a visit to the Trevi fountain for this purpose. By 1883, he says (quoting from Baedeker's *Rome*, 8th edition), the custom was to drink the water and throw in a coin. Today, everyone has heard of the custom of throwing in the coin, though few practise the additional rite of drinking the water. This can, however, still be done, thanks to a supply of *Acqua Vergine Nuova* provided by the municipality at one corner of the fountain.

In 1858 also, Edward Lear returned to Rome, and stayed two years. His visit demonstrates the truism that a place dearly loved in youth may mysteriously lose its loved qualities when seen again after a long interval and through the eyes of middle age. Since he left Rome ten years earlier, he had travelled all over the Balkans and Greece, had visited Egypt, Gibraltar, Switzerland, Germany and the Middle East, and had lived in Corfu and in England. But he was less prosperous than before, more prone to melancholy, more sensitive to any environment that did not suit him. He found Rome impossibly expensive, the city crowded, the atmosphere of "forced art-quackery" uncongenial and depressing. Although he finally found suitable rooms in the Via Condotti, he had to pay more for them (£20 per quarter) than he should have done, and had to take them on a three years' lease. He fitted up one of his rooms as a "gallery", and sold some pictures. But the social invitations interfered with his work. He particularly abhorred the "late mixed tea-parties" that Thackeray had been unable to attend often enough. Then, in April 1859, war broke out again: the war that began with Garibaldi's attack on the Austrians in Lombardy, and was followed by the establishment of the Kingdom of Italy in 1861, and the selection of Florence as its first capital.

All the British art patrons reacted in the usual way to the war – they left Rome as fast as they could, depriving most of the resident artists of their main source of income. Lear was left with no alternative but to go back to England. When he returned to Rome at the end of 1859, the place seemed empty and dead. Most of the hotels and lodging houses were shut, and the only notable people in the city were Robert and

Elizabeth Browning. In 1860 he decided to leave Rome altogether, even though this meant sacrificing a year's rent for the rooms in Via Condotti. During all the rest of his life (he died in 1888, at San Remo) he only came once more to Rome, in 1871, and that was merely a holiday interlude.

The decade of the 1860s, even more than the previous ten years, was a period when Rome had a very special character all its own. In one sense, Rome was then rather in the position of Vienna after the end of the Austro-Hungarian Empire in 1919. It was the only city of any size within a truncated hinterland whose resources were quite inadequate for the support of such a capital. Rome had lost control of the Papal States of Romagna, Ferrara, the Marches and Umbria, which had joined the new Italian Kingdom, and was left only with the Patrimony of St. Peter, consisting of Rome, Viterbo, the one port of Civitavecchia, and the countryside in between. There were 400,000 people in the countryside of the Patrimony; 200,000 in Rome itself; and scarcely any industries. Into Rome there came a great influx of priests who were also civil servants; they had formerly administered the papal government in the other states. For most of them no work could now be found, though they all drew their pensions. There were still fifteen bishoprics in the Patrimony, as well as the suburban sees that were traditionally given to the Cardinals.

Rome remained politically backward, and all Italian patriots (with whom the English liberals now ardently sympathized) looked forward to the day when the city would take its rightful place as the capital of a united Italy. Nearly all the population of Rome was crowded into the insanitary, low-lying districts along the banks of the Tiber; but further away, above Piazza di Spagna and around the ruined Forum and out towards the Aurelian Wall, were picturesque old buildings, country lanes and quiet gardens; the Rome of the artists and the winter visitors. David Mathew described the Rome of the 1860's thus:

The city lay unprosperous, inert and beautiful. The deserted Campagna formed a timeless setting. Across it stretched the paving stones of the Via Appia, then still uncovered. Within Rome itself the ancient churches arose among the trees and bushes. A view of the Roman Forum, now in the Louvre and painted by Corot a few years before this time, catches very perfectly the light on the wall spaces of the ancient city. The domes and towers and pine trees rose in the warm weather. There were many priests and monks; it was their kingdom.[19]

Rome in this decade was the Rome of Joseph Severn, who after living in England between 1841 and 1860 (also in Jersey, in order to escape his creditors), returned to Rome as British Consul to the Papal States. He held this office until it ceased to exist in 1872. It was also the Rome of William Wetmore Story, whose *Roba di Roma* was published in 1862.

The Rome of the 1860s was also the Rome of Augustus Hare, to whom few would deny the honour of having written, in his *Walks in Rome*, the best guide-book to the city that has ever been published in English. It was certainly the first book of its kind. Although the guide only became popular in the next decade, the Rome described in it is really the Rome of 1860-70 – the Rome that middle-aged Edward Lear detested, but that Augustus Hare, then in his thirties, would later look back upon with the nostalgic certainty that *this* had been the perfect time to be living in Rome.

Augustus Hare was born in Rome, in 1834. The Hare family were inveterate winterers in Italy: Augustus' brother William and his sister Ann had both been born in the vicinity of Lucca, in 1831 and 1832 respectively; while his father and his grandfather had both been born abroad, as well as his uncles Augustus (after whom he was named), Julius and Marcus. His father, Francis Hare, had lived almost continuously on the Continent ever since 1817. He occupied himself in travelling, in building up (like his son after him) a reputation as a conversationalist, in collecting books and selling them, in cultivating the acquaintance of such varied notables as Walter Savage Landor, the Earl of Bristol and the King of Bavaria, and in courting and eventually marrying Anne Paul. Anne was the great-granddaughter of the 8th Earl of Strathmore. She had come to Italy with her mother and three sisters "partly for the sake of completing their education, partly to escape with dignity from the discords of a most uncongenial home." This connexion on his mother's side with the Strathmore family was a source of great pride to Augustus Hare in later life, though his own indiscretion in revealing one of the skeletons in the family cupboard, in *The Story of my Life*, can hardly have made them equally proud of him.

The birth of a third child to Mr and Mrs Francis Hare, in the Via Strozzi in Rome, aroused no enthusiasm in either parent. Mrs Hare, having ascertained that her sister-in-law, widow of the other Augustus Hare (who had died a month previously in Rome), would be willing to adopt the child, lost no time in disposing of her offspring – as of an unwanted kitten. "My dear Maria, how very kind of you!" she wrote. "Yes, certainly, the baby shall be sent as soon as it is weaned; and, if anyone else would like one, would you kindly recollect that we have others."

It was typical of Augustus that, after he grew up, he should have ferreted out this information, pigeon-holed it, and in due course published it for the edification of the world in general.

So young Augustus was packed off to England in the charge of an English nurse, and later joined his adoptive mother in Sussex, where she had decided to settle. After a peculiarly unhappy childhood and boyhood, without either toys or playmates, he eventually proceeded, via a series of private tutors, to Oxford. There, the Master and Dean of Balliol were puzzled as to the best way of rendering "born in Rome" in the matriculation book. They finally settled for *de urbe Roma civitate Italiae*. Here, as at school, what he learnt was of more value than what he was taught. He left the university in 1857 with a degree and without regret, but with a great amount of self-taught history, French and Italian.

Mrs Hare, his adoptive mother, had been advised to nurse her delicate health abroad. Augustus, who was devoted to her, of course accompanied her on the journey. From June 1857 to November 1858 they travelled together in Switzerland, Austria and Italy. Augustus Hare was 23 when he revisited Rome for the first time since babyhood. The description of his approach to his birthplace is as vivid as anything that has been penned on that immemorial subject:

> *Breathlessly interesting was the first approach to Rome – the characteristic scenery of the Campagna, with its tufa quarries, and its crumbling towers and tombs rising amidst the withered thistles and asphodels; its strange herds of buffaloes; then the faint grey dome rising over the low hills, and the unspoken knowledge about it, which was almost too much for words; lastly, the miserable suburb and the great Piazza del Popolo.*

In Rome he first visited his real mother, nicknamed Italima, and his sister. Although Italima had never shown him any affection, it was awkward having two mothers in the same city, and jealousy quickly arose in both maternal hearts, Italima resenting it if he did not visit her, Mrs Hare being alarmed if he did. He resolved this difficulty as best he could, and most of the time he remained, as usual, with his adoptive mother:

> *My normal life was a quiet one with my mother, driving with her, sketching with her, sitting with her in the studio of the venerable Canevari, who was doing her portrait, spending afternoons with her in the Medici gardens, in the beautiful Villa Wolkonski, or in the quiet valley near the grove and grotto of Egeria.*

In the mornings they generally walked on the Pincio. In February – a bitterly cold February that year – they made the excursion to Naples, Amalfi and Salerno. In May they returned to England by way of Florence, Lucca, Switzerland and Paris.

This first adult visit to Rome with his mother was followed by five more between 1863 and 1870, in every case for the entire winter season. There can be no doubt that these early visits were the happiest of his life. He had no financial cares, no need to earn money by writing or lecturing. For human company he had all he required – his mother. Beyond that, he had the quiet picturesque Rome of the pre-1870 era to explore and record. In 1863 he wrote in his journal:

> *The first days in Rome this winter were absolute Elysium – the sitting for hours in the depth of the Forum, then picturesque, flowery, and 'unrestored', watching the sunlight first kiss the edge of the columns and then bathe them with gold; the wanderings with different friends over the old mysterious churches on the Aventine and Coelian, and the finding out and analysing all their histories from different books in the evenings; the very drives between the high walls, watching the different effects of light on the broken tufa stones, and the pellitory and maidenhair growing between them.*

Two years later he was describing the same sort of scene in very similar words:

> *Most delightful was it, after the fatigue and the intense anxieties of the journey, to wake upon the splendid view, with its succession of aerial distances, and to know how many glorious sunsets we had to enjoy nightly behind the mighty dome which rose on the other side of the brown-grey city. And then came the slow walk to church along the sunny Pincio terrace, with the deepest of unimaginable blue*

skies seen through branches of ilex and bay, and garden beds, beneath the terraced wall, always showing some flowers, but in spring quite ablaze with pansies and marigolds.

By 1865-66 he had begun to establish a reputation as an expert on Rome. That winter he received so many invitations to go out sketching that he circulated his artistic acquaintances with a list of times and places, and fixed a standing rendezvous on the steps of Trinità dei Monti at 10 a.m. To his astonishment the first day produced no less than "forty ladies, in many cases attended by footmen, carrying their luncheon-baskets, camp-stools, etc." This particular series of sketching parties had to be abandoned after a few months because all the ladies had by then ceased to be on speaking terms with one another. But they foreran the lectures and the personally conducted tours round Rome that in due course established Augustus Hare as the leader in the highest class of unpaid Roman guide.

Walks in Rome itself belongs essentially to the years after 1870, and will therefore be discussed in the next chapter. But throughout the 1860s Augustus Hare was collecting material, at first unconsciously and later deliberately, that he would use in his book. It is first mentioned, in his autobiography, in relation to his sixth visit to Rome, in 1870:

It seems as if Walks in Rome *would some day grow into a book. Mother thinks it presumptuous, but I assure her that though of course it will be full of faults, no book would ever be printed if perfection were waited for. And I really do know much more about the subject than most people, though of course not half as much as I ought to know.*

A son was born to another expatriate British family in 1834 (the year of Augustus Hare's birth), not in Rome this time but in Naples. John Emerich Edward Dalberg Acton, later first Baron Acton and Professor of

The English Road To Rome

Modern History at Cambridge, and remembered now chiefly for his aphorism "Power tends to corrupt, and absolute power corrupts absolutely", did not in fact have very close family links with Italy. His father had a *palazzo* in Naples (hence his birth there). One of his uncles, Charles Edward Januarius Acton, was elected a Cardinal at the early age of 39, in 1842 (he also had been born at Naples). Another relative, Sir John Acton, who died in 1811, had been Prime Minister of Naples and commander of the Neapolitan army and navy. However, John Emerich Acton's family ties were more with Germany (his mother was of German origin), where the Actons also owned property. He was in fact a man, as his election agent once put it, "of a princely income and respectable lineage", who could afford to live in any place that suited him.

Acton was brought up in England, coming under the influence of Bishop Wiseman at Oscott College. Between 1860 and 1870 he spent a good deal of time in Rome, attending the Vatican Council as an observer, and developing his views, which – although he was a Roman Catholic – were sharply opposed to those of Pope Pius IX. In 1869-70 he was in Rome for seven months (his longest stay there) for the meetings of the Vatican Council, which he reported in detail to W.E. Gladstone. The main business of the Council was to discuss the doctrine of Papal Infallibility, a doctrine which, naturally enough, was strongly condemned by British Liberals, whether they were Protestant or Catholic.

W.E. Gladstone was himself in Rome several times as a tourist. The last occasion was in 1866, when he arrived by train from Ancona with his wife and two daughters. They stayed near Piazza di Spagna. But Mr Gladstone was not much interested in archaeology and preferred to spend his time going round the Italian churches and listening to the preachers. The Gladstones had a Papal audience, and Mr Gladstone found that the Pope made a pleasant impression, though his daughter recorded that there was "something excessively ludicrous about the whole thing".

Towards the end of the decade, the modern world was encroaching steadily upon Rome. It was not merely a question of when the temporal rule of the Popes would end, but when Rome would be linked to the rest of the world as regards such mundane things as a railway system and modern sanitation. In 1847, Edward Lear had prophesied "railroads, gaslight, pavements" in Rome by 1960, thanks to the beneficent influence of Pius IX. In fact, Pius IX turned out to be more of a hindrance than a help. Nevertheless, much less than a century was to pass before these amenities were to be found in Rome as well.

During the 1840s, the railway had only just ceased to be a rich man's toy or a visionary's pet idea. But, despite the railway fever of that decade, the hundreds of new lines, embankments, cuttings, tunnels and stations that were beginning to transform the British and the European landscape, the railway might have continued to be a relatively expensive means of travel had it not been for the genius of Thomas Cook, the first to realize, and to act upon his realization, that "it might be easier to find one thousand persons prepared to pay five shillings" for a journey by rail, "than to find a dozen ready to pay five pounds each".[20]

At first in England, later on the Continent, Cook ran his excursions not for those who had plenty of money, but for the millions of people who had never before had the opportunity of travelling. In doing this, he altered the character of the British visit to the Continent, becoming courier, tutor, governor and *vetturino* to thousands of travellers – "the man from Cook's", whom every tourist would dutifully follow.

Cook's efforts, beginning with the world's first excursion train in 1841, were at first concentrated wholly within the British Isles. It was not until 1856 that he sent a party on a circular tour abroad, crossing the North Sea from Harwich to Antwerp, and visiting Brussels, Cologne, the Rhine, Strasbourg and Paris.

In 1858 a railway was authorized from Pimlico (in due course, Victoria Station) to Dover. In 1863, after the Scottish railway managers had decided not to recognize his excursion tickets, Cook turned his attention to France, Switzerland and Italy. In 1864 he was carrying passengers from London to Paris, via Newhaven and Dieppe. In the same year he personally conducted a tour to Switzerland, and went on to reconnoitre a route into Italy. There was still no direct link under or through the Alps between the railway systems of France and Switzerland on one side, Italy on the other. So Cook crossed the Mont Cenis pass in a diligence to Susa, then went on by rail to Turin, Milan and Florence, returning via Leghorn, Genoa and the Riviera coast to Marseilles and so to Paris.

This was the route that he chose for his first Italian guided tour, in July 1864. At Easter 1866, he escorted the first party of English railway excursionists to Rome. When the party reached Florence, Cook was informed that there was not a hotel room to be had in Rome, since it was Holy Week. Undaunted, he went on alone, hired the palace of Prince Torlonia for ten days for £500, returned to Florence for his tourists, brought them to Rome and installed them in the palace, with meals supplied by nearby restaurants.

In 1866 it was possible to buy through railway tickets from London to any station in Italy. The same year even that rigid conservative Augustus Hare resolved to leave Rome by rail at the end of the winter season, i.e. in April. He arrived in Rome from Spoleto just too late to make the connexion. He ordered a carriage, and reached Perugia – 138 miles from Rome – ahead of the train.

In 1868 the railway systems on the two sides of the Alps were finally connected, with the completion of the tunnel under Mont Cenis. Soon after this, for the first time in history, it was possible to enter a railway carriage at Calais and not leave it until, some sixty hours later, the train arrived in Rome – and for a very reasonable charge. The first class single fare from London to Rome at that time was £12.9.0.

If Thomas Cook was chiefly responsible for bringing the ordinary British traveller to Rome, it was another Englishman who takes much of the credit for supplying him, while he was there, with gas and water. During the 1850s an English engineer, James Shepherd, built Rome's first gasometer on the Circus Maximus. Ten years later the same enterprising man, together with G.H. Fawcett, formed the Anglo-Roman Water Company with a capital of £200,000. They were granted a lease of 99 years from 1865, in order to bring the Acqua Pia Marcia along a cast iron aqueduct from its source 60 miles east of Rome into the city. The company changed its name to Società Anonima dell'Acqua Marcia in 1867, and in September 1870 the water flowed along the aqueduct and into Rome for the first time, there to be welcomed by Pope Pius IX.

This, as H.V. Morton has pointed out[21], was the last occasion on which a pontiff appeared at any public ceremony as the sovereign of the Papal States. Ten days later, on 20 September 1870, the Italian Army broke through the walls of Rome at the Porta Pia, and after a plebiscite on 2 October, Rome was annexed to Italy and became, at long last, its capital.

THE MODERN WAY TO ROME

FROM 1870 TO 1944

Throughout the seventeenth, eighteenth and much of the nineteenth centuries, the population of Rome had altered relatively little. At the beginning of the seventeenth century, Rome had 114,000 inhabitants and was smaller than Venice. In 1676, reported the census, the total was 150,000 people; and in 1764, according to figures quoted by Gibbon, 172,000 people lived in Rome – not counting about 10,000 Jews who were not included in the census. The figure dropped to 123,000 in 1809, during the French occupation, rose again to 145,000 in 1829 and to 170,000 in 1847; shortly before 1870 it exceeded 200,000 for the first time. After that came an enormous expansion. The 1870 total had more than doubled by 1890; and in 1921 the population of Rome exceeded 660,000. In 1929 it was 902,500; and today it is more than two million.

Although, as we have seen, the Romans themselves in the last years of Papal Rome were mostly crowded into the low-lying areas adjacent to the Tiber, the rest of the city still retained, in 1870, the quiet and picturesque character that had charmed the foreign visitor for so many winter seasons. Up on the Esquiline, between Santa Maria Maggiore and St. John Lateran, were quiet gardens and vineyards, and lonely country lanes. Beyond the Aurelian Wall the almost uninhabited Campagna still stretched away towards the hills on both sides of the

Appian Way, still patrolled by unkempt shepherds, still a place to be avoided in high summer on account of the malaria. Residents near the edge of Rome could hear the owls hooting at night, and smell the new-mown hay during the summer evenings. In the autumn they could watch the sheep being driven into the city for the winter; and in the spring they saw them being herded out into the Campagna again. The foreign artists used to drive out once a year to hold an elaborate picnic in the Campagna; but they returned to the safety of the city at night. Within the walls, the Jews' ghetto still stood, the peasant girls still waited on the Spanish Steps to be hired out as models: the Tiber was not yet embanked, and in times of flood the Pantheon could be seen reflected in its waters.

In 1870, however, Rome became the capital of a large modern State. Such capitals are noted for their bureaucracies; but since bureaucracies are composed of men, with their wives and children, they have to live somewhere; and therefore houses have to be built for them. There was no room for the new houses in the crowded districts near the river; and it was therefore decided to develop, first of all, the area between the new railway and the Esquiline Hill – the triangle of which the three angles were Piazza della Repubblica, St. John Lateran and Porta Maggiore, and the three sides Via Merulana, Viale Carlo Felice (and the Aurelian Wall) and Via Giovanni Giolitti (and the railway). Large grey *palazzi* (the word had now also come to mean apartment houses, or blocks of flats), bordering straight wide streets, rapidly filled all this district, of which the centre-piece was the new Piazza Vittorio Emanuele, and all the pretty gardens and winding lanes in that area were built over. The 'modernization' unfortunately, was an unusually tasteless one, which was castigated by *The Times* in a leading article of 1888 as the "most pretentious, commonplace, unspiritual and dull" housing plan ever produced for a great city, a plan which gave Rome merely "a paltry and spurious copy of Paris boulevards", displaying a "poverty of artistic ideas almost amounting to genius", besides defying "all the rules of recent sanitary science in a manner incomparably its own."[1]

Augustus Hare, who quoted this thundering diatribe in the Introduction to his *Walks in Rome* (16th edition), heartily concurred. Piazza Vittorio, he wrote with ferocious gloom, was "a square of unspeakable hideousness", and the buildings in Viale Carlo Felice were "cracked and villainous houses in the worst style". After a while, the passions aroused by the modernization cooled and were then forgotten; Eleanor Clark, describing this same district in *Rome and a Villa* (1953), wrote that it has "a solid and quite pleasant middle-class look of about eighty years ago," while Piazza Vittorio seemed to her "airy, sensible and bourgeois . . ." but then, perhaps, she did not actually live in the district herself. The author of the present book did.

The railway brought into Rome not only the bureaucrats and their families, but also the immigrants from the south, in search of more menial jobs; as well as an ever-growing number of foreign visitors from the north, who, thanks to the railway, were now enabled, if they wished, to spend relatively short vacations in Italy. Although the age of the paid holiday and the inclusive tour had not yet arrived, the Italian visit was no longer the prerogative of the rich, and it is already possible to discern the pattern of modern travel from the facts that Thomas Cook established his first office in London in 1865 (by which time a million passengers had passed through his hands): while Dean & Dawson's tours began in 1871, Frame's in 1881, Lunn's in 1892, and Polytechnic (as a separate travel organization) in 1911.

English admiration for Garibaldi had been intense, and this admiration focused on the Kingdom of Italy when the latter came into being. For the first time, English visitors were actually prepared to meet and get to know individual Italians, and they entered into Italian everyday life to a degree that would have been inconceivable fifty years earlier – though there certainly still lingered the feeling that foreigners were not, of course, quite on the same plane as those who had had the good fortune to have inherited the British way of life.

The "English quarter" in Rome was still Piazza di Spagna and the environing district. Many winter visitors (for the prevailing pattern was still to winter in Italy, rather than to take a brief trip there) stayed at the

Pension Smith, run by three English spinsters at 93, Piazza di Spagna, and reputed to cater for a quiet, respectable class of boarder. Anglo-Catholics preferred the Pension Bethell, in Via del Babuino; and there were many others. The Caffè Greco still flourished on the corner of Via Condotti, though it was patronized more by artists and writers than by the quiet and respectable visitors, for whom, after 1894, Babington's Tea Room, at the foot of the Spanish Steps, would cater. According to Axel Munthe in *The Story of San Michele*, there were about this time no less than forty-four foreign doctors practising in Rome, of whom eleven were English-born and twelve American. Not all of them were entirely reputable, however:

> *We were indeed a sad crew, shipwrecks from various lands and seas, landed in Rome with our scanty kit of knowledge. We had to live somewhere, there was surely no reason why we shouldn't live in Rome as long as we didn't interfere with the living of our patients.*

There was also an English chemist in Via Condotti, and another chemist who could dispense English prescriptions, in Piazza Mignanelli. Dr. Munthe himself had his consulting rooms in the house where Keats died. There was also (again according to Dr. Munthe) an English baker.

On Sundays the English residents went dutifully to church. The Anglican church had been outside the city walls, beyond Porta del Popolo; but in the eighteen-eighties there was constructed the new Anglican Church of All Saints, whose incongruous steeple now dominates the flat-roofed Roman houses in Via del Babuino. And, near Porta San Paolo, the vacant spaces in the Protestant Cemetery gradually filled up with more or less eminent Victorians who had either accepted that they would die in Rome, or had been caught there by death unawares – for example, the sculptor John Gibson, who was buried there in 1866; William Howitt, who wrote a *History of Discovery in Australia*, and died in 1879; his wife Mary, with whom he collaborated in writing poetry (she lived till 1888); and J.A. Symonds, whose *History of the Italian Renaissance*, in seven volumes, was published between 1875 and 1886; he died in 1893.

The *vade mecum* of the English visitor to Rome between 1871 and 1914 was, of course, Augustus Hare's *Walks in Rome*. Its two volumes bound in black and red, and containing six hundred pages of closely packed information about the city, ran into sixteen editions before the author's death in 1903; and there were more editions after that, revised by St. Clair Baddeley, who continued to edit the work until its final impression in 1925. Rather to its author's surprise, it was "the one of my works which pays best"; and it did this on its own merits. It had three characteristics that set it in a class by itself.

First (and without this any guide-book would be useless) the information contained in *Walks in Rome* was meticulously accurate and always up to date. Augustus Hare paid what he called a "professional" visit to Rome about every three years for this purpose, allowing no change in the Roman scene to go unrecorded. He always prided himself on the accuracy of his facts, upon which his opinions – even if one disagreed with them – were always based.

Second, there was the clarity of his descriptions of Rome, and the skill he used in linking them together. He claimed that the book aimed at "nothing original . . . only a gathering up of the information of others, and a gleaning from what has already been given to the world in a far better and fuller, but less portable form". This was true in a sense, but the "gathering up" itself was superbly done. The book dealt with what some might consider dull facts, but to Hare himself the facts were never dull. Yet in his mastery of the subject he never forgot how differently it must appear to someone approaching it for the first time. He advised his readers not to try to see everything in Rome, but to return again and again to particularly loved spots – "to watch them, to live with them, to love them, till they have become a part of life and life's recollections". Because he himself did this, *Walks in Rome* could not fail to endure.

Thirdly, there were the quotations from other writers on Rome that were scattered throughout the work. These were as skilfully "gathered up" and slipped into the text as were the linking passages and the basic information on the ruins, churches, monuments, fountains and buildings; and the impression they collectively give is of a multiplicity of people of all kinds and of all nations who have visited Rome and gained something from their visits; yet one also feels that none of these visitors is as great and enduring as the city itself. In the Introduction to the 16th edition of the book, Hare quoted from sources as diverse as Dr. Arnold, Byron, Clough, Lanciani, Montaigne, Ouida, Mme de Staël, J.A. Symonds, *The Times* and *Popolo Romano*. In chapter II he brought in quotations also from De Brosses, Dickens, Lady Eastlake, Sir George Head, Lanzi, Merivale, Mendelssohn, Plutarch, Suetonius and Zola, among others; while other writers whose comments appeared in other chapters included Balzac, Goethe, Mrs Anna Jameson, Samuel Rogers and Cardinal Wiseman. This wide representation of writers on Rome constitutes the human element that is missing from nearly all guidebooks; yet the quotations never obtrude themselves, because Augustus Hare was able to subordinate them to the encyclopaedic richness of the memories enshrined in the buildings of Rome.

Hare himself, however, took little pleasure in his "professional" visits to Rome after 1870. Dreading the return to Rome without his adoptive mother, who had died in 1870, he refused to be romantic about his first journey, in 1873, through the Mont Cenis railway tunnel, that wonder of the age. It was "exactly like any other tunnel", he decided, and Rome was now like Paris or New York.

> *The absence of pope, cardinals and monks, the shutting up of the convents; the loss of the ceremonies; the misery caused by the terrible taxes and conscription; the voluntary exile of the Borgheses and many other noble families; the total destruction of the glorious Villa Negroni and so much else of interest and beauty; the ugly new streets in imitation of Paris and New York, all grate against one's former Roman*

associations. And to set against this there is so very little – a gayer Pincio, a live wolf on the Capitol, a mere scrap of excavation in the Forum, and all is said.

Next season it was even worse, with an incongruous Swiss chalet on the Pincio, the Quirinal Chapel "a cloak-room for balls, and the cloak-tickets kept in the holy water basins"; while such ruins as survived were being washed and scrubbed until they looked like "sham ruins built yesterday".

Throughout the later pages of his Journal, Augustus Hare continued to deplore the disappearance of old Rome. Soon there was no society left, he complained, except the "most inferior American" kind, the sort of society that flocked to see pictures by 'Leonard Vinchey'. In 1892 there was even an electrically illuminated fountain for a royal visit, where twenty years previously there would have been on such occasions a line of torches "on every step of the great staircase". Even the working class was beginning to come to Rome. He took a party of fifty-eight artisans and schoolmasters from the Toynbee Hall Institute, with some of their wives, over the Palatine. Generously, he found them "most delightful companions, and the most interested and informed audience I have ever known". He concluded that one should visit the East End "for really good, intelligent, high-minded society".

There were probably, on average, two thousand British people in Rome every winter between 1871 and 1914. No European war occurred to hinder their regular visits; the Italian internal political crises were not serious enough to interfere with their comings and goings. Europe in general was so stable that no British national required a passport at all unless he were bound for Russia or Turkey; and his handfuls of golden sovereigns could be exchanged without difficulty for almost equally stable foreign currencies.

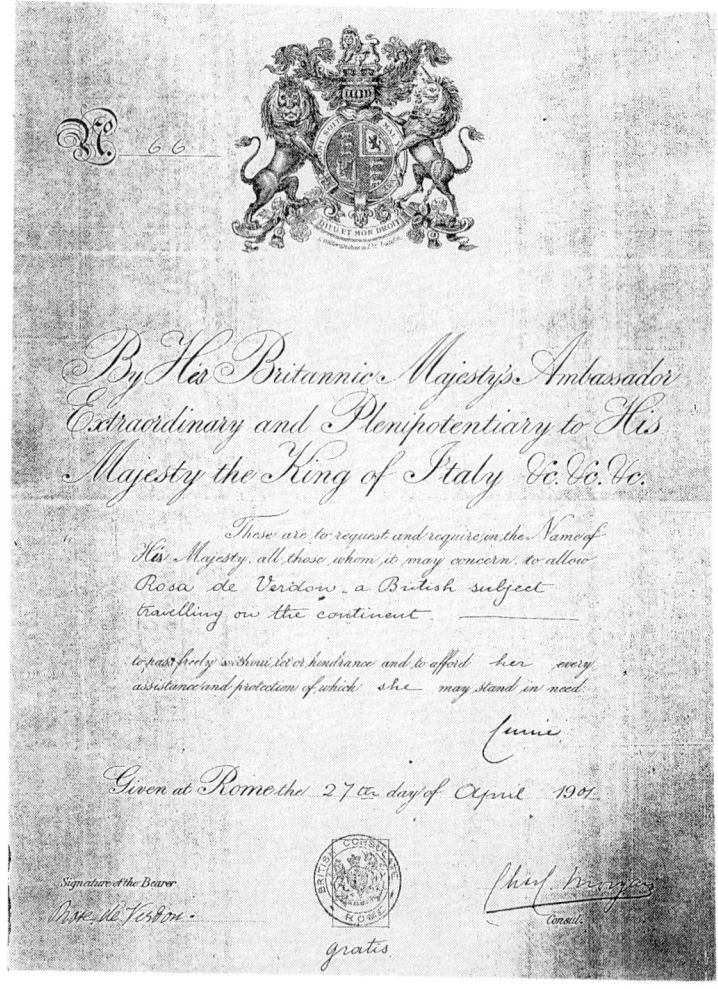

Even three months into the reign of Edward VII (1901), it was still far from customary for British subjects to hold a passport. Regulations for the issue of passports were not set until 1846; not until 1915 did a passport for foreign travel become a usual document, and even today it is not a strict legal requirement, as was convincingly argued by A.P. Herbert in one of his Misleading Cases *(1935), in which his character Albert Haddock refused to exhibit a passport when intending to travel to Calais, and subsequently was awarded damages from the Southern Railway and Constable Boot. Indeed, the right to leave the country freely (without* let or hindrance*) was a privilege established by the Magna Carta and suspended only in wartime.*

In the late nineteenth century, and in Italy especially, a few hundred pounds of unearned income went a very long way indeed. No one felt ashamed of living on it, as people are inclined to do today. The unmarried daughters of business men could and did spend their winters in Roman or Florentine *pensioni*, comfortably insulated by etiquette from the nobility above and the working class below, maintaining their accepted place in society, dabbling a little in the arts, neither needing nor wishing to augment their incomes by a wage or salary.

Such was the Anglo-Roman society in which, every year from 1871 to 1900, the two sisters Matilda and Anne Lucas moved, recording for the benefit of their Hitchin relatives the events of each winter season. Matilda Lucas was twenty-three when she first came to Rome with her sister, fifty-six when the annual habit came to an end: nearly ninety when she was persuaded to publish the edited letters in book form.

This society, rigid in its internal subdivisions, yet allowed plenty of opportunity for social intercourse. It was only a question of whom one was permitted to meet in society, and under which circumstances.

At the top of the ladder, and quite beyond the reach of the English middle class in Rome, was royalty. Members of royal families could be observed in fashionable spots, described and criticized, and the sisters would wait hours to see one; but they were the first to recognize that they did not belong at that level. They were dubious even about asking Axel Munthe to dinner, not because of his literary reputation, but because "he is the friend of Crowned Heads, and we have none to meet him." (Dr. Munthe came, however, and the dinner was a success).

Next in order of importance came the Pope and the Catholic hierarchy. The Pope was a perpetual source of interest to the English people in Rome. Even non-Catholics liked to discuss the comings and goings at the Vatican, the chances of Leo XIII being more liberal than Pius IX, the robes that the pontiffs wore, their expressions as they pronounced benediction, the prospects of their living a while longer or dying from the exhaustion induced by their perpetual duties. The Misses Lucas were delighted when they obtained their audience with

Leo XIII in 1881, and had no qualms at all about receiving the papal blessing.

Eminent priests and the minor Italian aristocracy were the highest categories in the sisters' acquaintance. Two very select people, an English Catholic *monsignore* and a noble Italian lady, had indeed to be invited separately to parties in which they were the only guests, since they could not be mixed with anyone of less social consequence. Below this level the groups were larger: "First priests, other Papalini, and the better class of English: second Liberals, chiefly Italians with a sprinkling of Italian titles, which we hold very cheap, and professional musicians: third artists, and people we had to put off from the other parties." The "better class of English" included some who were there for the season, as well as permanent residents. They were all middle class people – judges, aldermen ("it takes great courage to dine an alderman"), military men, clergymen, Oxford tutors, their great friend Mr Mangles, who had private means and had been a clerk in the India Office – and innumerable maiden ladies. Fifteen of the latter came to tea one New Year's Day, and thoroughly enjoyed themselves, "laughing and chattering over their tea, and great merriment over a round game until eleven, when as Anne said 'their broomsticks were ordered'."

Below this level came the English excursionists whom they might occasionally encounter (but did not invite), such as the English lady who came to that "most guarded place", Pension Smith in the Piazza di Spagna, on a four-day visit to Rome:

> *On the fourth day she complained that there was nothing left to see, but we think she was not doing it in an intelligent way, for she told her cabman to drive her to 'Don Giovanni' and when he looked bewildered she said: "Why, to Don Giovanni in Laterano of course."*

That completed the range of their acquaintanceship in Rome, except for one wretched man who had to be invited on his own, because he dropped his 'h's; and at the very bottom, of course, came the English servants, who were quite out of their depth in Rome, and were not encountered socially. One of them was under the impression that she and her mistress were wintering in Jerusalem.

The Lucas sisters' feelings towards Italians were of that blend of conscious effusive admiration but unconscious superiority that the English abroad usually adopted. As English commoners, they felt themselves to be undoubtedly better than the Italian aristocracy; but, not having been presented at Court in London, they could not be invited to Italian court functions.

The word 'snob' may rise easily to the mind in connexion with the Lucas sisters, but the temptation to apply it should be resisted. It is their absolute conformity with the ideals of their society, together with their original, amusing comments, that gives them their period charm. They had no use for anything in which their society was not interested, nor in any system of thought that might conceivably weaken it. Busy as bees round the honeypot of Catholicism, inviting friars and *monsignori* to tea, even on one occasion drinking the Pope's health in marsala, they still remained lifelong Protestants. Roman Catholicism represented no threat to them; but they had to take a thoroughly good look at it. But other religious faiths received short shrift. One winter there was a prominent Brahmin in Rome, giving a course of lectures on Buddhism. "We have not been to hear him" wrote Matilda Lucas briefly. "We have no time for Buddhism." It would not have been the same if they had been wintering in Peking.

Similarly with political systems. They had no inkling of the imminence of the socialist revolutions which, within fifty years of their final departure from Rome, were to eliminate their privileged society almost completely. Their only contact with a "socialist" message was at a stylish tea-party given by a wealthy American woman who expounded "Christian Socialism, not the bomb-throwing kind." One wonders what they would have said if they could have been told the future of two "unusual and charming girls" whom they met several times during the season 1881 and thought "remarkably original and clever." These girls were the sisters Beatrice and Theresa Potter, who became respectively Lady Passfield (Beatrice Webb) and Lady Parmoor (mother of Sir Stafford Cripps).

They also met Judge Hughes, author of *Tom Brown's Schooldays*, who came to Rome in 1895; George Musgrave, the Dante scholar, who was there in 1894; J.R. Green, the historian; Stillman, correspondent of *The Times*; the artist Henry Coleman; Mark Twain, whom they met in 1892, when he was at the height of his success, and whom they described as being like "a very large mop on a very small stick"; and Augustus Hare, who was "a little, dark-haired man who sits near us in church . . . he has an affected manner and rather a trying voice, which one would have to get used to . . . He is small and round-shouldered, with hair as glossy as his hat, and a very prominent nose."

They were eye-witnesses of two significant events in Anglo-Roman history. The first of these occurred in 1875, when Cardinal Manning was installed as Cardinal-Vicar of San Gregorio, the first Englishman ever to achieve this office, despite that church's almost immemorial association with the Christianization of England. On that occasion the church was crowded with English people, mainly sightseers and not many of them Catholics. The Cardinal "looked very imposing in his new robes."

> *He wore a scarlet biretta and cassock, a white fur hood and gold chain, a girdle with a gold tassel, and a most gorgeous scarlet silk cloak with a train yards long. Anne's involuntary thought was 'What a splendid evening dress it would make for Mrs Manning!' forgetting the impropriety of the idea. The Cardinal looked very thin and ascetic . . . He walked round the Church blessing us. After him came Monsignore Howard, looking much more like a Guardsman than a priest, with his great big shoulders. You know he left the Army to go into the Church.*

On Manning being read in and kissed by the four abbots of the

Augustinian convent, Matilda Lucas wrote: "I felt for him; but noticed that they had been well scrubbed up for the occasion." And afterwards:

> *He said a few words in Italian to the monks, and then made a most impressive address in English. He began by saying that he was sure it was not curiosity which had brought us here, at which I took down my eyeglass . . .*

The other event was the re-burial of Joseph Severn's body alongside that of John Keats, in 1882.

The Victorians had long been in a dilemma regarding Keats' grave. They had to respect the poet's own desire for anonymity; but at the same time they were never happier than when according honour where they considered honour was due. So Keats' tombstone itself could not be touched; but could there not be a pointer of some kind nearby, which would make it quite clear to the passer-by that here one of England's greatest poets was buried?

A retired general, one Sir Vincent Eyre, who used to winter in Rome, was the first to make the attempt. He wrote an inept five-line acrostic, each line beginning with a letter of Keats' name, had it cut in stone and inserted in the inner wall of the cemetery near Keats' grave. But the poor taste of this effort was widely criticized even at the time. Oscar Wilde (who, however, wrote a singularly embarrassing sonnet about Keats' grave) called it "a marble libel."

A much better opportunity was offered to Keats' admirers in 1879, when Severn died and was buried in the newer part of the cemetery. If they could not have Keats' name cut on Keats' own tombstone, at least they could get it on to Severn's; and to clarify matters to posterity beyond any possible doubt, they could dig up Severn's body and bury it again next to that of his friend. By 1882 these plans had been brought to fruition. The Roman authorities had given permission for the re-interment: the inscription on Keats' tombstone was completely re-cut (but the wording still not amended) in order to conform to the inscription on Severn's; and with due ceremony, marked by speeches from Adolphus Trollope and William Wetmore Story (as well as by a violent hailstorm which delayed proceedings), a mauve pall was removed from the twin tombstones to reveal the inscriptions. Severn's epitaph read as follows:

> *To the Memory of*
> JOSEPH SEVERN
> *Devoted Friend and Death Bed Companion*
> *of*
> JOHN KEATS
> *Whom he lived to see numbered among*
> *The Immortal Poets of England*
> *An Artist eminent for his Representations*
> *of Italian Life and Nature*
> *British Consul in Rome from 1861 to 1872*
> *and Officer of the Crown of Italy*
> *In Recognition of his Services to Freedom and Humanity*
> *Died 3rd August, 1879*
> *Aged 85*

Matilda Lucas wrote:

> *The ceremony ended by planting a small tree, a stone pine, which will need at least fifty years to develop. Severn's body had, by special permission, been removed from the newer part of the old cemetery. I wish they had removed Shelley instead.*

A hundred years after that re-burial, the Romantics are out of fashion, and though everyone respects Keats, few read him, while the English who used to winter in Rome in their thousands have vanished. For the benefit of the modern tourist, a slit has been cut in the wall of the Protestant cemetery, so that the two famous graves can be quickly glimpsed without unnecessary waste of time; but those who are interested can still make their way through the cemetery to the extreme north-western corner, where they can ponder over the graves of the poet, the artist, and one of the artist's children; the retired general's well-meant acrostic; a bed of violets that flowers every spring – and the two stone pines now towering fifty feet above this peaceful scene where, at last, Keats' grave has recaptured something of the obscurity he sought for it.

When Matilda and Anne Lucas lived in Rome, they often used to go sketching or botanizing in the Campagna, which then abounded in anemones, crocuses, jonquils, narcissi, bee orchis, rosemary, daphne, cyclamen, cowslip, borage, wild gladioli and autumn daisies, and offered innumerable subjects to the water-colourist:

> . . . *a mass of peach blossom against a middle distance of blue Campagna, and beyond it a gold band of sea in the afternoon sunlight, is one of the loveliest sights I ever saw.*

But they did not visit the Campagna during the height of summer, nor did they ever stay in Rome then. The traditional dangers of the Campagna at that season were still feared. As late as 1875 two English ladies had been "intimidated" and robbed by bandits in the Campagna, though this was admitted to be an exceptional occurrence. It seemed that nothing would ever eliminate either the malaria or the heat.

The associations of the English with Roman malaria had indeed lasted almost immemorially long. There is a tradition that Rahere, jester of Henry II, who was on a pilgrimage to Rome in the twelfth century and fell ill with malaria there, vowed that he would found a church in London should he recover – which was the origin of St. Bartholomew the Great and, later, St. Bartholomew's Hospital. At least one English writer (J.C. Eustace) died of the disease in Italy. So did Hugh of Evesham, a thirteenth century cardinal whose titular church was S.

Lorenzo in Lucina. He had been summoned to Rome by the Pope (Martin IV) to act as his personal physician – and to rid Rome of malaria. On the contrary, malaria got rid of him.

It seems appropriate, therefore, that when, right at the end of the nineteenth century, the "noxious vapours" theory of the origin of malaria was finally disproved, the credit should have been equally shared between British and Roman scientists. In 1897, Sir Ronald Ross discovered the malaria parasite in the body of the *Anopheles* mosquito. The following year Giovanni Grassi, in Rome, proved that this is the only mosquito that can transmit malaria. The matter was clinched in 1900 by the work of Sir Patrick Manson, in the newly-formed London School of Tropical Medicine. In that year, infected mosquitoes were brought from Italy to London and allowed to bite Manson's son, who duly developed malaria. At the same time, three of Manson's assistants spent the malaria season in a mosquito-proof hut in the Campagna – and remained in perfect health. Thereafter, scientific control of the *Anopheles* mosquito quickly eliminated the disease from the Campagna, one of the first malarial areas of the world to be so freed. Artists and tourists (and suburban developers too) could visit it with impunity. Thus Rome needed to be avoided in the summer only by those who disliked heat *per se*. Separated from the association with disease, the Roman summer heat began to be regarded as more of a friend than an enemy. The way was being paved for the sunburned tourists, the overcrowded Lido di Roma, the excavations at Ostia Antica and the petrol filling stations and ice-cream bars spreading inexorably over the Campagna.

The season of 1893 was a particularly splendid and gay one. In that year Pope Leo XIII celebrated his episcopal jubilee, and received the Princess of Wales, later Queen Alexandra, while King Umberto and Queen Margherita celebrated their silver wedding. There were so many British visitors that the inauguration of Babington's Tea Room – first in the Via dei due Marcelli in 1893, then in the Piazza di Spagna the following year – filled a long-felt want. The Tea Room was started as a business by Miss Anna Maria Babington (a descendant of Andrew

Babington, a Catholic who had been executed in 1586 for leading a conspiracy against Elizabeth I), in partnership with Miss Isobel Cargill, a New Zealander, whose ancestor Donald Cargill had also been executed for treason – though he was a Protestant who preached in Scotland against Charles II. Babington's Tea Room stepped immediately into its proper place in the life of the foreign colony in Rome, attracting all those who could not but feel slightly out of place in the Bohemian setting of the Caffè Greco.

At the turn of the century, one of the last of the determinedly unconventional journeys to Rome was undertaken, by Hilaire Belloc, who described his pilgrimage in detail in *The Path to Rome*, first published in 1902.

The Path to Rome was unconventional in that it was a throwback; a deliberate recession to the habits of much earlier centuries. Hilaire Belloc chose to go to Rome on foot, as a pilgrim, in fulfilment of a vow made in the church of his native valley, in Lorraine.

> *I said: "I will start from the place where I served in arms for my sins; I will walk all the way and take advantage of no wheeled thing; I will sleep rough and cover thirty miles a day, and I will hear mass every morning; and I will be present at high mass in St. Peter's on the feast of St. Peter and St. Paul."*

Not one of these resolutions was he able, finally, to keep, except the last; and he made the journey still more artificial by deciding to keep a straight line between Toul, his starting point, and Rome; he did not, like the early pilgrims, follow a well-travelled route along which travelled many other pilgrims who walked because they could not afford to ride.

The first stretch of Hilaire Belloc's journey was not difficult, since by a happy chance the valley of the Upper Moselle points directly towards Rome; and the Vosges, where this river rises, are easy mountains. But after crossing the Belfort Gap and advancing towards the Jura, Belloc soon found himself in extreme difficulties when he tried to cross the Alps in a dead straight line. His shoes worn through at the soles, his thin clothes quite inadequate for high mountains, he yet struggled to climb ridges, descend escarpments, and face the ice-cold, towering proximity of "these magnificent creatures of God, I mean the Alps." He had seen them for the first time when sixty miles away; stretching, it seemed, across the sky, barring his way:

> . . . *peak and field and needle of intense ice, remote, remote from the world. Sky beneath them and sky above them, a steadfast legion, they glittered as though with the armour of the immovable armies of Heaven.*

The Alps defeated him. He had to compromise, and follow a tourist route for some miles of the way. Then he made forced marches towards Milan, where money awaited him; finally he had no option but to complete the last twenty-five miles to Milan in a "wheeled thing", namely, a railway train, paying the last of his francs for a single ticket, and thereby becoming:

> . . . *that rarest and ultimate kind of traveller, the man without any money whatsoever – without passport, without letters, without food or wine; it would be interesting to see what would follow if the train broke down.*

The straight line from Toul and the Moselle valley to Milan does, when protracted, rather surprisingly continue almost exactly through Piacenza, Siena, Viterbo and Rome. This was the route that Belloc now followed as nearly as he could. He crossed the flat and muddy Lombardy plain, passed through Piacenza (where it rained continually), and after crossing more rivers and finding himself on the Via Emilia, he arrived in Tuscany where, still not very proficient in Italian, he conversed in Latin with a village priest, while the villagers looked on admiringly. He went through Lucca ("and of that also I will say nothing") and, succumbing once more to temptation by the "wheeled thing", took the train to Siena ("where the railway ends and goes no further."). Then finally he walked to Viterbo and to Rome.

But concerning Rome itself he kept a deliberate silence, much to the disappointment of his character 'Lector', who jumps into the pages of the book from time to time in a vain attempt to call 'Auctor' to order, and keep his thoughts in as straight a line as his course through Europe:

> *LECTOR: But do you intend to tell us nothing of Rome?*
> *AUCTOR: Nothing, dear Lector.*
> *LECTOR: Tell me at least one thing; did you see the Coliseum?"*

And yet 'Auctor' did reveal one fact, which dates the book. There were at that time horse-trams in Rome.

> *At the foot of the hill I prepared to enter the city, and I lifted up my heart.*
>
> *There was an open space; a tramway; a tram upon it about to be drawn by two lean and tired horses whom in the heat many flies disturbed. There was dust on everything around.*

Despite its artificiality, its conscious archaisms of style and vocabulary, *The Path to Rome* is a moving, vivid book, with a sense of purpose that never leaves its author nor his readers. It is also one of the last descriptions written of a journey to Rome before the coming of the internal combustion engine – an invention that would once more profoundly alter the timing, the routes and the social habits of all English travel to Italy. Through Belloc's eyes, we look almost for the last time on the bucolic scene of village inns, meals at a franc a time, wheeled carts and sad horses, that still covered all of Europe where the railway did not run – a scene that the modern tourist can discover only in the remotest districts, fleetingly, and usually by chance.

A new "path to Rome" was opened up early in the twentieth century, with the establishment of the British School at Rome. Although English-speaking theological students had for many centuries enjoyed the opportunity of institutional study in Rome – first at the Schola Saxonum, then at the English Hospice from the twelfth to the sixteenth century, later at the Venerable English College that succeeded the Hospice, since 1852 also at the Beda College, founded by Pius IX for the training of convert Anglican clergymen and Nonconformist ministers, which in its early years occupied the fourth floor of the English College – there had not, so far, been any equivalent place of study for students of the fine arts and archaeology.

This began to be remedied in 1901, when the British School at Rome was originally founded as a School of Archaeology; and ten years later a complicated set of circumstances brought about its transformation into a school of archaeology, fine art and medieval history. In 1911, an International Exhibition of Fine Arts was held in Rome, on the outskirts of the Villa Borghese; and the temporary façade of the British Pavilion there, designed by Sir Edwin Lutyens, made such a favourable impression in Roman artistic circles that an unexpected offer was received from the municipality of the site temporarily occupied by the Pavilion – on condition that a building should be constructed there, embodying the admired façade in permanent form, and that the building should be used for some purpose of cultural character.

The opportunity, too good to miss, was taken to establish in Rome a British national Academy of Arts. The existing school of archaeology became in 1912 the Faculty of Archaeology, History and Letters of the new institute; and at the same time Faculties of Architecture, Painting, Sculpture and Engraving were established. The School received a Royal Charter, and work started the same year on the new building. Because of the first World War, the building was not ready for occupation until

1916, and not in fact occupied until after 1918. Subsequent additions completed the building programme in 1938 – a year before another World War again interrupted the free flow of Anglo-Italian artistic relations, and removed Rome once more from the English traveller's map.

In the meantime, in 1917, the Beda College moved to new premises in the Via San Nicolo da Tolentino, with about forty-five students. Two years after that, another English Cardinal, Francis Neil Gasquet, became Vatican Librarian. He had lived in Rome since 1907, and at the time of his appointment as librarian was 72 years old. In 1920 he published the *History of the Venerable English College*.

During the twenty years between the two world wars, there were still many English, and still more American, tourists in Rome; and Piazza di Spagna remained the centre of English-speaking life in the city. E.V. Lucas wrote, in *A Wanderer in Rome* (1926):

> *English is heard sporadically all over Rome . . . but in the Piazza di Spagna it may be said to be the only tongue. For the Piazza di Spagna has the libraries, the tourist bureaus, the tea rooms; it is the capital of the artists' colony; it has antiquity shops and apartment agents; it is close to the Pincio with its gardens and views, and it is one of the parts of old Rome nearest to the new Ludovisi quarter with the fashionable hotels in the latest manner and the elegant and sumptuous flats.*

The patrons of the fashionable hotels and the tenants of the sumptuous flats could even keep their money in a bank with an English name; for in 1925 an Italian company, Barclays Bank S.A.I., opened a branch in Piazza di Spagna, which continued in existence until it was sold to the Banca Commerciale Italiana at the end of 1950.

Most of the between-wars visitors to Rome travelled there by train, arriving at the new terminal station after a wide sweep round the southern suburbs, so that they really approached the city from the south; a circumstance which deprived the English traveller of the traditional distant first view of the dome of St. Peter's, clearly visible above the vague outlines of the city around it. E.V. Lucas thought it worthwhile to mention, in the Preface to *A Wanderer in Rome*, that the rail journey from London to Rome now only involved one night in the train. If this fact were more widely known, he pointed out, there would be more visitors to Rome.

There were more visitors in the short term, but the tradition of wintering in Rome, which had achieved such a long history, was now practically dead. Prices had risen; few people could live on the interest from their investments any more. When Rome was so quickly and easily accessible, there was no reason why the ordinary visitor should prolong his stay more than was necessary or financially practicable. Once more, as at the start of the Grand Tour period, only those visitors who had professional reasons for a prolonged visit – artists and theologians in particular – were there for any length of time.

Many writers and artists were now much more attracted to France than to Italy; and of those who still loved Italy best, not many were drawn to Rome. Arnold Bennett was a 'Florentine' rather than a 'Roman' (he completed one of his novels there, and thought that "Florence is certainly an ideal place to write a novel in, or at least to arrange your ideas for a novel in"). Norman Douglas wrote chiefly about Calabria and Capri. D.H. Lawrence, although he was a frequent visitor to Italy, and lived in various parts of that country for some six years of his life (a year or two each at Lerici, Florence, Capri and Taormina), was not at all attracted to Rome. In December 1919 he had expressed interest in going there, on the somewhat naive grounds that he might be better or happier as a result, since "one seems drawn to the great historic past, now that the present has become so lamentably historic". But after visiting it for the first time, in December 1919, he wrote briefly: "Rome was tawdry and so *crowded*, I hated it." He scarcely ever referred to the place in his later letters except as somewhere to collect money, letters or a new passport; as a mere staging-post, in fact, between

Florence and Naples.

Mussolini was certainly partly responsible for the antagonism felt towards Italy by many intellectuals in the nineteen twenties and thirties; they felt little enthusiasm, for example, for the construction of the wide new approach to St. Peter's instituted by the Fascist government about the time of the Vatican Treaty in 1929, which involved the demolition of innumerable old buildings; or for the grandiose processional thoroughfares that were built in 1933 on both sides of the Capitol and the Forum, leading up to the Victor Emanuel Monument.

One English minor novelist, however, felt quite at home in Rome, and indeed he died there. He was Ronald Firbank, dilettante, epigone, yet a principal innovator of the inconsequential dialogue that characterized early twentieth century novel-writing. One of his novels, *Concerning the Eccentricities of Cardinal Pirelli*, was published in 1926, the year of his death. It has one chapter set in Rome, "at the season when the oleanders are in full perfection", in the Pope's apartments, from where:

> *. . . it was charming to catch from time to time the distant sound of Rome – the fitful clamour of trams and cabs, and the plash of the great twin-fountains in the court of St. Damascus.*

Firbank died in a Rome hotel in May 1926, having, it is said, discouraged his friends from visiting him, owing to the dreadfulness of the wallpaper in the bedroom. He was buried in the Protestant cemetery in error (he was a Catholic), and was later removed to the *Monumentale*, the vast, ornate, Roman Catholic burial ground beyond the Porta San Lorenzo.

One more link with the Anglo-Roman past was severed in 1926, with the demolition of the Villa Mills which used to stand at the top of the Palatine. This building, described by E.V. Lucas just before it was pulled down, dated from the seventeenth century. It was bought by

Charles Andrew Mills, a West Indian sugar planter who arrived in Rome in 1817; and the house then became known as the Villa Mills. C.A. Mills died in 1846, at the age of 86, and was the last private resident of the Palatine Hill. The Villa subsequently became a convent and then stood in ruins, "yet another – but compared to the Caesars' palaces how flimsy – monument to Decay!" as E.V. Lucas put it.

Between 1939 and 1944, Rome again became virtually inaccessible to British travellers; designs to visit it had an inescapably military flavour. "I look forward" wrote Lt.-Gen. Montgomery in February 1943, "to leading the Eighth Army into Rome. By Jove, what a party!"[2]

It is not given even to generals, however, to forecast their future movements across battlefields with absolute accuracy. After Mussolini's dismissal, in July 1943, and Italy's subsequent peace overtures, it was finally decided that Rome and Naples should be captured. But President Roosevelt was not in favour of an Allied advance much beyond Rome, and he insisted, in opposition to the Chiefs of Staff, that Rome should be regarded as an open city. After the Eighth Army had crossed the Strait of Messina at Reggio di Calabria, in September 1943, and the American Fifth Army had occupied Naples the following month, a decision was taken to prepare elsewhere than in Italy for the main attack on Germany. General Montgomery, together with four American and three British divisions, was moved to Britain with this in view.

So it was not until the following year that Rome was occupied by the Anglo-American armies. The British landing at Anzio, in January 1944, one of whose objects had been the capture of Rome, resulted only in the establishment of a beach-head; not until nearly the end of May, after the taking of Monte Cassino, was the road to Rome open. On 4 June 1944, American troops of the Fifth Army were the first to enter Rome. Appropriately, one of the Roman squares that they occupied was Piazza di Spagna. H.V. Morton described how the arrival of the Allied troops appeared to the Italian curator of the Keats-Shelley Memorial:

It was a calm moonlit night. The last Germans had gone; the last bursts of machine-gun fire were over. The silence was unearthly as even the usual sound of La Barcaccia *was stilled, for the conduits had been bombed and, like all the fountains of Rome, it was dry. Suddenly a voice was heard calling from one of the windows in the Piazza di Spagna that the Allies were coming! She heard the rumble of approaching tanks. Then two files of armed figures passed silently in the moonlight. Then an order was given and a halt was made. The Piazza was crowded. There in the moonlight the soldiers slept: on the pavements, in the dried-up fountain, on the Spanish Steps. For a moment it seemed to Signora Cacciatore that all these men were dead, victims of a silent battle fought in the piazza.*[3]

The following morning, at six o'clock, the Keats-Shelley Memorial received its first Anglo-American visitors of the post-Fascist era – A.C. Sedgwick, a *New York Times* correspondent with the Fifth Army, and Captain Morgan, a British officer.

CONCLUSION

It is time to pause, to look back over the centuries, and to look around Rome with a view to discovering what traces have been left in the city by two thousand years of "English-speaking" travel.

What better place to start than Piazza di Spagna itself? For more than three hundred years this has been the place to which English travellers to Rome have first turned for lodging, for social life and for their reminders of home. There can be no city square in Europe so crammed with British and American associations, although it is not in fact a "square", being shaped more like an hour-glass: two open spaces joined by a connecting, truncated, slightly narrower space in which the fountain of La Barcaccia provides a focal point for the whole concept.

The fountain has been here since 1627, a hundred years before the so-called "Spanish Steps" were constructed, leading up to Trinità dei Monti. The history of the fountain runs parallel to that of the English who made the Piazza so much their own that the Italians used to refer to it as "the English ghetto". The fountain had been in position only eleven years when the brothers Nicholas and Henry Stone rented a house in this district; seventeen years when John Evelyn, directed to what he called "Piazza Spagnola", also lodged here during his Roman winter.

If we stand at the foot of the steps, near the fountain, on the spot where the peasant girls and young men used to wait to be hired out as models for the English artists, and where Augustus Hare used to meet the ladies who arrived for his sketching-parties, with their footmen and their luncheon-baskets, we are within sight of a number of places with Anglo-Roman associations: the Keats-Shelley Memorial – no. 26 Piazza di Spagna, where in 1814 John Mayne lodged, and where later Axel Munthe advised the hypochondriacs of Anglo-Roman society; on the other side of the steps, Babington's Tea Room (no. 23); across the *piazza*, on the corner of Via Condotti (no. 86, via Condotti) is the Caffè Greco – modernized, but still full of memories. One of the last of its Bohemian habitués, the poet C.H. Geoghegan, self-styled *bardo errante*, died as recently as 1941.

In the Piazza are also the British Consulate-General, the bank that for twenty-five years bore the name of Barclay's, Anderson's picture shop and the American Express.

Our first 'Walk in Rome' is a relatively short one, and will cover the points of interest contained in the triangle formed by Via del Babuino, Via del Corso and Via del Tritone. All this area owes its inception to the town planning schemes of Sixtus V (1585-90). It was uninhabited (except for the newly-completed Via Sistina) in 1587, but very rapidly became popular first with the artists, then with the tourists, then with the various trades that cater for and batten on the tourist – a sequence of events not unfamiliar in the modern world, both in Italy and elsewhere. When this occurs in tourist resorts nowadays, the artists usually pack up and leave as soon as the hotel managers move in. But in Rome there are still some artists' studios in the Via Margutta, parallel to Via del Babuino.

In Via del Babuino (the street where Edward Lear lived when he first came to Rome) are the Anglican church of All Saints, and the English "Lion Book Shop" (no. 181). At the northern end of this street is Piazza del Popolo, which dates from 1589, though the celebrated "twin churches" were built almost a hundred years later. Until the coming of the railway (and since the coming of the motor-car) this square was the traditional point of entry into Rome from the north. Here Gibbon, Smollett, Wilkes and Boswell were in turn held up at the Custom

House; here Belloc, last of the great pedestrians, observed the horse-trams; here everyone noted the three straight streets that led out of the *piazza* into the heart of the city – Via Ripetta, the oldest, which dates from 1518, Via del Babuino, and Via del Corso, along which the Carnival processions and races passed.

Coming down the Via del Corso on the other side of our triangle, we note, at no. 375, the plaque put up by the municipality of Rome to commemorate (on the centenary of his birth) Percy Bysshe Shelley's stay in a house where he wrote *Prometheus Unbound* and *The Cenci.*

Reaching Via del Tritone and turning left into it, we turn left again to arrive at Via della Mercede (near the Post Office), where there is another of the municipality's blue plaques on the lodgings briefly occupied by Sir Walter Scott in 1831. In the heart of the triangular area, there is another plaque to mark the flat, in Via Bocca di Leone, where Robert and Elizabeth Barrett Browning lived. From there we return to Via Condotti (where Edward Lear had his rooms in 1859-60), and so back to Piazza di Spagna.

If time permits, we can climb the steps up to Trinità dei Monti, and a little distance to the south-west, where Via Sistina is joined by Via Crispi, is the place where the "green and gold chariot" stood outside the house occupied by Robert Adam. The gardens of the Pincio (where John Keats, on doctor's orders, unwillingly rode on horseback, and where Augustus Hare so often walked to admire the view over towards St. Peter's) and of the Villa Borghese (designed by Jacob More, "More of Rome") should perhaps be included in this walk, though they lie outside the triangle and are some distance from Piazza di Spagna. In the Borghese gardens, near the Porta Pinciana, at the *Casina delle Rose* restaurant, is the statue erected to the memory of Lord Byron. In the gardens of the Villa Giulia (adjoining the Borghese gardens) is the building of the British School at Rome.

The second walk will require a full day, since it will take us from Piazza di Spagna to St. Peter's and the Vatican City, then up on to the Janiculum and down again into Trastevere. Again starting from the foot of the steps in Piazza di Spagna, we cross Via del Tritone and come immediately upon Via Poli (where Nathaniel Hawthorne lodged) and the Trevi Fountain, familiar to every tourist. A few streets and squares further on is the Pantheon, and the maze of little streets and squares where Inigo Jones wandered. In one of these is the French church of S. Luigi dei Francesi, and just beyond this church is a street with the unusual name of *Via del Pozzo delle Cornacchie* – the Street of the Well of the Crows. Georgina Masson has pointed out[1] that this name is derived from the arms of Cardinal Wolsey, which were two crows standing on either side of a rose. The Cardinal built here a palace in which he never lived. A well in the courtyard of the palace probably bore his arms.

Returning to the Pantheon, we strike southwards to the Corso Vittorio Emanuele and on into the district of which Via Giulia used to be the principal street. Running parallel with Via Giulia (on the side distant from the river) is Via Monserrato, in which is the Venerable English College, established six hundred years ago (1362) and claiming to be the oldest English institution abroad. Here can be seen the memorial to the students of the College who suffered martyrdom for their faith, the library, which contains the archives of the English Hospice and of the College. In the College church of S. Tommaso di Canterbury is the tomb of Cardinal Bainbridge, Henry VIII's first ambassador to the Holy See; he died in Rome in 1514.

Next we proceed northwards along the bank of the Tiber, and cross the river by the Ponte Vittorio Emanuele II, which brings us into the district once known as the Schola Saxonum and as the *burh*. The modern church of S. Spirito in Sassia ("modern" in that it dates only from the sixteenth century) stands on the site of St. Mary of the Saxons, but of the earlier building no trace remains. The name Borgo, however, has been perpetuated in the street names hereabouts – Borgo S. Spirito (on the site of the Saxon quarter), Borgo S. Angelo, Borgo Pio, Borgo Vittorio and Borgo Angelico, as well as Lungotevere in Sassia.

Approaching St. Peter's by the Via della Conciliazione, we see on the right the Palazzo Torlonia, which was built between 1496 and 1504 and served, until the Reformation, as the seat of Henry VIII's Embassy. In St. Peter's itself the best known monument of Anglo-Roman interest is the elaborate tomb designed by Canova in 1819 for the Old Pretender and his sons. One of the oldest is the tomb of Pope Adrian IV in the Crypt. One of the least known (discovered by H.V. Morton and described in *A Traveller in Rome*) is a room in the office of the *Sanpietrini* (who look after the fabric of St. Peter's and dig the Papal graves), of which the doors bear the Royal Arms of England above a Cardinal's hat. These doors once formed part of a house belonging to Cardinal York, Henry Stuart. In the Vatican Library, an interesting item on display to the public consists of the love letters written by Henry VIII to Ann Boleyn. There is also a signed copy of his book *Assertio Septem Sacramentarum*, for which he was awarded the title of Defender of the Faith.

Returning to the Borgo S. Spirito, and climbing the hill of the Janiculum, the next place of interest we come to is the Garibaldi Monument, where one of that hero's followers who is commemorated is John Whitehead Peard, "Garibaldi's Englishman". He, on one occasion, was mistaken for Garibaldi himself, and hailed by the population of an Italian town as their liberator. A little further on, in the Via delle Mura Gianicolense, is the Salvator Mundi International Hospital, known to many present day members of the British and American colonies in Rome. Then the church of S. Pietro in Montorio, where are buried the Earls of Tyrone and Tyrconnel, who led a conspiracy against Elizabeth I and fled to Rome when it failed. At the bottom of the hill is the district of Trastevere, in whose best known church, S. Cecilia in Trastevere, is the tomb of Adam Easton, of Hertford, who was titular cardinal of the church. The tomb is decorated with the arms of the Plantagenets.

The next walk is also a long one. It will take us from Piazza di Spagna southwards to the Capitol and the Roman Forum, and right out to the Lateran Palace and the Aurelian Wall. Half way between our starting point and the Capitol is the Piazza dei Santi Apostoli, where stands the Palazzo Balestra (formerly Palazzo Muti), above whose main

The English Road To Rome

door used to stand, for almost fifty years in the eighteenth century, the Royal Arms of England, Scotland and Ireland, when the palace was rented to the Stuarts. On the Capitol, we shall find no memorial plaque in the church of S. Maria in Aracoeli to remind us of Gibbon's moment of inspiration. But perhaps we do not need one. A lesser degree of inspiration is recalled, in the Capitoline Museum, by the marble faun that gave Nathaniel Hawthorne the idea for his fantasy of the same name. In the Palazzo dei Conservatori, opposite, is the last surviving fragment of Claudius' triumphal arch commemorating the invasion of Britain in A.D. 43. The first four letters of the word BRITannia can still be seen. All the rest of the arch now forms part of the transept of St. John Lateran. On the way from the Forum to the Colosseum, the church of S. Francesca Romana and the Arch of Constantine are in themselves sufficient memorials to Inigo Jones, measuring, admiring and rediscovering there the principles of classical architecture. The church of S. Francesca Romana, however, does contain a picture, above the sacristy door, which is of interest to the English traveller. It shows Reginald Pole in conversation with Pope Paul III. The Colosseum might remind us of the 1820 Romantics in its moonlit ruins, or of Dr. Deakin carefully searching for and describing the 420 species of plants growing on the six acres of ruined site.

The church of S. Gregorio Magno is a real place of pilgrimage for the English traveller. Here St. Gregory built his original church about 575, next to his own palace. From here St. Augustine left in 596 on his mission to convert the English. Here Sir Edward Carne is buried; also another religious exile, Robert Pecham. Here Cardinal Manning was installed in 1875 as Cardinal-Vicar. And very close to S. Gregorio is another church with English associations – the church of SS. Giovanni e Paolo, in the Piazza of the same name. This church was rebuilt by Adrian IV during his term of office, and of the twelfth century work there still remain today the apse, with its graceful gallery of columns (the only example of Lombard architecture in Rome); the porch, with a tablet recording further restoration by Cardinal Spellman of New York, in the 1950 Holy Year, and the two stone lions couched one on either side of the main door. The campanile dates from the thirteenth century; the small dome is of a later date. All the buildings in the *piazza* are part of the church, which thus dominates the square not in the way that the Trevi fountain dominates its square, or St. Peter's dominates Rome – the church *is* the *piazza*, and the yellow ochre and dark red *piazza* (the city colours of Rome and the characteristic hue of her buildings), seen for example on a warm afternoon, with hardly a sound to be heard apart from the hourly chiming of the bell, makes the Middle Ages extremely real for the traveller. But all this part of Rome, leading towards St. John Lateran, has retained to a remarkable degree the peaceful, half-deserted air that so greatly appealed to the English visitor before 1870. This may be one reason why there are so many buildings with English and Irish associations here – first the church of S. Stefano Rotondo, containing a chapel where Donough O'Brian, King of Cashel and Thomond, and son of Brian Boru, is buried; then the hospital and convent of the English Blue Sisters, and finally the Irish College (which has only been on its present site since 1927).

Then comes the Lateran Palace, and St. John Lateran (one of the few churches outside England so familiar to English-speaking visitors that its name has become anglicized), and in one of the few open spaces spared by the post-1870 "urbanization" of this quarter, the Villa Wolkonsky which houses the British Embassy.

From here we might return to Piazza di Spagna via Stazione Termini, known to countless British visitors in modern times, and near the spot where the Acqua Pia Marcia was brought into Rome by James Shepherd's limited company.

The fourth and final walk really requires not a stout pair of shoes but a helicopter, since we still have to make a rapid round trip on the periphery of Rome. Far away on the right bank of the Tiber, on the Monte Mario, is the Villa Mellini. This was once occupied by that starry-eyed character the Earl-Bishop of Bristol and Derry, and is now the home of the Astronomical Institute. Nearly as far from Piazza di Spagna in the other direction, beyond the University City and the Church of S. Lorenzo fuori le Mura, is the cemetery of Campo Verano, where Ronald

Firbank is buried. Further to the south, just beyond the well known chapel of Domine Quo Vadis, on the Via Appia Antica, is a much less well known small circular chapel, built by Cardinal Reginald Pole to mark the spot where St. Peter's vision may have occurred.

Directly to the south is the modern building of the FAO (Food and Agriculture Organization of the United Nations), visited by many British and American scientists and administrators in our own day. Also to the south, but nearer the Tiber, is the church of San Paolo fuori le Mura, near where, since 1959, the Beda College has finally moved into its own collegiate building.

Finally, and appropriately, there is the Protestant Cemetery, close to the San Paolo Gate and the Pyramid of Caius Cestius. Here we might take the trouble to go round to the main gate, and walk slowly past the closely-packed tombstones, half concealed by the cypresses and bay trees, that stretch steeply up to the inner side of the Aurelian Wall. Here, if anywhere in Rome, can something of the essence of romantic poetry be found, something of the Arcadia that Keats, Shelley and Byron came to Italy to find. There can be few more beautiful cemeteries in the world. In this silent place the dead easily outnumber the few living people who come to visit them. Although the physical elements (the trees, plants, marble, earth) that make up its sad beauty are unmistakably Italian, the site belongs spiritually not to the noisy, sunny, public civilization of the Mediterranean, but to the cool, dark North. Many of the inscriptions on the gravestones are in English; but not all of them. There are some in German (Goethe's son August is buried in the cemetery), Dutch, Swedish, French, even Italian and Russian. Among the English and American celebrities whose names can be found here are Keats, Severn, Shelley, his friend Trelawney, R.M. Ballantyne who wrote *Coral Island*), William Wetmore Story and his wife, William Howitt and his wife Mary, John Addington Symonds, Rosa Bathurst (who, with her horse, was swept into the Tiber in 1824) and C.A. Mills of the 'Villa Mills'. Just across the road from the cemetery is another one of a different character, the British Military Cemetery, which contains the graves of some four hundred British soldiers who died in the vicinity of Rome in 1944.

Considering the number and variety of these English memorials scattered throughout Rome, not to speak of the many thousands more English-speaking visitors who came to Rome during one century or another, but left no monument or specific association with a street or building, it is a little surprising to find so few comments by Italians on this perennial presence of travellers from the North, who claimed the city of Rome as part of their own historical, literary or artistic heritage, yet would have so little to do with the native inhabitants. I have come across only one book – *Roma e gli Inglesi*, by Livio Iannatoni – that deals specifically with the subject of the English in Rome, from the Italian point of view. This is essentially an illustrated description of a few Anglo-Roman monuments, and attempts no critical evaluation. There is an astonishing dearth of satirical comment, considering that the Grand Tourist in particular was the ideal subject for satire. Now and then a little gentle fun has been poked at this type of visitor (the character who says that the Colosseum will be a fine building when it is finished, or who covets a marble angel on a Papal tomb). But even the Roman satirical poet G.G. Belli (1791-1863) only has a few sly and harmless references to "all the English of Piazza di Spagna". The satire has never been savage.

Perhaps they hardly noticed us, after all, though there were many more *inglesi italianati* than *italiani inglesiati*, at least until the nineteenth century, when political persecution led to a steady influx of Italians into England. After the revolutions in Piedmont and Naples in 1820-21, for example, some Italians came as refugees to England. They could only earn a living by competing with one another as teachers of their native tongue. So little scope was there for this kind of work that even the most successful of them, Antonio Panizzi, who became Professor of Italian at London University, and British Museum librarian, could only secure half a dozen students at a time. Later in the nineteenth century came the first wave of restaurateurs who gave Soho a character which was at the same time quasi-Italian and entirely typical of London. In the second half of the twentieth century came the purveyors of *espresso* coffee and *pizze*. They had some effect on English social and gastronomic habits, but can hardly be said to have influenced the course of British culture.

One of the few *italiani inglesiati* who achieved a little celebrity was Giuseppe Barretti, a friend of Samuel Johnson, who wrote *An Account of the Manners and Customs of Italy* (1768) in order to counter the erroneous ideas put about by certain English writers (now happily forgotten) on the subject of Italy. Even he was remarkably courteous and restrained; saddened rather than moved to anger by the conventional behaviour of the English tourist:

> *No English traveller that ever I heard ever went a step or two out of those roads, which from the foot of the Alps lead straight to our most favoured cities. None of them ever will deign to visit those places whose names are not in every body's mouth. They travel to see things, and not men.*

Do they still? It would seem so, though today, the Autostrada del Sole has supplanted the winding roads that used to carry the creaking carriages of the Grand Tourists from the foot of the Alps to the "most favoured cities". The favoured cities are, perhaps, less likely to be Venice, Florence and Rome than the crowded beaches of the Adriatic or of the Riviera, or the Isles of Capri and Elba.

What is left of the traditional visit to Rome? Not much, it appears. Apart from Rome Scholars at the British School, employees of international organizations such as FAO, students of the Roman Catholic colleges, the employees of airlines and members of the Foreign Service, few British people now have the opportunity to spend even one complete winter in Rome. Rome does not yield her secrets easily to the transient visitor, of whom there have been more and more as twentieth century transport facilities have improved. On the other hand, that very transport expertise has not been entirely a bad thing. In the eighteenth century, it was scarcely possible to contemplate more than one visit to Rome in a single lifetime; today, it has become perfectly possible to visit Rome repeatedly, to refresh one's knowledge of odd corners or aspects of it, to look at districts omitted on a previous visit.

The trouble is that there is so much to see. Somerset Maugham, who set some of his stories in Rome, once complained that the worst thing about growing old is the intolerable burden of individual memories that the old man has to carry about with him; a burden from which death will at last, and perhaps not unwelcomingly, set him free. It is rather like that with Rome (except that Rome itself seems incapable of dying). The more visitors Rome has had, the more innumerable the memories. the more marked the feeling that the weight of history there is just more than can be grasped or borne. C. Day Lewis seems to have been trying to express this, in his poem *An Italian Visit*, written in 1948/49, but not published until 1953:

> *... The place has had*
> *Over two thousand years of advance publicity*
> *For us, which clouds the taste and saps the judgment.*
> *What are you to do when Catullus buttonholes you*
> *On the way to St. Peter's?*

And again:

> *... Words here can only scrabble*
> *Like insects at the plinth of a colossus,*
> *Scrabble and feebly gesticulate and go elsewhere.*
> *Mere ingratitude one might deal with, or pure and simple*
> *Meaning; but both in one, they give no purchase.*

Rome was just too much for him, he implies. But Florence, "the nonpareil city", was easier to understand. Here the past was still visible and tangible, and did not overpower either the visitor or the native Florentine.

Eleanor Clark, in her *Rome and a Villa* (1953) carries the same train of thought to a deeper level:

> *The city has its own language in time, its own vocabulary for the eye, for which nothing else was any preparation; no other place was so difficult, performed under the slow action of your eyes such transmutations. So the ordinary traveller runs off in relief to Florence, to the single statement, the single moment of time, the charming unity of somewhat prison-like architecture, and is aware later of having retained from his whizz tour of Rome some stirring round the heart: those images, huge, often grotesque, were what he had been looking for, only it would have taken so long . . . Those who stay in Rome, where nothing is single or simple and the aesthetic experience is always subordinate to something else, unless they are too handicapped to start with begin to change: an awful spectacle, which can go on for years, as though some queer yeast were working on an elephant . . .*

It was Ampère, the nineteenth century electrician, who claimed that everyone is spiritually either a Roman, a Florentine or a Venetian – in other words, that we have a natural predilection for either the Classical, the Gothic or the Renaissance way of culture. Whether this is anything more than a striking aphorism is, perhaps, doubtful. But it is not difficult to list the characters in this book who have expressed strong preferences for one or other of these cities. The "Romans" include nearly all the artists, and the two greatest of our architects – Inigo Jones and Robert Adam – together with Addison, Thomas Gray, Gibbon, Samuel Rogers, J.H. Newman, Hilaire Belloc and Ronald Firbank. Among the "Florentines" are Walpole, Hazlitt, Browning (both the

Brownings), Arnold Bennett and D.H. Lawrence. Only Ruskin (somewhat doubtfully) and Sir Henry Wotton are prominent among the "Venetians".

It does not tell us very much, after all, except to confirm the words of Ernest Rhys, who, in his biography of Lord Leighton, described Rome as a place where "sooner or later the steps of all men who work for religion or for art tend, and where so few stay." Yet always some have stayed. One of these, Joseph Severn, referred to his adopted home in a phrase that can hardly not have been echoed by any of his compatriots who have been to Rome, whether for a week, a month, a year or a lifetime:

Thanks, thanks, to the end of my days, for making me come to Rome.

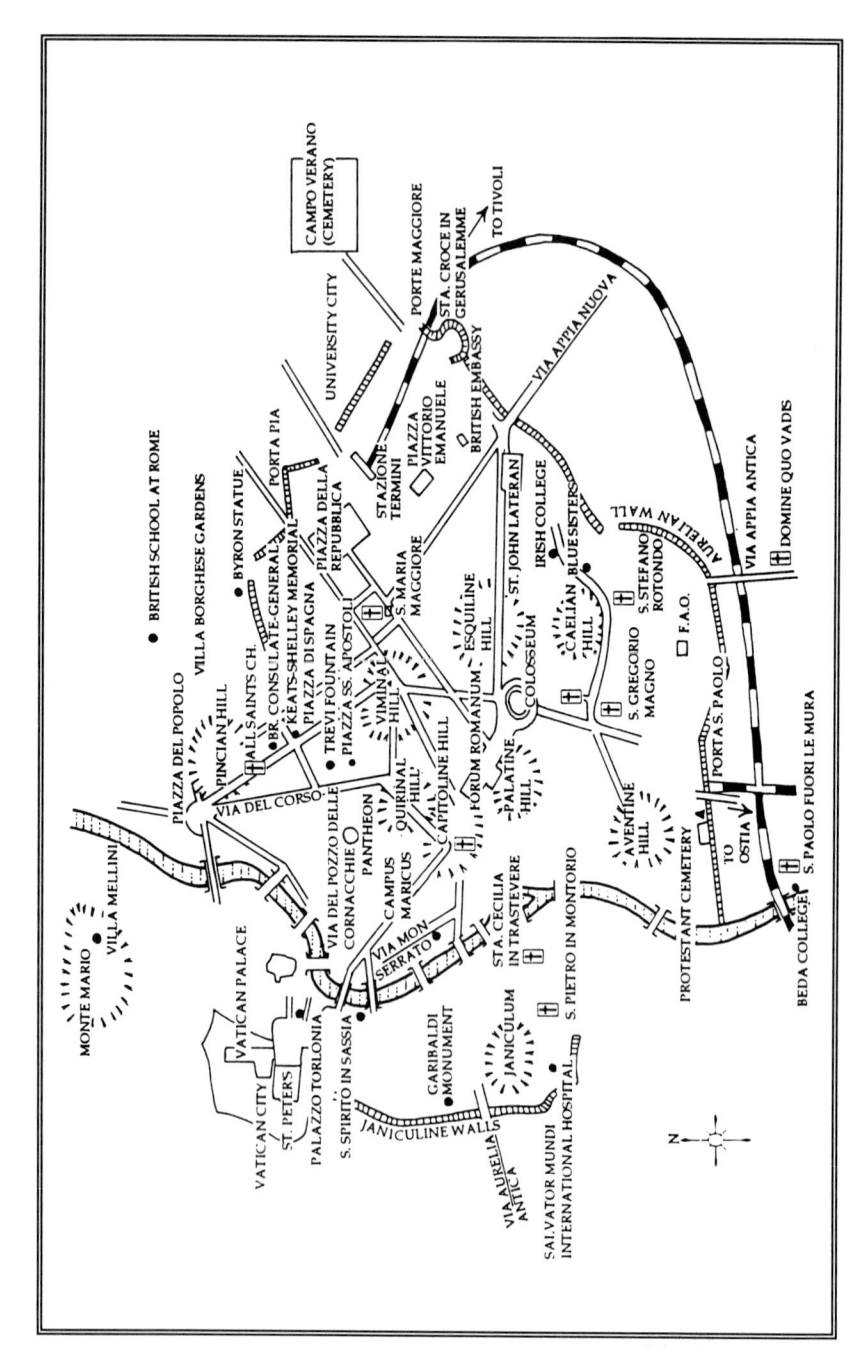

Showing Sites of Anglo-Roman interest

NOTES

THE PILGRIMS' ROAD

1. *Life and Letters in the Fourth Century*, T.R. Glover.
2. *Piedmont and the English*, P. Nichols.
3. *Letter of Abbess Eangyth*, in Boniface, Epist. no. 78, quoted by Levison, England and the Continent in the Eighth Century.
4. I.A. Richmond, *Roman Britain* (Penguin History of England, vol. I.)
5. Stubbs, *Seventeen Lectures*.
6. J. J. Jusserand, English Wayfaring Life in the Middle Ages.
7. Ibid.
8. There is still a Maison Dieu Road in Dover – pronounced locally "Mason Dew".

REDISCOVERY OF ITALY

1. The construction of St. Mark'S Palace (now the Palazzo Venezia) was started in 1465, and of Farnese in 1514.
2. E.A. Adair, *Tudor Studies*.
3. L. Einstein, *The Italian Renaissance in England*.

4. Manchet – a small loaf of fine white bread (Samuel Johnson's Dictionary).
5. Forks, napkins and wine-glasses were still in the seventeenth century regarded as exotic Italian novelties.
6. *Cal. State Papers Foreign, 1582.* No. 134, July 3.
7. According to the Oxford English Dictionary, the word passport first came into use about 1500. The Privy Council exercised the power to grant passports from 1540 until 1685, but between 1685 and 1794 two forms of passport existed – one signed by the monarch and the other by the Secretary of State. Except in wartime, however, few British citizens needed passports, and the familiar "blue" passport was not issued until 1921.
8. The implication of this remark, supported by recent research, is that Inigo Jones had already visited Italy.

GIRO D'ITALIA AND GRAND TOUR

1. cf. p. 144.
2. Quoted by Peter de Polnay in *Death of a Legend.*
3. Walpole Society, vol XXXII.
4. This and the subsequent quotations, as well as most of the facts made use of in this section, come from John Fleming, *Robert Adam and his Circle in Edinburgh and Rome* (1962).
5. Quoted by Peter de Polnay in *Death of a Legend.*
6. The quotations are from a letter to J-J. Rousseau, in *Boswell on the Grand Tour* (1953).
7. Gibbon's Journey from Geneva to Rome, ed. Georges A. Bonnard (1961).
8. It was actually the temple of Juno – i.e. the church of S. Maria in Aracoeli. The temple of Jupiter used to stand on the other side of

the Capitoline Hill.

9. Lesley Lewis, *Connoisseurs and Secret Agents in Eighteenth Century Rome* (1961).
10. H.V. Morton, *The Fountains of Rome* (1970)

TO ROME FOR THE WINTER

1. The population of England increased from six and three-quarter million in 1760 to twelve million in 1821 (W.F. Reddaway).
2. H.V. Morton, *A Traveller in Rome.*
3. J.R. Hale, *The Italian Journal of Samuel Rogers.*
4. *Matthew Todd's Journal*, ed. G. Trease.
5. Ibid.
6. J.R. Hale, *op. cit.*
7. *Paradise Regained*, Book IV, 11.44 ff.
8. J.C. Eustace, *Classical Tour.*
9. This and subsequent quotations are from *A Journey to Florence in 1817*, by Harriet Charlotte Beaujolois Campbell, ed. G.R. de Beer, F.R.S.
10. Stendhal, *Rome, Naples et Florence* (tr. Richard N. Coe, 1959).
11. Not at 5 p.m. on 23rd February as is sometimes stated. In Papal Rome the day ended with the Angelus, i.e. at 6 p.m., so that for the purposes of the official records, Keats died at 05.00 hours on 24th February, or at 11 p.m. on the 23rd by modern reckoning. Thus the date on his tombstone (24th February) is correct according to the usage of the period. The Romans were commendably patient with foreigners who were confused by this way of recording dates, and specified "French time" where necessary. Thus, the *vetturino* who conveyed Matthew Todd from Rome to Florence in 1814 stated in the contract that they

would leave "demain matin à cinq heures de France."
12. *Diary of an Ennuyé* (1826).
13. *Letters of Lord Macaulay.*
14. Mrs Uwins, *Memoirs of T. Uwins*, quoted by C.P. Brand *Italy and the English Romantics.*
15. John Ruskin, *Praeterita.*
16. Mona Wilson, *Grand Tour: a Journey in the Tracks of the Age of Aristocracy.*
17. A new edition was published in 1964, under the title of *Edward Lear in Southern Italy.*
18. H.V. Morton, *The Fountains of Rome.*
19. David Mathew, *Lord Acton and his Times.*
20. W. Fraser Rae, *The Business of Travel.*
21. H.V. Morton, *The Fountains of Rome.*

THE MODERN WAY TO ROME

1. *The Times*, Jan. 10, 1888.
2. Quoted by Arthur Bryant in *The Turn of the Tide, 1939-1943.*
3. H.V. Morton, A Traveller in Rome.

CONCLUSION

1. In *The Companion Guide to Rome*, which I found very useful in compiling this section of my book.

BIBLIOGRAPHY

So many subjects have been touched upon in this book that a complete list of references would be virtualy impossible to compile. The following bibliography, therefore, is not intended to be exhaustive; it is, rather, an expression of my indebtedness to the authors of the works concerned, and only those books and papers that I actually consulted have been included.

Some of the books in this list have already been mentioned in footnotes to the text. In the interests of readability I tried to keep the number of footnotes to a minimum, though when an actual passage from another book was quoted, it was obviously necessary to provide an acknowledgement.

In the bibliography, sources of major importance have been marked with the symbol *. All the books mentioned were published in London unless otherwise stated.

INTRODUCTION

RICHMOND, I.A. *Roman Britain* (Penguin History of England, vol. 1). (2nd edition, 1963).

WEBSTER, G. and DUDLEY, D.R. *The Roman Conquest of Britain, A.D. 43-47.* (1965).

THE PILGRIMS' ROAD

AMUNDESHAM, Joannes *Annales Monasterii Sancta Albani, 1421-142?.* (ed. H.T. Riley) (Rolls ed., 1870-71).

BREWYN, William *A XV Century Guide-Book to the Principal Churches of Rome, compiled c.1470 by William Brewyn.* (tr. and ed. C. Eveleigh Woodruff (1953)).

CAPGRAVE, John *Ye Solace of Pilgrims: a Description of Rome circa A.D. 1450, by John Capgrave, an Austin Friar of Kings Lynn.* (ed. C.A. Mills) (Oxford 1911).

CUNTZ, O. (ed.) *Itineraria Romana* (Leipzig, 1929) (In Latin).

DOUGLAS, David and GREENAWAY, George W. *English Historical Documents. II 1042-1189* (1953).

GASQUET, Cardinal *A History of the Venerable English College* (Rome, 1920).

GLOVER, T.R. *Life and Letters in the Fourth Century* (1901).

HEATH, Sidney *Pilgrim Life in the Middle Ages* (1911). Later republished as *In the Steps of the Pilgrims.*

HODGE, C.E. *The Abbey of St. Albans under John of Whethamstede* (unpublished thesis, 1933).

HUGHES, G.M. *Roman Roads in South-east Britain* (1936).

*JUSSERAND, J.J. *English Wayfaring Life in the Middle Ages* (4th edition, 1950)

*LEVISON, W. *England and the Continent in the Eighth Century* (Oxford, 1943).

MACAULAY, Rose *Pleasures of Ruins* (1953).

MASSON, Georgina *The Pilgrimage Road of Italy.* Geographical Magazine, vol. 30, p.473 (1958)

MILLER, C. (ed.) *Itineraria Romana: Römische Reisewege an der Hand der Tabula Peutingeriana* (Stuttgart, 1916).

*McKILLIAM, A.E. *A Chronicle of the Archbishops of Canterbury* (1913).

NICHOLS, P. *Piedmont and the English* (1967).

*PARKS, G.B. *The English Traveller to Italy, Vol. 1. The Middle Ages (to 1525)*. (Rome 1954). (This book gives details concerning almost every known Englishman who travelled to Italy during this period).

POOLE, R.L. 'The Early Lives of Robert Pullen and Nicholas Breakspear', in *Essays in Medieval History presented to T.F. Tout* (1925).

RICHMOND, I. A.*Roman Britain* (op. cit.)

ROMANI, Mario *Pellegrini e Viaggiatori nell'Economia di Roma dal XIV al XVII Secolo* (Milan, 1948).

SMITH, R. Maynard *Pre-Reformation England* (1938).

STUBBS, Wiliam *Seventeen Lectures* (Oxford, 1886). *Memorials of St. Dunstan* (Rolls series, pp.392-395).

WEISS, R. *Humanism in England and the Fifteenth Century* (revised edition, Oxford, 1957).

YOUNG, Norwood *Rome* (Mediaeval Towns series). (Revised edition, 1953).

REDISCOVERY OF ITALY

ADAIR, E.A. 'William Thomas, a forgotten Clerk of the Privy Council', in *Tudor Studies*, ed. Seton-Watson (1924).

*BATES, E.S. *Touring in 1600; a study in the development of travel as a means of education* (Boston & New York, 1911).

*EINSTEIN, L. *The Italian Renaissance in England* (New York, 1902; reprinted in London, 1935).

FLYNN, V.J. 'Englishmen in Rome during the Renaissance' in *Modern Philology*, vol. 36 (1938).

*GOTCH, J.A. *Inigo Jones* (1928).

*HALE, J.R. *England and the Italian Renaissance* (1914).

HERVEY, Mary *The Life, Correspondence and Collections of Thomas*

Howard, Earl of Arundel (1921).

*HOWARD, C. *English Travellers of the Renaissance* (1914).

LEES-MILNE, James *The Age of Inigo Jones* (1953).

LYTTON SELLS, A. *The Paradise of Travellers: the Italian Influence on Englishmen in the 17th Century* (1964).

MATHEW, David *The Jacobean Age* (1938).

MITCHELL, R.J. *John Free: from Bristol to Rome in the Fifteenth Century* (1955).

MORISON, Fynes *An Itinerary containing his Ten years Travel, etc.* (Glasgow, 1907. First published, 1617).

*MUNDAY, Anthony *The English Romayne Lyfe* (1582) was reprinted in 1925 with an Introduction by G.B. Harrison. See also J. Payne Collier's Introduction to Munday's *John a Kent and John a Cumber* (1851).

SMITH, H. Maynard *op. cit.*

SMITH, L. Pearsall *The Life and Letters of Sir Henry Wotton* (1907).

*STOYE, J.W. *English Travellers Abroad, 1603-1667; their influence on English society and politics* (1952).

TURNER, Celeste *Anthony Munday: an Elizabethan Man of Letters* (Berkeley, Calif., 1921).

*THOMAS, William *The Historie of Italie* (1549), and *The Principall Rules of the Italian Grammar* (1550). See also *The Works of William Thomas*, ed. d'Aubant (1774). Only short excerpts from these works have been reprinted in modern times.

GIRO D'ITALIA AND GRAND TOUR

ALBION, G. *Charles I and the Court of Rome* (1935).

ANDRIEUX, Maurice *Daily Life in Papal Rome in the eighteenth Century* (1968).

BARRETTI, Joseph *An Account of the Manners and Customs of Italy* (1768).

BONNARD, Georges (ed.) *Gibbon's Journey from Geneva to Rome* (1961).

BOSWELL, James *Boswell on the Grand Tour* (1953).

*BURGESS, A. and HASKELL, F. *The Age of the Grand Tour* (1967).

BURNETT, G. *Travels through Switzerland, Italy and Germany* (1689).

*CHILDE-PEMBERTON, W.S. *The Earl Bishop* (1924).

COGAN, Henry *The Court of Rome* (1654). (The section entitled 'Directions for such as shall travel to Rome').

DAVIDSON, Angus *The History and Treasures of Ickworth, Suffolk* (Pitkin Pictorials series).

EVELYN, John *The Diary of John Evelyn* (Everyman's Library edn.)

*FLEMING, John *Robert Adam and his Circle in Edinburgh and Rome* (1962).

FORD, Brinsley 'A Portrait group by Gavin Hamiton: with some notes on portraits of Englishmen in Rome' (Burlington Magazine, XCVII, Dec. 1955, p.372. the same author's 'Richard Wilson in Rome', Burlington Magazine, XCIII, May 1951, p.157).

GRAY, Thomas *The Correspondence of Thomas Gray*, ed. P. Toynbee & L. Whibley (1935).

GUNTHER, R.G. *The Architecture of Sir Roger Pratt* (1928).

*HALE, J.R. *op. cit.*

HANFORD, J. Holly *John Milton, Englishman* (1950).

*HIBBERT, Christopher *The Grand Tour* (1969).

*HOWARD, C. *op. cit.*

HUDSON, Derek *Sir Joshua Reynolds: a personal study* (1958).

(JONES, Thomas) *Walpole Society*, vol. xxxii (1946-48).

LASSELS, Richard *An Italian Voyage; or a Compleat Journey through Italy* (1670).

LEES-MILNE, James *Roman Mornings* (1956) (On William Smith).

LEWIS, Lesley *Connoisseurs and Secret Agents in Eighteenth Century Rome* (1961).

MACAULAY, Rose *They went to Portugal* (1946). (On Thomas Flecknoe).

MAUGHAM, H. Neville *The Book of Italian Travel* (1903). (Chiefly an anthology compiled from descriptions of Italy in the eighteenth and nineteenth centuries).

*MEAD, W.E. *The Grand Tour in the Eighteenth Century* (Boston and New York, 1914).

MILLER, Lady Anne (anonymously) *Letters from Italy . . . in the Years 1770 and 1771* (1776).

MISSON, F.M. *New Voyage to Italy* (1739).

NUGENT, T. *The Grand Tour* (1778).

OMAN, Carola *David Garrick* (1958).

(PATCH, Thomas) *Walpole Society*, vol. xxviii (1939-40).

*POLNAY, Peter de *Death of a Legend: the True Story of Bonnie Prince Charlie* (1952).

*PRINCE, F.T. *The Italian Element in Milton's Verse* (Oxford, 1954).

QUENNELL, Peter *Four Portraits: studies of the eighteenth century* (1945). (On Edward Gibbon).

RAY, J. *Travels through the Low Countries, etc.* (1738).

RAYMOND, J. *An Itinerary contayning a voyage made through Italy in the Years 1646-7* (1648). Also known as *Il Mercurio Italico*.

RICHARDSON, Jonathan (senior and junior) *An Account of some of the Statues, Bas Reliefs, Drawings and Pictures in Italy, with Remarks* (1722).

SMITH, J.T. *Nollekens and his Times* (republished 1949 with Introduction by G.W. Stonier).

*SMOLLETT, Tobias *Travels in France and Italy* (1949 edition).

STONE, Nicholas and STONE, Henry *Walpole Society*, vol. vii (1919).

SUTTON, Denys (ed.) *An Italian Sketchbook by Richard Wilson, RA* (1968).

*TREASE, G. *The Grand Tour* (1967).

WALPOLE, Horace *Letters of Horace Walpole*, (ed. P. Toynbee). (1903-5).

WARNER, Rex *John Milton* (1949).

WATERHOUSE, E.K. *Painting in Britain, 1530-1790* (Pelican History of Art, 1953).

WEDGWOOD, C.V. *The King's Peace, 1637-1641* (1955).

WEDGWOOD, C.V. *The Thirty Years War* (1938).

*WILSON, Mona *Grand Tour: a Journey in the Tracks of the Age of Aristocracy* (1935). (This popular work arose out of a series of BBC talks on the Grand Tour. The two sections consulted were by Mona Wilson and Sir Osbert SITWELL).

WRIGHT, E. *Travels through France, Italy, etc.* (1730).

TO ROME FOR THE WINTER

ARTOM TREVES, Guiliana *The Anglo-Florentines, 1847-1862* (1956). (Although the subject of this book is Florence rather than Rome, it helps to put the years of this period into proper perspective, particularly since it is written from the Italian point of view).

BEYLE, Henri (STENDHAL) *Rome, Naples and Florence* (tr. Richard N. Coe, 1959).

*BRAND, C.P. *Italy and the English Romantics* (Cambridge, 1957).

CAMPBELL, Harriet Beaujolois *A Journey to Florence in 1817*, ed. G.R. de Beer (1951).

CARPENTER, Maurice *The Indifferent Horseman: the Divine Comedy of S.T. Coleridge* (1954).

COLVIN, Sir Sidney *John Keats* (1920).

CROSLAND, Margaret (ed.) *A Traveller's Guide to Literary Europe, vol. III; Southern Europe* (1967).

*DAVIDSON, Angus *Edward Lear* (Penguin edition, 1938).

DEAKIN, R. *Flora of the Colosseum of Rome* (1855).

DICKENS, Charles *Pictures from Italy* (1846).

EUSTACE, J.C. *A Classical Tour through Italy* (4th edition, 1817).

GITTINGS, Robert *John Keats: The Living Year* (1953).

*HALE, J.R. *The Italian Journal of Samuel Rogers* (1956). (The Introduction, entitled 'English Travellers in Italy, 1814-1821', was particularly useful).

*HARE, Augustus *The Story of my Life, in six volumes* (1896-1900) and the 16th edition of *Walks in Rome* (1903).

HAWTHORNE, Nathaniel *Passages from the French and Italian Notebooks of Nathaniel Hawthorne* (1871).

HAZLITT, William *Notes of a Journey through France and Italy* (1826). (The edition consulted was Volume 10 of Hazlitt's Complete Works, ed. P.P. Howe, 1932).

HEWLETT, Dorothy *A Life of John Keats* (2nd Edition, 1949).

HERMANN, Luke *The Twilight of the Grand Tour* (Catalogue of the drawings of James Hakewill, British School at Rome, 1992.)

HILLARD, George *Six Months in Italy* (1853).

HUMPHRIES, H. Noel *Rome and its Surrounding Scenery* (1840).

JAMESON, Anna *Diary of an Ennuyée* (1826).

LESLIE, Shane *Men were Different: five studies in late Victorian biography* (1937).

LESLIE, Shane *Cardinal Manning* (1953).

MATHEW, David *Lord Acton and his Times* (1963).

MAUGHAM, H. Neville *op. cit.*

MILNES, R. Monckton *The Life and Letters of John Keats* (Everyman's Library edition, 1953).

MORTON, H.V. *The Fountains of Rome* (1970).

QUENNELL, Peter *Byron in Italy* (1941).

READE, Brian Introduction to the catalogue of the Edward Lear exhibition held in London (1958).

RHYS, Ernest *Frederick Lord Leighton; an illustrated record of his life and work* (1900).

ROBERTS, Cecil *The Remarkable Young Man.* (A postscript to this historical novel about Joseph Severn gives biographical details of some of the English men and women who were in Rome at the same time as Severn.)

RUSKIN, John *Praeterita* (1949 edition, ed. Kenneth Clark).

THACKERAY, W.M. *Letters and Private Papers of William Makepeace Thackeray*, ed. Gordon M. Ray (1945).

TREASE, Geoffrey (ed.) *Matthew Todd's Journal* (1968).

TREVOR, Meriol *Newman: the Pillar of the Cloud* (1962).

UWINS, Mrs *Memoir of T. Uwins* (1858).

WHITESIDE, James *Italy in the Eighteenth Century contrasted with its present condition* (1848).

THE MODERN WAY TO ROME

BARCLAY, Brig. C.N.in *A Concise History of World War II*, ed. Vincent J. Esposito (1964). Ch. 9: Mediterranean Operations.

BELLOC, Hilaire *The Path to Rome* (1902).

BENNETT, Arnold *A Florentine Journal, 1910* (ed. D. Cheston Bennett (1967).

BRYANT, Sir Arthur *The Turn of the Tide, 1939-1943* (1957).

CLARK, Eleanor *Rome and a Villa* (1953).

CROSLAND, Margaret (ed.) *op. cit.*

FIRBANK, Ronald *The Complete Ronald Firbank*, with a preface by Anthony Powell (1961).

GUTHRIE, Douglas *A History of Medicine* (1945). (On the elimination of malaria from the Campagna).

*HARE, Augustus *Walks in Rome* (op. cit.)

HERBERT, A.P. *Misleading Cases* (1935).

IANNOTONI, Livio *Roma e gli Inglesi* (Rome, 1945).

JAMES, Henry *William Wetmore Story and his Friends.*

LAWRENCE, D.H. *The Letters of D.H. Lawrence* (ed. Aldous Huxley) (1932).

LEWIS, C. Day *An Italian Visit* (1953).

LUCAS, E.V. *A Wanderer in Rome* (1926).

*LUCAS, Matilda *Two Englishwomen in Rome, 1871-1900* (1938).

LYALL, Archibald *Rome sweet Rome* (1956).

*MASSON, Georgina *The Companion Guide to Rome* (1965).

MUNTHE, Axel *The Story of San Michele* (1929).

MORTON, H.V. *A Traveller in Rome* (1957).

MORTON, H.V. *The Fountains of Rome* (op. cit.) This book was originally published in 1966 under the title *The Waters of Rome.*

PIMLOTT, J.A.R. *The Englishman's Holiday* (1947).

PISANI, Saverio *A Week in Rome: a new Guide to Rome and its Environs* (1953 edition). A tourist guide book, published in Rome.

RAE, W. Francis *The Business of Travel* (1891).

ACKNOWLEDGEMENTS

During the initial research on this book – much of it carried out many years ago – I was particularly helped by the library staff of the Hertfordshire County Library, the Kent County Library, the British Museum Library, and the libraries of the British Council in Rome and of the Royal Geographic Society in London. I also received valuable individual assistance from the following: Maurice Bond, then of the Record Office, House of Lords, for constructive help with the *Pilgrims' Road* chapter; Bernard Hamilton, in relation to the Anglo-Saxon Period; Georgina Masson, who guided me through the scanty documentation of those earlier centuries; my brother, Peter Barefoot, for helpful criticism of the section on Inigo Jones; Sir Alan Bowness, for information about eighteenth century British artists in Rome; and Angus Davidson, for encouragement and advice regarding the Earl-Bishop of Bristol and Derry, and regarding Edward Lear.

More recently, during the work of preparing this book for publication, I am glad to acknowledge the help and expertise of Tony Harold of Images Ltd., Sue Wilson and Cintia Stammers. Assistance was also given by the staff of the U.K. Passport Agency and the Public Record Office, by Andrew Norris of the Drawings Collection of the Royal Institute of British Architects, and by the British School at Rome, owners of the collection of drawings by James Hakewill, several of which are illustrated here. The photograph of my Piranesi engraving of the Appian Way in Rome was expertly taken by Simon Ferguson; and

Peter Barefoot once more helped by contributing his photograph of the church of St Paul, Covent Garden, and of what should have been the Covent Garden Piazza.

Crown copyright material in the Public Record Office is reproduced by permission of the Controller of Her Majesty's Stationery Office, REF. FO 655/266.

The cover illustration, The Piazza di Spagna, Rome by Piranesi is reproduced by permission of the British Architectural Library R.I.B.A., London.

In the bibliography I have listed all the books and articles consulted during the research, the more important ones being marked with an asterisk (*). I have quoted short passages from many of these books and hope that any copyright holders not directly approached will accept this "umbrella" acknowledgement.

INDEX

A

Acton, Emerick Edward, Dalberg, First Baron Acton, 191-192
Adam of Usk, journey to Rome in 1402, 41
Adam, Robert, 110-116
Addison, Joseph, 96
Alcuin, Northumbrian scholar, 19
Alfred the Great, King 19
Appian Way, (*see* also Via Appia), 17
Arundel, Earl of, 74, 78, 80
Atkins, Richard, Protestant fanatic, 67
Augustine, St., 15, 21

B

Babington's Tea Room, 212-3, 224
Bainbridge, Christopher, Archbishop of York, 47
Becket, Thomas, 30
Belloc, Hilaire, 213
Bernini, 84
Biscop, Benedict, Northumbrian nobleman, 19
Boswell, James, 117-118
Breakspear, Nicholas, 27-28; becomes Pope Adrian IV, 28; dies and is buried in St. Peter's, 30

Brewyn, William, 41-43
British School at Rome, 148, 150, 216, 225
Browning, Elizabeth Barrett and Robert, 182
Byron, Lord, 153-155

C

Caedwalla, King of Wessex, 19
Caelian Hill, 15
Caesar, Julius, 11, 13
Caffè Greco, 154, 171, 200, 213, 224
Campbell, Beaujolois, 150-153
Canute, King, 24
Capgrave, John, 45
Caratacus, 11
Carne, Dr. Edward, later Sir Edward Carne, 49-52
Cateryck, John, 46
Clark, Dr. James, 155-157
Clenock, Dr. Maurice, 62
Coenrad, King of Mercia, 19
Cogan, Henry, 94
Coleridge, S.T., 136-138
Con, George, 83
Cook, Thomas, 193

Countess of Albany, daughter of Prince Charles Edward, 126, 128
Covent Garden Piazza, 76, 252
Cuthbert, 21

D
Dalton, Richard, 107
Deakin, Dr. Richard, 172
Duchess of Albany, wife of Prince Charles Edward, 126

E
Earl of Arundel, 74, 78, 80
Easton, Adam, 36
English College, (see also Venerable English College), 44, 47, 52, 60, 67, 70, 88, 136, 138, 165, 178, 216, 226
English Hospice, 52
Ethelheard, Archbishop of Canterbury, 21
Eustace, J.C., 145-148
Evelyn, John, 90-92

F
Firbank, Ronald, 219
Flecknoe, Richard, 92-93
Flemmyng, Robert, 55
Free, John, 54-55

G
Gardiner, Stephen, 47
Garrick, David, 118
Gibbon, Edward, 118-120
Gibson, John, 158
Gladstone, W.E., 192
Gray, Thomas, 100-104

H
Hakewill, James, 148-151, 154, 173
Hamilton, Sir William, 83, 127
Hamilton, Lady (Emma Hart), 127, 130

Hare, Augustus, 187-191, 201-203, 224
Hawkwood, Sir John, mercenary General, 38, 47
Hawthorne, Nathaniel, 182-184
Henry VIII, 48, 50
Henry, Duke of York, 99
Hervey, Frederick, Earl of Bristol and Bishop of Derry, 127-133
Hillard, George, 181
Hone, Nathaniel, 107, 108

I
Ickworth House, 130
Ine, King of Wessex, 19, 23

J
Jones, Inigo, 73-80, 84, 89
Jones, Thomas, painter, 109

K
Keats, John, 156-159, 209, 211
Keats-Shelley Memorial, 224
Kent, William, landscape gardener, 95
Kilwardby, Robert, Archbishop of Canterbury, 30

L
Langton, Stephen, Archbishop of Canterbury, 26
Lassels, Richard, gentleman's tutor, 93
Lear, Edward, 169-176, 185
Linacre, Thomas, 55-56
Lithgow, William, 71
Louis, Thomas, 136
Lucas, Matilda and Anne, 205-211

M
Macaulay, Lord, 160
Manson, Sir Patrick, 212
Milton, John, 85-90
Mole, John, 71

Index

Morison, Fynes, 67-68
Munday, Anthony, 60-66
Munthe, Axel, 200, 205

N
Newman, J.H., 165, 178
Nollekens, Joseph, 116

O
Offa, King of Mercia, 23

P
Pantheon, 76
Patch, Thomas, engraver, 107
Peckham, John, Archbishop of Canterbury, 31
Pelagius, 12
Piazza di Spagna, 85, 91, 109, 112, 124, 141, 157, 171, 181, 192, 199, 206, 212, 217, 220, 223, 224, 229
Piranesi, G.B., 112, 113, 115, 127, 139, 142, 155, 251
Pole, Reginald, 50
Pratt, Sir Roger, architect, 90
Prince Offa of Essex, 19
Protestant cemetery, 219
Pullen, Robert, 27

Q
Queen's House at Greenwich, 77, 84

R
Raymond, John, 92
Reynolds, Sir Joshua, 106, 107
Richardsons, Jonathan, 105
Rogers, Samuel, 138, 139
Ruskin, John, 167-168

S
Scott, Sir Walter, 164
Severn, Joseph, 162, 187, 209

Shelley, Percy Bysshe, 155
Shepherd, James, engineer, 194
Shepherd, John, first warden of English Hospice, 44
Sigeric, 21
Smollett, Tobias, 120-125
Stone, Nicholas, 84
Stuart, James Edward, "The Old Pretender", 97-99, 125
Stuart, Charles Edward, "The Young Pretender", 99-100, 104-105, 125-126
Stuart, Henry, Duke of York, 99, 126

T
Thackeray, W.M., 179-181
Thomas, William, 57-59
Twain, Mark, 208

V
Venerable English College, 44, 52, 70, 226
Via Appia, 187, 230
Via Condotti, 171, 185, 186, 200, 224, 225
von Stosch, Philip, 11, 97

W
Walpole, Horace, 100-101, 104
Wethburga, 19
Wheathampstead, John of, Abbot of St. Albans, 41-43
Whiteside, James, 175
Willibald, 20
Wilson, Richard, 108
Winchelsea, Robert, 31
Wiseman, Cardinal, 165, 177
Wolsey, Thomas, 47
Wotton, Sir Henry, 68, 87
Wright, Michael, 95

255